A GUIDE TO ORGAN MUSIC

A GUIDE TO ORGAN MUSIC

by

Viktor Lukas

Translated by Anne Wyburd
from the Fifth, Revised and Enlarged Edition

With Addenda by Lee Garrett, Region 8 Councillor
American Guild of Organists

Reinhard G. Pauly, General Editor

AMADEUS PRESS
Portland, Oregon

ISBN 0-931340-10-1

Printed in Hong Kong

Amadeus Press
9999 S.W. Wilshire
Portland, Oregon 97225

Library of Congress Cataloging-in-Publication Data

Lukas, Viktor.
[Reclams Orgelmusikführer. English]
A guide to organ music / by Viktor Lukas ; translated by Anne Wyburd from the fifth, revised and enlarged edition ; with addenda by Lee Garrett.
p. cm.
Translation of: Reclams Orgelmusikführer.
Includes index.
ISBN 0-931340-10-1
1. Organ music--Analysis, appreciation. I. Title.
MT140.L8413 1989
786.5'01'5--dc19 89-30795
CIP
MN

Contents

Preface

Today's music lover is familiar with instruments such as violin, piano and saxophone—indeed, knowing them forms part of general knowledge—but while these instruments and the music written for them are popular today, the organ remains in the background of concert life. Is it not taken seriously because it primarily functions as part of religious services? Is the organ repertory out of date, or accessible only to a small circle of initiates? These questions have been answered positively by composers and organists in this century, and as a result of a revival which began with Reger and was strongly supported by the "organ movement" and various liturgical efforts, the organ has been awakened from its magic sleep and is now well on the way to reconquering its place as a concert instrument.

The instrumental construction of the organ seems too complicated to many people, but when its mechanism is studied it is found to be straightforward and easy to grasp. Organists generally are ready and glad to open the doors and give anyone interested a glimpse into the heart of the king of instruments.

Anyone reading this book as a chronological journey through history will at once realize that the 17th century was exceptionally rich in composers of organ music and celebrated a unique climax of the development which began in the 15th century and found its apogee in Bach. Nevertheless this golden age of organ music must not keep us from appreciating, playing, and listening to the masters of earlier centuries and of our own. Only then can the whole wealth of organ composition be revealed. The task of this guide is to demonstrate this wealth and help people to listen to it. Since organ music predominantly consists of fugues and other imitative forms, the numerous examples given here make it possible to hear each respective theme even in the densest musical texture, thereby putting the listener in a position to share in the experience offered by the composer's own kind of structure.

As regards the sound of the organ, its new and unexpected tonal colors can surprise listeners who are perhaps accustomed to conventional impressions. The more they pursue this phenomenon, however, and try to penetrate the world of these tone colors, the more ravishing will organ music seem.

Bayreuth, October 1963 *Viktor Lukas*

For the Fifth Edition

In the Preface to the first edition of this book in 1963 I lamented that in comparison with other instrumetns, the organ remained in the background of concert life. This picture has changed: everywhere today, in cities and in the suburbs, in churches and concert halls, we find recitals and even complete cycles performed on historical and modern instruments, and also master classes and workshops, in such profusion that one wonders whether they should be welcomed or deplored. A whole generation of young, newly-trained organists has contributed to this growth of interest, as has the upsurge in organ-building in the post-war years. Nor has this development been confined to Germany, where the organ has traditionally been popular. On concert tours in the Soviet Union I have become aware of a revival in Baroque music, directly manifested in a thirst for organ works, and it may be symptomatic that this *Guide to Organ Music* was recently published in a Japanese translation (by Pax of Osaka), that is, in the language of a country with no tradition of organ music.

Does this indicate that the stream is broadening?

In the first edition it seemed appropriate to refer particularly to French organ music—the merry, relaxed, often somewhat frivolous sister of its serious-minded German brother. Out of this stimulus to acquaint oneself with something new has developed a trend, even an obsession, with novelty, as is often characteristic of Germans. For contemporary and especially avant-garde music the question was then as it is now: What will last, and what will only have a brief experimental effect? History will undoubtedly classify our era as eagerly receptive, if not uncritical. This could have a positive side, provided that contemporary organ music profits from it, because it still needs assistance. This applies particularly to those parts of the repertory not under the umbrella of box-office names or anniversary years.

Jean Paul wrote that books were "long letters to friends". May this book appeal to lovers of organ music and promote their understanding of the art of the organ.

Cologne and Bayreuth, October 1985 *Viktor Lukas*

Composers and Their Works

PAUL HOFHAIMER

b. Radstadt, Tauern (Austria), January 25, 1459; d. Salzburg, 1537

Hofhaimer came from a family of organists, worked at several princely courts—but mainly in the court chapel of Emperor Maximilian I in Augsburg—and finally became cathedral organist in Salzburg. He was widely known as one of the great organists of his time. He left only a few vocal and instrumental pieces, which create melismatic effects through the decoration of individual parts.

The music of Hofhaimer and his contemporaries (cf. KOTTER and BUCHNER) is consistently polyphonic: each individual voice is independent to an extent not found in later centuries, and therein also lies the charm of these works. On the one hand they reflect their origin in purely vocal music or are actual songs rewritten for the instrument; on the other hand the ornamentation, which stresses their instrumental and decorative character, gives rise to a somewhat stiff exuberance often resulting in mechanical phrases. The slightly veiled beauty of this music can only be truly revealed on a good instrument, and even then listeners need time to accustom themselves to it, but the quiet splendor and clear lines of these works will repay the effort.**Salve regina** (duration 9 minutes). I "Salve", cantus firmus in the tenor, upper part highly ornamented. II "Ad te", cantus firmus in the upper part:

III "Eya ergo", cantus firmus in the middle part. IV "Nobis post", cantus firmus again in the upper part:

V "O clemens", cantus firmus in the middle part. VI "O dulcis Maria", cantus firmus in the upper part:

Other works (some with sacred cantus firmus, some with secular): **Recordare,** in three parts, cantus firmus in the soprano; **T'Andernaken,** in four parts, cantus firmus in the tenor; **Carmen magistri Pauli** and **Ave maris stella** in three parts.

Publishers: Peters—*Orgelmusik aus drei Jahrhunderten (Organ music from three centuries)* Vol. 1, ed. T. Fedtke; Breitkopf—*Frühmeister der deutschen Orgelkunst* (*Early masters of the German organ*) ed. H. J. Moser; Doblinger.

JOHANNES KOTTER

b. Strasbourg, c. 1480; d. Bern, 1541

Pupil of Hofhaimer, organist in Torgau, Freiburg im Breisgau and Fribourg, Switzerland: finally schoolmaster in Bern. His only surviving work is the tablature for Bonifatius Amerbach, which contains both secular and sacred songs and dances.

Salve regina. In three parts throughout. I "Salve", cantus firmus in the tenor with ornamented upper part. II "Ad te clamamus", cantus firmus in the upper part with final ornamentation. III "Eia ergo", cantus firmus in the upper part. IV "O clemens", cantus firmus in the tenor. V "O dulcis Maria", cantus firmus in the lower part.

Aus tiefer Not schrei ich zu dir (Out of the depths of my misery I cry unto thee). In three parts with richly ornamented chorale melody after Wolfgang Dachstein, 1525. The boldness of his use of decoration is illustrated by juxtaposing the second

and last lines of the chorale.

See also HOFHAIMER.

Other works: Prooemium in D; Fantasia in C.

Publishers: Breitkopf; Merseburger—*Orgelmusik der Reformationszeit*(*Organ music of the Reformation period*) ed. J. H. Schmidt.

JOHANNES BUCHNER

b. Ravensburg, October 27, 1483; d. Konstanz, ? early March, 1538

Pupil of Hofhaimer, and before his appointment in 1506 at Konstanz cathedral may have been a member of Emperor Maximilian's court chapel. His theoretical work Fundamentbuch (Book of rudiments) *gives instructions on improvisation and composition for the organ. Apart from his organ works, a small number of motets and songs have survived.*

For the type of composition of the circle to which he stylistically belongs, see HOFHAIMER.

Kyrie eleison. In four parts with cantus firmus in the tenor, but anticipated in the upper part, albeit in a very veiled form:

Recordare. Cantus firmus in the bass:

In the second part of the work, "Ab hac familia", the cantus firmus appears in the upper part.

Es gieng ein man den berg uff (A man went up the mountain). The setting of this song is interestingly constructed: at the beginning the anticipatory form ("head imitation") assumes an almost fugal character:

and this presentation of the motifs, almost in the style of an exposition, continues later in a similar vein.

Further works: Arrangements of Gregorian melodies such as masses for organ, organ settings of sequences, hymns and the Magnificat; preambles and other free organ pieces.

Publishers: Peters—*Orgelwerke (Organ works)* ed. J. H. Schmidt; Breitkopf; Hinrichsen; Merseburger.

The following composers also belong stylistically to Hofhaimer's circle:

HEINRICH ISAAC (b. c.1450; d. Florence, March 26, 1517). Known as Arrigo Tedesco at the Florentine court of the Medici (after 1480–94); court composer to Emperor Maximilian (1497–1514). Particularly noted for his well-known song "Innsbruck, ich muss dich lassen" (Innsbruck, I must leave thee), which was written in tablature like other vocal pieces and thus set for a keyboard instrument. It was published by Merseburger, together with other pieces. Further works were published by Breitkopf—*Alte Meister aus der Frühzeit des Orgelspiels (Old Masters of early organ-playing)* ed. A. Schering, and *Frühmeister der deutschen Orgelkunst (Early masters of the German organ)*; Hinrichsen—*Alte Deutsche Orgelmeister* (*Old German masters of the organ*) ed. P. Marr.

ARNOLT SCHLICK (b. in the Rhineland-Palatinate, c.1455; d. Heidelberg, c.1525). Blind organist and theorist whose *Spiegel der Orgelmacher und Organisten (Mirror of organ builders and organists)*, published in 1511, is the earliest known work on organ-building and playing. His organ compositions from the *Tabulaturen etlicher Lobgesang und Liedlein uff die Orgeln und Lauten (Tablature of some hymns and little songs for organ and lute)* which came out in 1512, have been published by Schott and Merseburger (Three settings of "Verleih uns Frieden" [Grant us peace]).

Other examples of early organ music are found in the *Fundamentum organisandi (Rudiments of the art of the organ)* of 1452–55 by the blind CONRAD PAUMANN (b. Nuremberg, October 23, 1409; d. Munich, January 24, 1473). A good selection is included in *Geschichte des Orgelspiels und der Orgelkomposition (History of organ playing and organ composition)*, a volume of examples, edited by G. Frotscher and published by Merseburger. Other examples occur in the *Buxheimer Orgelbuch,* which also appeared in the middle of the century, ten pieces from which, including a complete **Salve regina** and a nine-part **Gloria de Sancta Maria Virgine,** were published by Hinrichsen.

In Italy two representatives of the early development of organ literature were MARCO ANTONIO CAVAZZONI (b. Bologna, c.1490; d. Venice, after 1570), and his son, GIROLAMO CAVAZZONI (b. Urbino, c.1510; d. Mantua, after 1565), who worked at the Mantua court and published two books of organ works. The first, *Intavolatura cioè recercari, canzoni, himni, magnificat . . . (Tablature, that is, ricercares, songs, hymns, Magnificat . . .)* appeared in 1541. His **Ricercares** are written in motet style with each section based on a single theme, treated fugally. His **Canzoni** are transcriptions of secular chansons. Publishers: Schott—new edition of the *Intavolatura,* ed. O. Mischiati; Peters—single pieces.

THOMAS TALLIS

b. c.1505; d. Greenwich, November 23, 1585

Tallis worked as an organist in Essex and at Canterbury before he attained the elevated position of organist of the Chapel Royal, which he held until his death. The surviving works of this early English composer consist predominantly of vocal music for use in church services—anthems, psalms, settings of the mass and motets—and are transitional in style, because after a short, sparse period of organ music towards the end of the 15th and beginning of the 16th century, of which little remains today, general interest was more strongly focused on other keyboard instruments such as the spinet, the harpsichord and the virginals, which replaced the organ for a long time. Tallis's principal instrumental compositions were written for the virginals (as were those of his great pupil, William Byrd).

Hymns on "Iam lucis orto sidere", "Veni redemptor", "Iste confessor", etc. are simple, contrapuntal pieces which only at the end may possibly be broken up by passage-work or cadences. The beginning of **Iste confessor:**

The **Antiphons** are also written in two parts and are lighter than the polyphonic composition, as for example the antiphon **Natus est nobis:**

Fantasies and other free, fundamentally simple, works—so-called "A points"—should also be mentioned.

Publisher: Hinrichsen.

ANDREA GABRIELI

b. Venice, c. 1510; d. ibid., late 1586

In 1536 he entered the choir of St. Mark's Cathedral as a singer, and after lengthy travels became second organist there in 1564 and principal in 1585, succeeding Claudio Merulo in each post. He wrote works of all musical genres and adhered particularly to the multichoral style. His organ works clearly bear the mark of their author's exceptional performing skill.

Ricercares. Gabrieli left a great number of such compositions, often monothematic, but sometimes introducing new motifs as well. A tranquil opening in which the theme is introduced in one part only is later fragmented into small note-values through melodic ornamentation, with occasional changes from duple to triple time.

Ricercar primo tono. This opens with the theme:

which is used and developed intensively and later enlarged in both soprano and bass parts. Its rhythmical structure changes with the time signature, but the intervals can still be recognized.

Only some of the **Canzone**—contrasting with the grave dignity of the ricercares—were original works by Gabrieli, a number having been adapted from French chansons and instrumentally ornamented for the organ or other keyboard instrument. Gabrieli also wrote ricercares on other song themes, as for instance the **Ricercari ariosi,** which probably derive from Italian melodies and of which the four that survive are particularly lovely examples of his art. This is the theme of the fourth:

His few toccatas still are very simple, with chords and homophonic phrases alternating with extended passage-work, mostly consisting of scales.

Pass' e mezzo antico. Variations on the dance of that name. The example below gives the opening:

The variations sometimes introduce passage work on sustained chords and sometimes part-writing with imitation. This is an attractive dance in elegant, courtly Venetian style.

Further works: Intonations for all eight modes.

Publishers: Bärenreiter; Peters.

ANTONIO DE CABEZÓN

b.? Castrillo de Matjudios nr. Castrojeriz, Burgos, 1510;
d. Madrid, March 16, 1566

Cabezón was blind. He first worked at the court of Emperor Charles V, and then until his death held the post of chamber musician and organist at the court of King Philip II of Spain. His instrumental works are of special value as the earliest tangible examples of their kind in Spain: he was the first to write variations on previously stated themes.

Tiento in hypophrygian mode, an example of several similar compositions. This opens with elaborate imitation which continues and increases later in the work. An arbitrarily chosen caesura shows this imitation in the shortest compass:

The Spanish "tiento" can be described as a prelude, in which imitation predominates. As the individual phrases are not very long there are many bridge passages and much dovetailing, in which a new motif or theme appears in one part and is at once treated in imitation. The change of time-signature in the last third breaks up this tiento and gives it an episodic character like a motet, with musically contrasting effects.

Hymn: Ave Maris stella. Verse 1: cantus firmus in the tenor, with alto, bass and soprano imitating. Verse 2: cantus firmus in the soprano, with head imitation. Verse 3: cantus firmus in the alto. Verse 4: cantus firmus in the bass but divided into lines, in contrast to the preceding verses. As in the tientos, the imitation plays the main part. Many of the head imitations are authentic fugal expositions.

Further works: Diferencias (variations) on *Llano del cavallero (Song of the knight)*, Milanese galliard, Italian pavan. Hymns: "Veni, creator", "Ut queant laxis", "Te lucis, Dic nobis, Maria", "Salve regina"; tientos.

Publishers: Bärenreiter; Schola Cantorum; Schott.

CLAUDIO MERULO

Bapt. Correggio, April 8, 1533; d. Parma, May 5, 1604

Organist at Brescia, St. Mark's, Venice, and at the Ferrara court; also an organ-builder. His importance lies in his organ compositions, above all in the foundations he laid for the toccata, though some of his other works also belong to the early, or even earliest, examples of their kind. He also composed choral works.

Canzone (1592). These instrumental pieces may have been intended for other instruments as well as for the organ, and are constructed as follows: exposition of the theme, which is replaced by other motifs in a somewhat improvisatory manner and ususally does not appear again. These pieces do not, however, acquire a compound character through the interchange of motifs. The ornamentation is written out, which makes the strict structure of the work obvious.

La gratiosa (Gracious lady):

La benvenuta (Welcome lady):

Merulo's toccatas are compound compositions which, rather than adhering to vertical part-writing, favor an element of free fantasy, enrich their development with ornamentation and passage-work and include short fugal sections. The resultant flow of iridescent music made up of several opposing elements is often exciting.

Toccata quarta del 6°tono

(Fourth Toccata in hypolydian mode, from the second book of his *Toccate d'intavolatura d'Organo* [*Toccatas intabulated for the organ*]). The opening is followed by a lengthy middle section with fugal treatment of the parts but bringing different motifs:

After only a few bars the fugato flows into the finale, which resembles the opening section.

Publishers: Bärenreiter; Ricordi.

COSTANZO ANTEGNATI (bapt. Brescia, December 9, 1549; d. ibid., November 14, 1624) belonged to a well-known family of organ-builders and compiled the *Arte organica,* a treatise on organ-building which also contained directions on registration for the player. In 1608 he published his *Intavolatura de recercari d'organo,* a collection of 12 ricercares in the church modes. These works, all strictly in four parts, are distinguished by their expressive treatment of melody, a single motif or a group of motifs being developed one after the other. Publisher: Zanibon.

GIOVANNI GABRIELI (b. Venice, 1554–1557; d. ibid., August 12, 1612 or 1613), nephew of Andrea Gabrieli (q.v.), wrote mostly multichoral vocal and instrumental music, but his lesser output of organ works—ricercares, fantasies, fugues, toccatas and intonations—are interesting pieces which present these existing forms in sharper rhythms and more thorough counterpoint. Publisher: Peters.

RODRIGUES COELHO (b. Elvas, c.1555; d. prob. Lisbon, after 1633) was organist in Lisbon from 1603 on and left mainly tientos and liturgical versets in his *Flores de musica (Flowers of music)* which appeared in 1620 (publ. Müller), while FRANCISCO CORREA DE ARAUXO (b. 1575–1580; d. Segovia, shortly before February 13, 1665) published both organ compositions and theoretical treatises. Publisher: Hansen—*Alte spanische Orgelmusik (Old Spanish organ music)* ed. C. Riess.

JAN PIETERSZOON SWEELINCK

b. Deventer, May 1562; d. Amsterdam, October 16, 1621

Sweelinck came to Amsterdam as a child and in 1580 succeeded his father as organist at the Old Church. The importance of his keyboard compositions cannot be overstated, and he also left some excellent vocal works, such as the Cantiones sacrae (Sacred songs) *and* Psalms of David. *He had learned from the Venetian masters and in turn passed his knowledge of composition to a wide circle of pupils, including Samuel Scheidt, who introduced his lasting influence into Germany.*

Fantasia chromatica (Chromatic fantasia). Starts fugally with the following theme:

which continues in a similar manner with various interpolations. The introductory part serves as an exposition and already contains stretti. Next comes new material to set against the same theme, a free interlude and then the theme in whole note-values in all four parts, one after the other. Then follow the chromatic modulations which together with the theme itself gave the work its name, because either the theme or its opening comes in immediately after the previous one on E, D, C, B-flat and G in the descant, and thereafter similarly in the bass. Towards the end the density is increased through stretto and diminution, so that by the end of the piece the theme has appeared in eighth-notes, quarter-notes, half-notes and whole-notes.

Like all early chromatic pieces, this sounds particularly enchanting and is a well-rounded and proportioned composition.

Sweelinck's other 11 fantasias are similarly constructed, with every theme easily distinguished as a result of the fugal introduction, and developed with varying counterpoint in the course of the work. Their structure, however, is not as complex as that of the above-mentioned chromatic fantasy.

The **Echo fantasias** derive their name from the echo effect achieved by alternating *forte* and *piano* registration for certain identical or similar motifs. Some dynamics are indicated in the autographs, but in other places the changes are self-evident.

The beginnings and ends of these six fantasias are either slightly imitative or homophonic, with the echoes occurring in the middle sections. Here are three examples of the echo effects from the Fantasia in D minor:

The Fantasia in C major has a clearly defined introductory passage of 42 bars, followed by the interplay between *forte* and *piano* which continues almost to the end of the piece.

The **Song Variations** are often classified as harpsichord works, but can be performed on any keyboard instrument, as at the time no general distinction between organ and harpsichord compositions had yet been established. One can equally imagine them being played on clavichord or harpsichord as on the portative and regal organs carried about for use at banquets and balls.

These *Song variations,* as those by Scheidt were to do later, extend from a four-part thematic section, through the bicinium, variations with runs and changing rhythms and time signatures to the closing verses, which are almost toccatalike in their changing figurations. The themes of the variations are the songs themselves: "Est-ce mars" (Is it Mars?), "Ich fuhr mich Über Rheine" (I crossed the Rhine), "Mein junges Leben hat ein End" (My young life draws to an end) and "Unter der Linden grüne" (Under the green lime-tree).

Chorale variations "Erbarm dich mein, o Herre Gott" (Have mercy on me, O Lord God). I Bicinium, with cantus firmus in the upper part, head imitation in the bottom part; transition to II in three parts, with the chorale in the bass. III, four-part movement with cantus firmus in the tenor, leading into IV, in four parts with chorale in the bass. V, for manuals only, with cantus firmus in the right hand, and two-part imitation in the left. VI, in three parts, for manuals only with cantus firmus in the soprano.

The following are similarly arranged: "Da pacem, Domine" (Grant peace, O Lord), 4 variations; "Nun freut euch lieben Christen gmein" (Rejoice now, dear Christians together), 3 variations; "Wir glauben all an einen Gott" (We all believe in one God), 3 variations; "Ach Gott, vom Himmel sieh darein" (O God, look down from heaven), 3 variations. Further works: Toccatas. Publishers: Breitkopf; Peters—*Ausgewählte Werke (Selected works),* ed. D. Hellmann; Schott.

JEHAN TITELOUZE

b. St Omer, 1563 (1564?); d. Rouen, October 24, 1633

Organist at the church of St. John in Rouen from 1585, and three years later at the cathedral, where he became a canon in 1610. He was one of the first great masters of the organ in France (where to this day composers are also organists and thus their own interpreters), and the forms he used were new. His collections of works were published at about the same time as those of Scheidt and Frescobaldi, and these three leading representatives of French, German and Italian music form an interesting group.

Hymnes de l'église (Church hymns, 1623). The 12 hymns Titelouze grouped under this title each consists of several versets in variation style on the Gregorian melody, and many show a typical ricercare character, with the motifs of the cantus firmus treated fugally. As all the hymns are developed in the same way it is enough to discuss one of them here.

Pange lingua (Weep, O tongue). 1st verset with cantus firmus in large note-values in the pedal. The three upper parts imitate the following theme thoroughly:

Later new motifs enter and are treated in the same way. 2nd verset, like a fughetta on the beginnings of each Gregorian line, with the transitions between the individual sections dovetailed together. The speed increases from 𝅗𝅥 ♩ ♩ | ♩ ♩ ♩ ♩ through ♩ ♩|♩ ♫ ♩|♩ ♩ to ♬ ♬♬ ♬♬ ♬♬ to give the piece its impetus. 3rd verset, also like a fughetta, with the cantus firmus introduced in large note-values, first in the soprano, then in the alto, then the tenor and again in the soprano. The other hymns are: "Ad coenam", "Annue Christe", "A solis ortus", "Ave maris stella", "Conditor alme siderum", "Exsultet coelum", "Iste confessor", "Sanctorum meritis", "Urbs Jerusalem", "Ut queant laxis" and "Veni, creator".

The Magnificat, 1626. The second collection of Titelouze's organ works contains Magnificats in the eight church modes. Each has seven versets and always develops each verse of the canticle twice. The composition of only six of the total of 11 verses recalls the earlier practice of performing Mary's hymn of praise antiphonally. The composition of these Magnificats is similar to that of the hymns, but here the cantus firmus appears less in the foreground because it is always the same, while the text changes from verse to verse.

Magnificat in the lydian mode, duration 10 minutes. Magnificat: fugal four-part section, beginning thus:

"Quia respixit:" fugal episodes in the following order: bass—tenor—alto—soprano. "Et misericordias eius:"

"Exposuit potentes:" first composed to the following theme:

Secondly:

"Suscepit Israel:" trio with fugal opening. "Gloria patri:" densely imitative section with the four parts entering in quick succession:

Publisher: Schott—Collected Edition, ed. A. Guilmant.

HANS LEO HASSLER

bapt. Nuremberg, October 26, 1564; d. Frankfurt-am-Main, June 8, 1612

Among his teachers in Venice was Andrea Gabrieli. From 1586 he was in the service of the Fugger family in Augsburg; in 1601 he went to Nuremberg as principal city Musician, and in 1608 to the Dresden court. As a highly esteemed musician of his time his special influence lay in his vocal compositions, above all the Lustgarten neuer teutscher Gesäng (Pleasure garden of new German song), *but also in his madrigals and masses. His organ works clearly show his dependence on Italian models.*

Introit in dorian mode. This introit clearly shows features of the toccata: introduction with chords and runs, fugal sections, each with a lively clausula at the end, and in the finale passage-work again, growing faster and faster towards the close, as in many similar compositions. The first fugal work after the introduction is on the following theme:

After the interpolation of short motifs this theme reappears in a somewhat altered form, though retaining the first six notes of the melody. The change to 3/4 time which follows soon after makes the flow of the music even livelier, until it leads through repeated chords reminiscent of contemporary vocal compositions into the final, homophonic section dominated by diatonic runs.

Ricercare in A. It is rare to find the theme dominating a piece as exclusively as here: no other strong ideas enter to change the color of the picture, as often occurs elsewhere.

The theme is in two parts, the second of which enters after the first five bars, and is sometimes developed as a single idea, though mostly divided into its constituent parts. By enlarging and contracting the note-values, and various other contrapuntal devices, Hassler created a technically impressive composition of over 250 bars. Its musical execution is not simple, but it is made easier by the same theme embracing all the sections in a tight grasp.

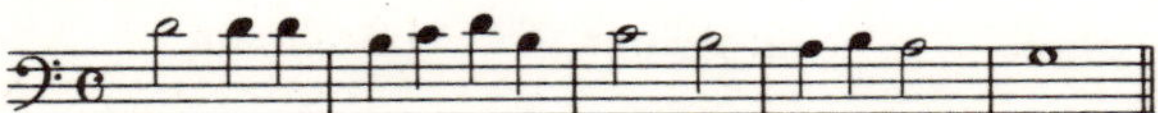

Canzona in G major. The canzona is related to the ricercare and not always strictly distinguished from it by the composer, but has a lighter, looser rhythm. After the expositional development there follows a further fugal section which leads into the homophonic finale.

Further works: ricercares, toccatas.

Publishers: Bärenreiter; Peters; Schott.

MICHAEL PRAETORIUS

b. Creuzburg on the Werra, February 15, 1571 (?1572);
d. Wolfenbüttel, February 15, 1621

While still a student at the University of Frankfurt-an-der-Oder he was already organist at the university church. From 1595 on he was organist to the Bishop of Halberstadt—later Duke Heinrich Julius of Brunswick—in Halberstadt and Wolfenbüttel. He travelled widely in central Germany as organizer of the festival concerts at the court, and visited Dresden, Halle, Sondershausen, Kassel, Magdeburg, Leipzig and Nuremberg. He shares with Heinrich Schütz the position of founding father of Protestant church music, and like Schütz he used the new, polychoral Italian style for his work, which was almost entirely dedicated to hymns and their arrangements. His three-volume work Syntagma Musicum *of 1614–20 is an invaluable source of information on everything to do with the music of his period.*

Hymns: 1. "Alvus tumescit virginis" for advent, to the tune "Veni redemptor gentium". 2a. "A solis ortus cardine" for Christmas; 2b. "Summo parenti gloria", 8th verse. 3. "Vita sanctorum" for Easter. 4a. "O lux beata Trinitas" for Trinity; 4b. "Te mane laudum carmine", 2nd verse. In all these works the cantus firmus is treated as a bass line in the pedals in large note-values and without rests. Above it lies the music for the manuals mostly in three parts, imitating the lines of the cantus firmus and also using free imitative material, much of which starts in canon. Sometimes the parts resolve into a unison line which runs through from the soprano to the bass, e.g. the finale of 2b. Those pieces resembling choral variations (intended for alternating singing by choir and congregation) are harmonically static. The harmonies are mostly heard to change with the main pedal notes, and all the figured flourishes remain within the framework of the basic harmony provided by the bass line.

Chorale fantasias. "Ein feste Burg ist unser Gott" (A mighty fortress is our God), "Christ, unser Herr, zum Jordan kam" (Christ our Lord to Jordan came), "Wir glauben all an einen Gott" (We all believe in one God). In each Fantasia one verse is set to music, starting in each case with a regular fugal exposition, the theme of which is the beginning of the chorale; and the following lines are divided either wholly or partly among all four voices, with the remaining ones imitating. "Christ, unser Herr' contains a charming change from 4/4 to 3/4 time reminiscent of a motet.

Further works: Symphony; 2 variations on "Nun lob mein Seel den Herren" (Now praise the Lord, my soul).

Publisher: Möseler.

GIROLAMO FRESCOBALDI

b. Ferrara, ?September 12, 1583; d. Rome, March 1, 1643

Early in his life Frescobaldi was drawn to Rome, where in 1604 he became organist and singer at the Congregation and Academy of St. Cecilia. From 1608 on he was organist at St. Peter's Cathedral, though he interrupted his work there by travelling and undertaking work elsewhere, e.g. in Florence in 1628. He was the first great Italian master of the organ, and his fame spread throughout Europe primarily through his pupils, among them Froberger, Kerll and Tunder, but a relatively small number of his works has survived. Apart from the organ compositions of this brilliant player and improviser, the sacred choral works and instrumental canzones are particularly noteworthy.

Fiori musicali (Musical flowers, 1635). This collection contains compositions of various kinds for use in church worship. Such works later became known, as in Couperin's case, as organ masses. Frescobaldi uses a usually very brief toccata, a canzona with the typical 3/4 middle section, a ricercare and even a Bergamasca and shorter imitative forms. The first of the three cycles contains the following pieces under the heading *In Dominicis infra annum:* "Toccata avanti la Messa" (Toccata before the mass), 2 Kyries, 4 Christes, 6 Kyries, some of which are interchangeable; "Canzon dopo l'Epistola" (Chant after the Epistle):

"Recercar dopo il Credo" (Ricercare after the Creed):

"Toccata cromaticha per l'Elevatione" (Chromatic toccata for the Elevation); "Canzon post il Communione" (Chant after the Communion):

Ricercare. This is an instrumental supplement to the motet and simultaneously represents a precursor of the fugue, which reached its apogee in the Baroque period. Thus it is composed in strict part-writing throughout, with various sections resembling developments. A second theme or motif often joins the main theme. The most striking change to the theme occurs by enlarging the note-values.

Recercar quinto. The theme:

Second theme:

The sections of the opening which resemble exposition and development are resolved in the middle section with a completely new thematic structure. After the transition to the last section all three themes appear in horizontal and vertical combinations.

The **Canzone,** which because of their themes are generally lighter and more fluid in composition and sound than the ricercares, are also looser in form, because the middle sections have a different time signature, as a rule changing from 2/2 to 3/2.

Canzon nona from the *Canzoni alla Francese,* 1645. The theme:

The middle section in 3/2

itself changes with this theme into common time and back again.

Toccatas. One finds among Frescobaldi's works pieces so described, the individual sections of which are admittedly musically clearly distinguished from one another, but often dovetailed, so that the caesuras are missing. The main component of these pieces is passage-work full of motifs, imitative in form and improvisatory in development. Fugal and homophonic sections are rarely encountered. There are 12 toccatas in the first book and 11 in the second.

Toccata nona from the first book of toccatas, publ. 1637; duration 5 minutes. The first bar contains two motifs (a and b) which dominate the entire first section:

Passage-work follows, with a cadence to A. Another motif makes a brief appearance, but dissolves into other phrases, and cadences to C. The calmer passage without figuration which follows elaborates on the motif shown below for longer than usual, ending with a cadence to E. The finale is a free improvisation without reference to what has gone before.

Toccata quinta from the second book of toccatas, publ. 1637. This work could be superficially divided up by the pedal points on G, C, F, A, D and G again. There are striking motifs in the F section:

The other sections such as G and D work with figuration and rhythmical groups:

Frescobaldi's prefaces to his works give detailed notes and instructions for executing ornaments and passage-work and for the tempos.

Further works: Partitas on "Aria della Romanesca", "Aria di Monicha", "Aria di Ruggiero", "Aria di Follia"; 3 arrangements of the Magnificat, "Aria detta Balletto", "Aria detta la Frescobalda"; Hymns: "Ave maris stella", "Iste confessor", "Della Domenica"; Capriccios; Fantasies.

Publishers: Bärenreiter—Collected Works, ed. P. Pidoux, also containing F.'s performing instructions; Peters.

CHRISTIAN ERBACH (b. Gau-Algesheim, c.1570; buried Augsburg, June 14, 1635), worked in Augsburg as an organist and in the service of the Fugger family. He continued Hassler's tradition. His **Canzone** are polyphonic and full of variety, and like his other works are stamped with the skill and delight in his art of a composer-organist. Publishers: Merseburger—*Acht Kanzonen,* ed. A. Reichling; Coppenrath—*Ausgewählte Kompositionen (Selected compositions),* ed. A. Reichling.

TARQUINIO MERULA (b. prob. Cremona, c.1590; d. ibid. December 10, 1665) produced both in his **Canzone** and in his **Sonata cromatica, Capriccio cromatico** and several **Intonations** concentrated pieces with very bold harmonic effects obtained by using chromatic phrases and scales.

In the **Sonata** he used inversion of the theme and stretti. Publisher: Bärenreiter—*Kompositionen für Orgel und Cembalo (Compositions for organ and harpsichord)* ed. A. Curtis.

All we know about GIOVANNI BATTISTA FASOLO's dates is that he was born in Asti in the first half of the 17th century. His *Annuale* appeared in 1645. It contains a collection of contemporary ecclesiastical music for use in church services: Versets for the mass, the Magnificat, the Te deum and hymns, but also ricercares, fugues and other free pieces to be played at the beginning of the mass, at certain points during it and at the end. There is a certain reserve and a simple gravity in the compositional technique of his sacred pieces, as shown in their modest imitation, but the free works reveal his virtuosity. Publisher: Müller—*Annuale,* ed. R. Walter.

MICHEL ANGELO ROSSI (b. Genoa, c.1602; d. Rome, July 7, 1656) was famous in his lifetime as a violinist and was Frescobaldi's most important student. Of his work **Toccatas** and **Correntes** survive. Rossi increasingly relaxed his teacher's toccata form by eliminating the individual bridge passages and relaxing the counterpoint. His complementary rhythms, e.g. in the 6th toccata, and chromatic accentuation of the closing passage of the 7th are particularly innovative:

Publisher: American Institute of Musicology—*Works for Keyboard Instruments,* ed. J. R. White.

ORLANDO GIBBONS

bapt. Oxford, December 25, 1583; d. Canterbury, June 5, 1625

From his youth until his death this scion of a great musical family was organist of the Chapel Royal, adding in 1623 the post of organist at Westminster Abbey. Most of his works are anthems, psalms, madrigals and motets, together with pieces for string and keyboard instruments, mostly the virginals. Gibbons's compositions form an important link in the development of English music between Tallis and the Baroque masters Blow and Purcell.

As do those of Tallis, Gibbons's compositions show the predominant influence of the harpsichord, and his technique of ornamentation is highly distinctive. It is stylistically interesting to note that a four-part **Fantasy** employs similar bridge passages, and even identical final phrases, to those in the toccatas of his contemporary Frescobaldi.

A **Voluntary in A** is clearly in two sections: the strict part-writing in the elaboration of a theme in the first gives way to freer, mostly ascending, diatonic scales in the second.

A Fancy for a double organ is written for performance on a two-manual organ, and indicates when manuals should be changed. Publisher: Hinrichsen.

SAMUEL SCHEIDT

bapt. Halle, November 3, 1587; d. ibid, March 24, 1654

In 1608, when he was organist at St. Maur's Church in Halle, Scheidt went to Amsterdam to study with Sweelinck. Subsequently he became court organist and master of the court music in Halle. Like Praetorius and Schütz he was one of the most important masters of his period. His compositions for the organ are very comprehensive and valuable, but his motets, sacred concertos, and Symphonien auf Concerten-Manier (Symphonies in the style of concertos) *also reveal his great mastery.*

Toccata on "In te Domine speravi" (In thee, Lord, have I hoped) is in three sections: one theme is stated and fugally treated, then this strict form dissolves into toccatalike runs. The same happens to a second and third theme, without any connection existing between the three ideas. Perhaps this comes from the cantus firmus? One cannot be quite sure. Theme of the second section:

Theme of the third section:

Fantasia on "Io son ferito lasso" (Fuga quadruplice—a quadruple fugue). From the heading it is clear that this must be in strict fugal form with four themes. The first two themes were frequently used at that time:

As usual in fantasias, the note-values of the themes are lengthened and shortened, and towards the end stretti often occur.

Among Scheidt's compositions his works with variations over a given cantus firmus surpass the "free" works both in number and in artistic and musical quality. These partitas are arrangements of German and Latin hymns and secular songs and dances. His settings of the Magnificat should also be mentioned here, although they depend on the text of the individual verses more than on a given melody.

The different methods of treatment can be basically described as follows: Works with secular cantus firmi have freely contrapuntal parts which mould each piece into an entity, while variations are free and full of coloring, ornamentation and passage-work.

Works with liturgical Latin cantus firmi usually treat it in individual lines, and the contrapuntal parts depend on the cantus firmus, which generally remains unaltered. Works based on German sacred songs come between these two methods, and their treatment of the liturgical tunes is enriched by borrowing from the style of secular variations. In the works with variations Scheidt truly shows his technical strength, accounting for the almost aristocratic detachment which often radiates from his music.

Passamezzo. As in a passacaglia, variations are heard over a fixed bass, but with one limitation: the exact original form of the bass is not retained, but only its spirit, i.e. its harmonies, and within these bounds can be treated freely. 1st variation: four-part piece, with simple melody and harmonies. 2nd variation: again in four parts, but relaxed principally by the motif quoted here.

3rd variation: in three parts with an almost perfectly consistent alternation between one bar in eighth-notes and one in sixteenths. The final motion consists of descending "steps". 4th variation: bicinium, with calm upper part and ornamented lower part. 5th variation: in four parts, with hints of motifs from the fourth. 6th variation: in four parts, with a distinctive upper part embellished by passage-work, and three lower parts in chords.

7th variation: in four parts, with the theme of no. 6 inverted. Ornamented bass and harmonic background in the upper parts. 8th variation: in three parts, with "Imitatio violistica" in the upper part. By this Scheidt meant "a particular manner, as a violist customarily draws his bow" and adds that "this produces on gently-voiced organs, regals, harpsichords and instruments a truly lovely and gracious harmony." Whether by this he just means a combination or a shortening or lengthening of some notes in a specific group is not clear.

9th variation: in four parts, with the voices running in pairs and therefore actually sounding like one. Examples:

10th variation: in four parts, with runs in thirds and sixths in both upper parts. 11th variation: in three parts, decorated in the upper part with broken sixths:

12th variation: in four parts, in triple time.

Cantio sacra "Vater unser im Himmelreich" (Our Father, who art in heaven). 1st verse: a four-part piece, with cantus firmus in the soprano. In the first choral line the other voices begin with head imitation. 2nd verse: in four parts, with cantus firmus in the tenor.

The other three voices imitate very densely, and in each new line of the chorale another motif taken from the music of the relevant theme appears, while similar pauses occur between them in the cantus firmus. See the last musical example. 3rd verse: in three parts, with cantus firmus in the soprano and echoes of the chorale in the lower parts. 4th verse: bicinium with interchangeable parts (double counterpoint). 5th verse: in three parts, with cantus firmus in the tenor and "imitatio violistica" occurring later in the upper part. 6th verse: in three parts, with cantus fermus in the bass. 7th verse: in three parts, with cantus firmus in the bass and imitative and ornamented upper parts. 8th verse: in three parts, with ornamented cantus firmus in the bass. The ornamentation is arranged so that the notes of the cantus firmus remain on the accented beats, marked x in this example.

9th verse: in four parts, with decorated cantus firmus in the soprano.

Niederländisch Liedchen "Ach du feiner Reiter" (Dutch song "Ah you fine cavalier"). The song:

Through the seven variations on this melody the cantus firmus is ornamented in the soprano in the 2nd and 4th variations, becomes a bicinium in double counterpoint in the 3rd variation and undergoes other changes. In the bicinium the same part of the cantus firmus is heard in the lower part after each line of the song has appeared in the soprano, thus executing the same counterpoint, mostly on the dominant, which previously belonged in the soprano.

In the 5th variation we find the peculiarity of the "imitatio tremula organi". By changing the fingering one should create the effect of a tremulant, which causes the wind to vibrate in the organ-pipes to make the sound more vital, but this is only possible on small organs.

Further works: *Geistliche Variationen (Sacred variations)* on "Wir glauben all an einen Gott" (We all believe in the one God), "Warum betrübst du dich, mein Herz" (Why are you troubled, my heart), "Da Jesus an dem Kreuze stund" (As Jesus hung on the cross), "Herzlich lieb hab ich dich, O Herr" (Dearly I love thee, O Lord), "Christ lag in Todesbanden", (Christ lay in death's grim prison), "Jesus Christus, unser Heiland" (Jesus Christ, our savior), "Gelobet seist du, Jesus Christ; Christe, qui lux es et dies" (Praise be to thee, Jesus Christ; Christ, who art light and day), "A solis ortus cardine", "Veni, creator spiritus", "O lux beata Trinitas". Secular variations: "Weh, Windchen, weh" (Blow, little breeze, blow), "Est-ce mars" (Is it Mars), "Soll es sein" (If it should be), "Also geht's, also steht's" (As it is, so it remains). 10 Magnificats; Echoes, fugues, fantasies, canons.

Publishers: Bärenreiter; Breitkopf; Peters—*Weihnachtliche Barockmusik (Baroque music for Christmas)* ed. T. Fedtke; Schott.

HEINRICH SCHEIDEMANN

b. Wöhrden, S. Dithmarschen c.1596; d. Hamburg, early 1663

He probably received his first musical education from his father, who was organist at St. Catherine's Church in Hamburg. After studying with Sweelinck in Amsterdam from 1611 to 1614, he succeeded his father and also became church clerk. Apart from his organ works, some ornamentation of motets by other composers and a few keyboard pieces have survived.

Most important are Scheidemann's 35 chorale settings and the settings of the Magnificat in four verses, with which his short preludes or preambles with fugues cannot compare.

A number of the **Chorale settings** follow Sweelinck's form: cantus firmus in long, sustained notes, in the first verse often in the pedal, later in the soprano in a three- or four-part piece or in a bicinium. Examples of this are "A solis ortus cardine", " Es spricht der Unweisen Mund wohl" (The mouth of the unwise speaks well), and "In dich hab ich gehoffet, Herr" (In thee have I trusted, Lord). Scheidemann broadened this traditional form by ornamenting the cantus firmus in the soprano of four-part pieces, not only by means of the formal motifs familiar from Scheidt's work, but in an expansion which above all does justice to the expression of this "solo" voice. He emphasizes the typical solo characteristic of the upper part by making the lower parts in the pedal and the left hand into a compact, harmonic accompaniment, rather than letting them just imitate and anticipate the chorale melody. Finally the form of his settings expands into a kind of fantasia, with individual sections no longer separated by lines at the end of each but welded into a compound whole with dovetailed bridge passages—a form which was frequently used in northern Germany in the following centuries.

Publisher: Bärenreiter.

FRANZ TUNDER

b. Burg, Fehmarn, 1614; d. Lübeck, November 5, 1667

Tunder worked at the court of Gottorf and in 1641 became organist at St. Mary's in Lübeck. Apart from his organ works his cantatas for solo and choir are noteworthy.

Four preludes and fugues in G minor, F major, G minor and G minor. All four are similarly constructed: a unison or homophonic beginning in the prelude, four-part fugue—with a subsequent contraction of the opening of the theme in the third and fourth works—and transition to the final cadence which ends the fugue in the manner of the prelude.

Variations "Jesus Christ, unser Heiland" (Jesus Christ, our savior). Duration 8 minutes. Verse 1: a difficult piece in five parts, with cantus firmus in the upper part of the pedal. The last two lines of the chorale are first developed in 4/4 time, then in 6/4. Verse 2: Imitative movement, with cantus fermus in the tenor. Verse 3: cantus firmus in the bass. The upper parts imitate a theme which first appeared in the soprano:

Fantasia "Komm, Heiliger Geist, Herre Gott (Come, Holy Ghost, Lord God). Lengthy development of the chorale by ornamentating it and breaking it into small motifs. Sequential treatment mainly in the soprano and the bass, while the two inner parts are played on another manual. Anticipation sometimes occurs in the lower parts when the upper one pauses.

Further works: Variations: "Auf meinen lieben Gott" (On my dear God). Fantasias: "Herr Gott, dich loben wir" (Lord God, we praise thee), "Jesus Christus, wahr Gottes Sohn" (Jesus Christ, true Son of God), "Was kann uns kommen an für Not" (What kind of distress can strike us), "In dich hab ich gehoffet" (In thee have I hoped).

Publishers: Breitkopf; Kistner; Schott.

JOHANN JAKOB FROBERGER

bapt. Stuttgart, May 19, 1616; d. Schloss Hericourt nr. Montbéliard, May 6(?7), 1667

Froberger spent most of his life in Vienna as court organist, but also travelled to many countries, both as a student—of Frescobaldi in Rome—and as a performer. As a result his importance lies in mingling various national styles and disseminating them in German-speaking countries. His organ works far outweigh his few sacred vocal compositions.

Toccata in C major. This is an important and typical work in the following sections: 12 bars of toccata opening with runs and ornaments, ending in G major; a 28-bar fugal section with the following theme:

Another fugato of 18 bars on the same theme, but with a different time-signature:

and lastly the seven-bar finale, which returns to the toccata style.

The swift changes and in particular the relatively short homophonic first and last sections are characteristic of this composer's innumerable toccatas, in which he continued the form used by his teacher Frescobaldi. The contrast between the individual parts of the work gives it a stronger and livelier effect.

Ricercare in C major. In strict fugal form the first section presents a theme with sustained counterpoint:

The second section adds a new motif:

and the third section yet another:

Froberger's countless other ricercares are constructed on similar lines.

Further works: Capriccios, always with frequent changes of time-signature; songs; fantasias.

Publishers: Bärenreiter—*Ausgewählte Orgelwerke (Selected organ works)* ed. K. Matthaei; Coppenrath—*Toccatas, fantasies, ricercares . . .* ed. R. Walter; Heinrichshofen; Kistner.

MATTHIAS WECKMANN

b. Niederdorla nr. Mühlhausen, Thuringia, 1621;
d. Hamburg, February 24, 1674

Weckmann, a pupil of Schütz and Praetorius, was court organist in Dresden, Copenhagen and Dresden again, before becoming organist at St. James's Church in Hamburg in 1655. In 1660 he founded the city's Collegium Musicum modelled on a court chapel. He mainly wrote keyboard music, but his cantatas are also expressive works and worth hearing.

Weckmann composed in the widest variety of forms with many modifications. Only his canzonas retain for the most part the existing form with duple time, changing to triple in the central section.

Fantasia in D minor. This title conceals a fugue in several parts with a toccatalike conclusion, similar to the next work mentioned, which is described as a fugue. The themes of the first and second parts of the fugue spring from the same basic idea:

The same technique is to be found in his **Fugue in D minor,** where the first section more or less states the general theme which the other sections then carry on and vary with changes of rhythm and figuration. As these fugues are wholly uncomplicated and regular, just the themes are given below: Theme 1:

Theme 2:

Theme 3:

Further works: Canzonas, preambles, toccatas.
Publishers: Bärenreiter; Kistner.

JOHANN KASPAR KERLL

b. Adorf, Vogtland, April 9, 1627; d. Munich, February 13, 1693

Kerll studied in Vienna, and in Rome with Carissimi and Frescobaldi. He was then for 17 years music director at the electoral court in Munich, a post to which he returned after working as organist at St. Stephen's Cathedral in Vienna from 1677 to 1684. He was a virtuoso organist, and devoted most of his attention to that instrument. Some of his church works still exist, but his operas have all been lost.

Capriccio "Cucu" (1679). This is an exceptionally spirited and witty piece based on the cuckoo's call, heard four times in succession in a sort of exposition and therefore almost seems to be the theme. It starts in duple time, later moving to 6/4

and finishes in the original meter with perpetual repetitions of the cuckoo's song

Canzona in G minor. Only the theme appears in the dorian mode. This composition is in four parts and several sections, and is enlivened with a later contrasting theme in eighth-notes.

Modulatio organica. A collection of versets for the Magnificat in the eight church modes, formerly used to alternate voices and organ when performing the canticle, and therefore each cycle contains settings for seven verses. These little compositions partly quote the Gregorian Magnificat melody, but often their thematic structure is completely free. Most of them are to be performed on the manuals; where pedals are added they only provide supporting notes or the cantus firmus, as for instance in verse 4 of the hypodorian mode.

Further works: canzonas, toccatas, chaconne.

Publishers: Coppenrath—*Modulatio Organica,* ed. R. Walter; Doblinger; Peters—*Barockmusik Italiens (Baroque music of Italy)*, ed. T. Fedtke, *Orgelmusik aus drei Jahrhunderten (Organ music from three centuries)* Vol. 2, ed. T. Fedtke, and *Spielbuch für die Kleinorgel (Music for playing on the small organ)* ed. W. Auler.

The Hamburg organist JOHANN ADAM REINCKEN (b. Wildeshausen, Oldenburg, April 26, 1623; d. Hamburg, November 24, 1722) was a typical north German representative of the music of this period, his work bearing the stamp of the Sweelinck school through his teacher Scheidemann. He is known for his **Choral fantasia "An Wasserflüssen Babylon"** (By the waters of Babylon), which is 327 bars long and has a decorated upper part supported by imitative lower ones. He was alluding to it in 1720 when he heard J. S. Bach improvising on the same chorale and said: "I thought this art had died out, but I see that it still lives in you." Reincken composed another, similar **Fantasia** on "Was kann uns kommen an für Not" (What kind of distress can come on us) and a **Toccata.** Publisher: Breitkopf—*Sämtliche Orgel-*

werke (Collected organ works) ed. K. Beckmann.

Opposite him stands the south German SEBASTIAN ANTON SCHERER, (bapt. Ulm, October 4, 1631; d. ibid., August 26, 1712), who worked in Ulm as a musician, music director and cathedral organist. Almost all his **Eight cycles of intonations** follow the same plan: the first intonation stands out in decorated form and sounds like a little toccata, while the other parts of the cycle are fugal. His eight **Toccatas** adhere to Frescobaldi's style. Publisher: Schott—*Orgelwerke* (*Organ works*) ed. A. Pirro.

NICOLAS-ANTOINE LEBÈGUE

b. Laon, 1631; d. Paris, July 6, 1702

Lebègue was organist at St. Merry's in Paris from 1664 and court organist from 1678. He wrote pieces for the harpsichord, and organ works which he collected into books.

Mass for organ from his second organ book, c.1678. It contains five sections for the Kyrie, nine for the Gloria, two for the Sanctus, one for the elevation and two for the Agnus Dei. The form, as in the works of all the French 17th-century composers, is very complex: fugue, duet, trio, solo parts for Cornet, Vox Humana and Trumpet. The pieces are partly composed over a Gregorian cantus firmus, and partly invented with complete freedom.

Noëls variés (Variations on Christmas carols), from the third organ book. Like Daquin, he based these variations on Christmas carols having tunes with the simplicity of folksongs. "À la venue de Noël" (At the coming of Christmas):

Examples of the variations:

Publisher: Bärenreiter.

The French organ tradition continued with NICOLAS GIGAULT (b. Paris, end 1626; d. ibid., August 20, 1707) and his organ book of 1685. This *Livre de musique pour l'orgue (Book of music for the organ)* contains a collection of specific pieces for liturgical use which very frequently employ the Gregorian chorale. Publisher: Schott—*Orgelwerke (Organ works)*, ed. A. Guilmant, and *Liber organi I (First book for the organ)*, ed. E. Kaller.

GUILLAUME-GABRIEL NIVERS (b. prob. near Paris, 1632; d. Paris, November 30, 1714) was more important as a theoretician than prolific as a composer. Source editions of his organ books 1–3 have been published by Schola Cantorum, edited by N. Dufourcq.

In Italy BERNARDO PASQUINI (b. Massa di Valdinievole, Pistoia, December

7, 1637; d. Rome, November 21, 1710) continued Frescobaldi's and Rossi's work. He was organist at Santa Maria Maggiore, Ara Coeli and other Rome churches, and wrote **Toccatas** in various styles. While number seven, for instance, still strongly recalls Frescobaldi's style, numbers one and four present a new aspect, because they lay stress on imitation and interpolate homophonic episodes. The sixth toccata in G minor is very original in character, because of its complexity and contrasts, and creates a model later used by G. Muffat. Publisher: Zanibon—*Sette toccate (Seven toccatas)*, ed. A. Espositio.

Pasquini's two **Sonatas for two organs**—or two harpsichords, or harpsichord and organ—in G minor and F major are very beautiful. They are both in three parts and their only notation is a figured bass, so that it is left to the players to use their imagination and gift for improvisation to fill in the melody and the inner parts. Suggestions are offered in Durand's edition of this work, edited by F. Boghen. At about this time the name Bach first features in the history of organ music, in the person of JOHANN CHRISTOPH BACH (b. Arnstadt, December 8, 1642; D. Eisenach, March 31, 1703), an uncle of Johann Sebastian. His **44 Choräle zum Präambulieren** (44 chorales for playing as preambles) are fugal chorale preludes for use in church services, clearly bearing the mark of the experienced organist. Publisher: Bärenreiter.

DIETRICH BUXTEHUDE

b. Oldesloe, Holstein, or Helsingborg, 1637; d. Lübeck, May 9, 1707

He was organist in Helsingborg and Helsingör and in 1668 succeeded Franz Tunder as organist of St. Mary's in Lübeck. He was an imaginative composer of organ music and cantatas, and was a leading figure in the north German organ tradition, by virtue of his grandly conceived, complex toccatas and his chorale settings, which developed into fantasialike forms.

Free Works

Prelude, fugue and chaconne in C major. The prelude divides clearly into three: after the introductory runs and chords there is a short fugal section which gives way to another, homophonic, prelude. The fugue opens with freely moving runs and leads into the chaconne, where the ostinato in the bass is taken from the beginning of the theme.

Prelude and fugue in D minor, duration 6 minutes. The prelude only lasts for a few fast-moving bars, with a series of sixth-chords before the cadence, and goes directly into a vigorous fugue. The theme leads from its second entry into a contrasting one which then repeats. There follows a stately recitative and a short imitation before a second fugal section starts, using for its theme a somewhat altered version from the first fugue, now appearing in 3/4 time. Some fast pedal figures and runs on the manuals conclude this delightful work.

Prelude and fugue in D major, duration 6 minutes. After a brief opening section, derived from the broken D major triad, comes the theme of the fugue which at first seems rather simple, but is developed with a wealth of variety and can sound enchanting when played on more than one manual and with the right registration.

After some bars marked adagio comes a relatively long, independent piece of a kind rarely found in Buxtehude's work, which basically only consists of sequences:

The toccatalike finale which begins on F-sharp has some surprising harmonic modulations.

Like many pieces in D major by J. S. Bach, this work has a radiant, festive feeling which makes it stand out prominently among Buxtehude's prolific output, as does his Prelude and fugue in E major.

Prelude and fugue in E major. This work should be played more frequently because of its key, which is rarely found in Baroque organ music, but it is also important both musically and technically. The stormy opening is caught up into the very strongly rhythmic theme of the fugue:

Recitative solos for manuals and pedals lead into the Presto, one of those quick, imitative pieces for the manuals which composers like to insert and which require of the organist a sparkling amd immediately speaking registration, so that they are preferably played on the Positive (Rückpositiv) or Regal (Brustwerk), those employing small mechanisms with a short action. Then come two bars which bear the pretty but unmistakable direction "con discrezione". After a further section for the manuals in 12/8 time and a connecting Adagio, the work finishes with the

Allegro finale, once again in fugal form. Describing the individual sections like this does not, however, imply that this is a very extended and lengthy composition; in fact all the parts of this magnificently sculpted chain of movements follow quickly on one another and are all very short. They form a prime example of the so-called "north German toccata", in spite of its title *Prelude and fugue.*

Toccata in F major. This work, after the opening, brings

broken chords, echo effects and runs, together with a polyphonic five-part movement. There follows a fugue which ends with a final cadence played twice, almost identically, on F and B-flat.

Prelude and fugue in F-sharp minor. After the customary scales and chords comes a four-part movement with interesting harmonies. The fugue moves from Grave to Vivace and ends with runs in the style of a prelude.

Prelude and fugue in G minor. Introduction with runs in thirds and sixths on the manuals, above a pedal ostinato which appears six times. The theme of the fugue has the same range of a minor sixth and almost the same intervals as the ostinato. After another quick passage for the manuals, with the pedals joining in halfway through, the second fugue follows and a few added bars bring the piece to an end.

Further works: Toccata in F major, Prelude and fugue in F major, Prelude and fugue in E minor, Prelude and fugue in A minor, Passacaglia in D minor, Chaconne in C minor, Fugues.

Chorale settings

Buxtehude wrote a quantity of large settings; some develop each line of the chorale separately and are called fantasias, while others present the different verses one after the other, as in a partita. The shorter preludes usually have a partly ornamented cantus firmus in the soprano, but an exception is found in "Erhalt uns, Herr, bei deinem Wort" (Preserve us, Lord, by thy word) in the bass. Head imitation is employed less elaborately than in the works of his contemporaries.

Wie schön leuchtet der Morgenstern (How brightly shines the morning star) opens in three parts with the cantus firmus in the bottom part. In the repeat the tune appears in the top part with similar treatment of the other lines. The motif given here introduces the second chorale section where the cantus firmus appears in the soprano and continues in triplets. In the next section of 6/8 time the triplets form a fluidly moving background for this cohesive movement, the theme of which is the last line of the chorale—a descending scale through the entire octave. A kind of fugato fantasy, whose quantity of lively motifs traces once more the individual lines of the chorale, brings to an end this early example of the chorale fantasy, which was subsequently to attain unprecedented eminence.

Partita "Nun lob, mein Seel, den Herren" (Now praise the Lord, my soul). I. Four-part development with head imitation and cantus firmus in the soprano. II. In three parts, with cantus firmus in the soprano. III. Development similar to II. IV. cantus firmus in the pedals, with two imitative upper parts.

Magnificat in the dorian mode. Each verse is treated fugally, or at least contains imitative passages. Examples of the themes of verses two, four, five and eight (the last) are given in that order.

Publishers: Breitkopf; Peters; Schott—*Antologia Organi (Organ anthology)*, Vol. 10, ed. S. Margittay.

JOHN BLOW

bapt. Newark, Nottinghamshire, prob. February 23, 1649;
d. London, October 1, 1708.

Blow may have studied with Christopher Gibbons, a son of Orlando Gibbons. He was Westminster Abbey organist and court composer from 1668 to 1680 and again from 1695, and from 1699 also organist of the Chapel Royal. Most of his creative work lies in vocal music, such as motets, anthems, songs and odes. He was the teacher of Henry Purcell.

The voluntaries and verses in the complete edition of Blow's organ works embrace the most widely varied forms. There are simple fugal and imitative movements, fugues, fugatos, toccatalike forms reminiscent of the developments on the Continent since Frescobaldi, and a dialogue form resembling contemporary French compositions. These movements are not necessarily strict, but rather lightly put together to conform to harmonic requirements, for inconsequential parts are often suddenly inserted into the fugues. Nevertheless it would be wrong to deny these delightful pieces their beauty, musicality and spirit. Blow wrote for organs with one or two manuals.

The **Fugue in D minor** serves as an example of his fugal compositions. The theme is developed in the four parts and, obviously inspired by the chromatic element, distant keys and fugal insertions are soon encountered. Strong rhythmic figures contrasting with the theme characterize the second section and lend it virtuosity, while the thematic material of the introductory section is only tentatively referred to. What begins as a strict and serious work finishes as a relaxed concertante.

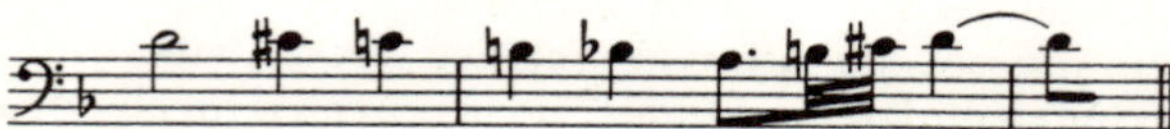

Voluntary for the double organ, in D minor. In the first movement the theme is treated fugally, with the bass part played sometimes on one manual, sometimes on the other. The second movement contains completely new thematic material which is imitated, and then rushes to its close in fast passage-work.

Verse for the Cornet and Single Organ, in A minor. The title indicates the desired registration: a solo part on the Cornet Mixture, i.e. 8′, 4′, 2 2/3′, 2′ and 1 3/5′, is contrasted with the other accompanying manual, on which the piece begins with the theme in dotted rhythms sounding like a march. Then the Cornet enters, also playing the theme at first, but later spinning out free figuration. The theme is thrown to and fro between the manuals like a ball and new ideas emerge, until the long and unusually static cadence brings the piece to a close.

Publisher: Schott.

CHRISTIAN RITTER

b. c.1650; d. prob. Hamburg, after 1725

Ritter was chamber musician and organist at the Halle court and subsequently in Dresden. From 1680 to 1682 and from 1688 to 1689 he lived in Sweden, where he was court music director. He wrote sacred choral music with and without accompaniment.

Sonatina in D minor. In this case the familiar title belongs to a compound work with strongly contrasting individual sections. It could equally well be called a toccata, and would in fact be more precisely described as such than as a sonatina. Its structure consists of passage-work with homophonic bars and a very colorful series of chords,

a fugue,

and a virtuoso bridge passage, mostly in two parts and in sixths, leading to an extended chordal cadence at the close. This work is obviously related to those of the north German school and is worthy of note for its technique of contrasting without causing a split in the music, and for its concentrated form.

Publisher: Kistner.

JOHANN KRIEGER

bapt. Nuremberg, January 1, 1652; d. Zittau, July 18, 1735

He was the younger brother of Johann Philipp Krieger, and was court organist in Bayreuth, music director in Greiz and finally church musician in Zittau. Apart from his organ and other keyboard works, many cantatas, songs and arias survive, but his instrumental works definitely occupy first place.

Toccata in C major. The introductory bars are homophonic with pedal solos. A chaconne-style section starts on the dominant, but its ostinato only appears in the soprano:

A long transition leads into the fugue which brings the piece to a close:

Prelude, ricercare, fugue and passacaglia. This is the only surviving work containing this rare combination of movements. It could be regarded as a suite if one substituted forms associated with organ music for the typical components of a suite. The prelude is not at all striking, but the ricercare is elaborated in strict, lucid style.

The *comes* appears immediately in inversion. The fugue works both with the main theme and with a second one introduced later, while the passacaglia consists of 16 variations over the ostinato motif:

Further works: Prelude and ricercare in G minor; toccatas; small preludes; fantasias.

Publishers: Kistner; Peters.

GEORG MUFFAT

bapt. Megève, Savoy, June 1, 1653;
d. Passau, February 23, 1704

Muffat received his musical education in France, Germany and Italy, where he studied with Bernardo Pasquini. After a period as organist at Molsheim in Alsace, he worked in Vienna, Prague and Salzburg, and in 1690 became music director at the court of the Bishop of Passau. He mainly wrote instrumental compositions and in that field was the most important south German composer of his time.

Apparatus musico-organisticus, 1690. His only published collection of organ music contains 12 toccatas, one chaconne, one passacaglia and two smaller pieces. In his toccatas he continues on the lines of Frescobaldi and Froberger with works which can be described as typically south German, in contrast to the north German style which reached its climax in Buxtehude. He uses the pedals very sparingly, and in fact they can be dispensed with altogether.

Seventh toccata, in C major, duration 9 minutes. The opening Grave goes at a solemn pace, like processional music:

and is followed by a fast section with a motif which alternates between the upper and lower parts, with simple supporting notes in the others, leading to several bars

of ascending and descending scales. Before the fugue a chordal section stands out in clear contrast to the other material. The compound fugue is a superbly fashioned work which gains momentum towards the end and has two themes separated by an interlude motif:

Second theme:

Both ideas are joined together artistically with the help of all available motifs and blend into an extremely dense close.

The eleventh toccata is constructed as follows: a homophonic introduction leads into a fugal section:

next comes a homophonic Adagio with slight imitation, a fugato with a two-part theme, and a final fugal Allegro.

Publishers: Coppenrath—*Apparatus,* ed. R. Walter; Peters; Schott—*Antologia organi,* Vol. 11, ed. S. Margittay.

JOHANN PACHELBEL

bapt. Nuremberg, September 1, 1653; d. ibid., March 3, 1706

After working in Vienna as assistant organist at St. Stephen's Cathedral, and then in Eisenach, Erfurt, Stuttgart and Gotha, he returned to his native city, where in 1695 he became organist at St. Sebald's. He was an important composer of organ music, especially because of his complex chorale settings.

Free Works

Prelude in D minor. This begins with the theme in the pedals, taken up and

imitated by both manuals. After this statement the theme is repeated almost identically in the dominant A major, and then dissolves into arpeggios. A peaceful middle section is followed by a strange passage in chords alone which leads in turn to the calm motion of the finale with its remote reference to the beginning of the work.

Aria Sebaldina. From the *Hexachordum Apollinis* which contains six of these arias. This aria consists of a simple, melodic theme with eight variations, mostly in

the upper parts, while the bass and its harmonies remain virtually unchanged. The variations are made in different ways: arpeggios with melodic top notes; two parts complementing each other and interrupted by rests in variation two,

rhythmic groupings (var. five),

fast runs in var. eight, and change of time signature in var. seven, which is in 9/8 time. This creates a wide variety of pieces, as in the **Ciaconas.** Here too the quantity of ornamental variations on a simple ostinato theme are a delight for both player and listener. Some of the themes:

Chaconne in D major

Chaconne in F major

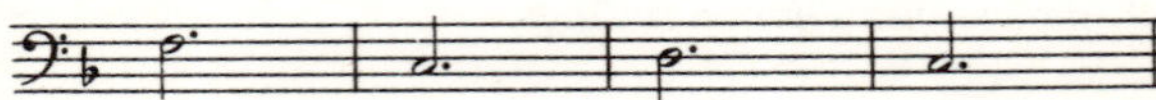

Chaconne in F minor

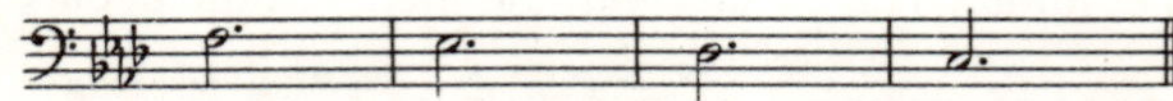

Ricercare in C minor. This form was already archaic in Pachelbel's day, but in this piece it enjoys a lovely and well-shaped late flowering: a chromatic theme is treated fugally and then reappears inverted, i.e. in a descending chromatic line. A new motif is also fugally elaborated and then both ideas are so joined together that the second theme is paired with the inversion of the first, and the first with the inversion of the second, the result being both convincing and most delightful.

Further works: preludes; toccatas; fugues; ricercares.

Pachelbel's countless **Chorale settings** are in a limited number of static forms, of which the most frequent is what we have already called "head imitation" and which was later to be called simply "Pachelbel form": Before the chorale opens in the soprano, or sometimes in the bass, the other parts start a fugue and develop the thematic material of the cantus firmus line before it appears in its entirety. There are also a number of choral fughettas in which the parts are fugally treated as in the previous form, not only at the beginning, however, but throughout, while the cantus firmus itself does not appear in its original form. The old bicinium and of course the partita also feature among these works.

A few examples of the form:

Vater unser im Himmelreich (Our Father who art in Heaven). Before each choral line appears in the soprano, the other three voices anticipate it (Pachelbel form), and the other lines are treated in the same way as the first, so that after all four parts have been heard together the work begins again in unison. The obvious danger of this form is that the continual stopping and starting again of the chorale lines can have a monotonous effect.

Wir glauben all an einen Gott. (We all believe in one God). Three-part development, the right hand embellishing the cantus firmus on its own manual and often rendering it unrecognizable, while the left hand sustains the two accompanying parts. Juxtaposing the cantus firmus and the part which develops out of it can illustrate the wealth of decoration:

Wie schön leuchtet der Morgenstern (How brightly shines the morning star). Three-part setting with head imitation. Cantus firmus in the pedals.

Nun lob mein Seel den Herren (Now praise the Lord, my soul). Cantus firmus in the middle voice of this three-part work.

Dies sind die heil'gen zehn Gebot (These are God's ten commandments). Fugue with the following theme:

The **Magnificat fugues** in all eight church modes are developed by Pachelbel with a great wealth of thematic shaping, for the themes are clearly distinguishable while the fugal development remains true to contemporary style.

Publishers: Bärenreiter—*Ausgewählte Orgelwerke in 6 Bänden (Selected organ works in 6 volumes)*, ed. K. Matthaei and W. Stockmeier; Kistner; Peters—*Orgelwerke (Organ works)*, ed. A. M. Gurgel; Schott—*Anthologia organi (Organ anthology)* Vol. 10, ed. S. Margittay.

VINCENT LÜBECK

b. Padingbüttel, Hanover, September 1654 or September 29 (Feast of St. Michael), 1656; d. Hamburg, February 9, 1740

As the son of an organist he was familiar with the instrument from an early age. In 1673 he was appointed organist in Stade and in 1702 at St. Nicholas's in Hamburg. His works—which include organ compositions, some cantatas and a Clavier Übung (Keyboard practice)*—clearly show Buxtehude's influence, but do not equal the latter's wealth of imagination and sense of form.*

Prelude and fugue in C major. The prelude's solo part is in the pedals, while simple harmonic sequences are played on the manuals. The first fugue has the following theme:

Thereafter comes a section for manuals only and the work ends with a second fugue.

Prelude and fugue in E major, duration 6 minutes. A brilliantly inspired opening, the theme of which continues in the left hand and pedals. After a short toccata comes a four-part fugue, a short episode on the manuals marked *Rückpositiv Scharf* (Positive, sharp mixture), a further four-part fugue with a sustained counterpart and a few additional final bars.

Partita "Nun lasst uns Gott dem Herren" (Now let us to God the Lord). Work with six variations, the first three and the last two verses leading into each other without a break as in a fantasy. Verse four has a freely constructed upper part, somewhat dependent on the cantus firmus.

Further works: Prelude and fugue in D minor; Prelude and fugue in G minor; Chorale settings.

Publishers: Bärenreiter; Breitkopf, ed. K. Beckmann; Kistner; Peters; Schott—*Antologia Organi (Organ anthology) Vol. 9, ed. S. Margittay.*

HENRY PURCELL

b. prob. London, summer or autumn 1659; d. London November 21, 1695

Purcell, a pupil of Blow, is acknowledged as the greatest English composer. In 1679 he became organist at Westminster Abbey and in 1682 at the Chapel Royal. The large catalogue of his works includes operas, odes, music for plays, cantatas, anthems and instrumental works for keyboard, strings and wind. In order not to paint a false picture of his magnificent compositions which were suffused with Baroque brilliance, it should be stressed that the few organ works of his which survive are virtually without importance in relation to his complete output, and are mentioned here for continuity's sake.

Organ setting of "Old Hundreth" (Praise God). The choral begins in the tenor, is imitated in the soprano and returns to the tenor. The cantus firmus is then fully developed in the bass, while in the second section the soprano carries the development. A distinctive tone-color is used for each recurrence of the cantus firmus, either by using another manual or dividing the same one.

The **Voluntary in C** should only be performed on two manuals, as it relies on dialogue and echo effects in the upper voice between Cornet and Soft Organ, which consists of Diapason and Flute. In addition the Sesquialtera should be used for the bass figure. The basic theme:

His other works are similarly constructed.

The **Trumpet tunes,** which are often played, are short pieces in the style of popular trumpet tunes and were originally intended for the harpsichord, but it should be said that with a blaring Trumpet stop they can sound brilliant on the organ.

Publishers: Breitkopf; Hinrichsen; Schott; Peters *(Orgelmusik aus drei Jahrhunderten (Organ music from three centuries),* Vol. 2, ed. T. Fedtke.

JOHANN KUHNAU

b. Geising, Erzgebirge, April 6, 1660; d. Leipzig, June 5, 1722.

Kuhnau was a "Kruzianer"—a pupil at the choir school of the Holy Cross Church in Dresden—and then studied law. In 1684 he became organist at St. Thomas's, and in 1701 cantor—as a predecessor of J. S. Bach—and music director of Leipzig University. His interesting keyboard sonatas were composed as a kind of program music for Biblical stories, and he also wrote many church cantatas.

Kuhnau's works are distinguished by their simple, clear lines. All his preludes are basically planned on chords, and his fugues are the good, workmanlike products of an experienced contrapuntalist, though with the exception of the toccata in A major they lack any great power to communicate.

Toccata in A major. This is a comprehensive and many-sided work built on manual runs, solo passage work for the pedals, homophonic intermezzi and recitativelike episodes. Each individual section introduces new motifs which admittedly often amount to no more than cadential formulas. There follows a regular fugue on a theme in 3/4 time, leading into a recitative, toccatalike finale.

Publisher: Kistner.

GEORG BÖHM

b. Hohenkirchen, nr. Ohrdruf, September 2, 1661;
d. Lüneburg, May 18, 1733

He was organist at St. John's in Lüneburg and wrote cantatas, piano suites, organ works and songs. He was well known and famous for his expressive chorale settings, highly decorated with coloratura in the manner which J. S. Bach was to bring to perfection a generation later.

Prelude and fugue in C major. Its structure is based on the north German models: pedal solo at the beginning, changing chords which can tempt a performer to create echo effects, and a fugue theme obviously inspired by Buxtehude. The fugue closes swiftly with a deceptive ending in A minor, some runs and a final cadence.

The **Prelude and fugue in A minor,** and the **Prelude and fugue in D minor** with two fugues, are constructed on similar lines.

Though on the basis of these works Böhm cannot be compared with Buxtehude, his short compositions are often vividly effective and their lines are expressive, as for instance his **Prelude and fugue in D major** in the form of a French overture, or the **Capriccio in D major.**

Further works: Prelude, fugue and postlude in G minor.

Böhm's **Chorale settings** are very much more noteworthy than his free works, and the "Böhm manner" of chorale treatment is even used to describe elaborate coloratura of the cantus firmus. Though significant, this is only one side of the chorale output which stems from his later years in Lüneburg; he also wrote chorale preludes in fugal form, and partitas which conform to contemporary fashion.

Vater unser im Himmelreich (Our Father, who art in heaven). This is in four parts throughout, i.e. the music of the lower parts is composed for either three or four voices, depending on whether or not the cantus firmus appears in one of them. The pedal-less beginning

already shows that ornamentation will be found in the other parts as well, since the cantus firmus only enters in the sixth bar. The following isolated examples give an idea of the ornamentation of the cantus firmus:

Another working of the **Our Father** consists of two verses, the first of which again contains coloratura, but for manuals alone, while the second carries the cantus firmus line by line in the pedals with the upper parts using head imitation.

Further arrangements with embellished cantus firmus: "Wer nur den lieben Gott lässt walten" (He who relies on God's compassion) and "Gelobet seist du, Jesu Christ" (Praise be to thee, Jesus Christ).

Partitas—i.e. variations on a chorale melody or a chorale text, usually employing imitatively worked motifs, include "Ach wie nichtig, ach wie flüchtig" (Ah how weary, ah how fleeting), "Herr Jesu Christ, dich zu uns wend" (Lord Jesus Christ, turn to us), "Freu dich sehr, o meine Seele" (Rejoice greatly, oh my soul), "Christe, der du bist Tag und Licht" (Christ, who are both day and light).

Publishers: Breitkopf; Kistner; Peters—*Weihnachtliche Barockmusik (Baroque Christmas music)*, ed. T. Fedtke; Schott—*Antologia Organi (Organ anthology)*, Vol. 9, ed. S. Margittay.

NICOLAUS BRUHNS

b. Schwabstedt, Schleswig, December 1665; d. Husum, March 29, 1697

Bruhns both travelled, and worked for a long time in Copenhagen as a violin and organ virtuoso, before he was appointed organist at the city church of Husum in 1689. He is said to have performed his cantata "Mein Herz ist bereit" (My heart is ready) for bass voice, violin, and continuo on his own, by simultaneously playing the continuo part on the organ pedals, the violin part with his hands and singing. Apart from his organ works his church cantatas should be mentioned, for in many of them his expressive powers enabled him to produce great and compelling effects.

Three preludes and fugues in E minor, G major and E minor. Bruhns was a pupil of Buxtehude's, and these three preludes, which can be more accurately described as toccatas, contain the typical north German alternation of passage-work, chords, short, slow phrases, improvised episodes and fugal sections. We find sustained counterpoint in the first fugue of I, a theme in varying time-signatures in the first and second fugues of II, and double pedals in the first fugue of II. The echo effects and the brilliant chains of broken chord arpeggios in I and II have great charm. The "great" prelude and fugue in E minor is a particularly splendid work of penetrating musical substance, and holds equal rank with the great works of Buxtehude.

Nun komm, der Heiden Heiland (Come, redeemer of our race), a chorale arrangement of 143 bars (!), is a somewhat drawn-out yet rewarding fantasy on the Advent chorale, and also Bruhns's only surviving chorale. As his teacher so often did, he wrote his solo top part for the Positive (*Rückpositiv*), two parts for the *Ober-*

werk and the fourth for the Pedals. The first line of the chorale alone appears six times in 29 bars and the second line 13 times in 50 bars. The third is fugally developed in the 6/4 rhythm of a gigue.

Publishers: Breitkopf, ed. K. Beckmann; Kistner; Peters.

JUAN CABANILLES (CAVANILLAS) (bapt. Algemesí nr. Valencia, September 6, 1644; d. Valencia, April 20, 1712), was cathedral organist in his home town. He was a master of 17th-century Spanish organ music by virtue of his many compositions, which include tientos, passacaglias, toccatas and batallas, which are literally "battle-music", using the Spanish Trumpet—a horizontal reed stop. Publisher: Müller—*Ausgewählte Orgelwerke (Selected organ works)*, ed. G. Doderer, which also contains batallas by other composers.

ANDRÉ RAISON (b. before 1650; d. Paris, 1719) continued the small-scale, practical and colorful forms of the French tradition in his two organ books of masses and other pieces. He was also a teacher, in that he clearly marked how provincial organists should play with the newly introduced registers, which may be why he changes his registration so frequently within a piece of music, and even from bar to bar. He loved to use dialogue and echo effects, which give his compositions an elegant, worldly air. The "Christe—trio en passacaille" (trio in passacaglia) of his **Mass in hypodorian mode** uses the theme J. S. Bach took up for his passacaglia BWV 582:

Publisher: Schola Cantorum.

JACQUES BOYVIN (b. Paris, c. 1653; d. Rouen, June 30, 1706), the organist of Rouen Cathedral, also collected his compositions in 1700 in two volumes entitled *Pièces d'orgue (Organ pieces)*. He made no new contribution to organ literature, but his works exude the transparency, concision and charm of late 17th-century French organ music.

DANIEL CRONER (b. Kronstadt, 1656; d. 1740) was one of the few organ composers in Transylvania, where he lived all his life, after his studies in Germany. His organ works survive in books of organ tablature and consist of choral preludes in imitative form, toccatas, fugues—which two descriptions often merge—preambles, fantasies and verses for the Magnificat, which together form a collection of briefly and graphically developed pieces for the organist. The resemblance to the organ compositions of J. E. Kindermann (1616–1655) gives rise to some doubt about the authenticity of Croner's work. Publisher: Breitkopf—*Altsiebenbürgische Orgelmusik (Old Transylvanian organ music)*, ed. A. Porfetye.

FRANZ XAVER MURSCHHAUSER (bapt. Zabern, July 1, 1663; d. Munich, January 6, 1738) was music director at the Church of Our Lady in Munich. His works introduce a genial element into organ music, as exemplified by his particularly lovely and heartfelt **Variations on "Lasst uns das Kindelein wiegen"** (Let us rock the little child), which introduces the cuckoo's song. He also wrote the customary preambles, toccatas and fugues. Publisher: Peters—*Spielbuch für die Kleinorgel (Music book for the small organ)*, ed. W. Auler.

JOHANN SPETH (b. Speinshart, Upper Palatinate, January 9, 1664; d. Augsburg, after ?1719) showed the same tendencies. His publication of organ music *Ars magna consoni et dissoni* was subtitled *Organisch-Instrumentalischer Kunst- Zier- und Lust-Garten (Garden of art, adornment and pleasure for the instrument of the organ)*, and he called the ten toccatas in it "Musikalische Blumen-Felder" (Musical fields of flowers)—another indication that organ music was gradually freeing itself from the severity of imitation and the tyranny of the cantus firmus. The toccatas are beautiful pieces which sound like improvisations, as the following example from the fourth one shows:

Publisher: Schott—*Zehn Toccaten (Ten toccatas),* ed. G. Klaus.

To the same stylistic trend belong JOHANN CASPAR FERDINAND FISCHER (b. nr. Schlackenwerth, Bohemia, c. 1665; d. Rastatt, August 27, 1746), who for instance published cycles in all eight church modes in his collection *Blumen-Strauss (Bouquet of flowers).* Publisher: Coppenrath—*Musikalischer Blumenstrauss (Musical bouquet),* ed. R. Walter; and GEORG FRIEDRICH KAUFFMANN (b. Ostramondra, Thuringia, February 14, 1679; d. Merseburg, early March 1735), with his imitative chorale preludes and fugues. Publisher: Peters—*Weihnachtliche Barockmusik (Baroque Christmas music),* ed. T. Fedtke.

JOHANN NICOLAUS HANFF (b. Wechmar nr. Mühlhausen, Thuringia, 1665; d. Schleswig, end 1711 or early 1712) left seven chorale arrangements, which all provide for the prominent cantus firmus to be played on a Solo, or Positive manual. Publisher: Breitkopf, ed. K. Beckmann.

FRANÇOIS COUPERIN

b. Paris, November 10, 1668; d. ibid., September 11, 1733

Like Bach, Couperin was the most important scion of a musical family with wide ramifications. At the age of 17 he was already organist at St. Gervais and at 25 one of the four organists of the royal chapel at Versailles. His work as a teacher resulted in L'art de toucher le clavecin (The art of playing the harpsichord) *of 1716—a work essential for understanding the music of that period, and with which J. S. Bach was also familiar. His works for harpsichord and his chamber music outweigh his organ compositions, and he also wrote sacred and secular vocal music.*

Organ pieces, consisting of **2 masses,** for parish and monastic use.

Each of these masses contains 21 individual items, including for instance five verses for the Kyrie and nine for the Gloria, each in a different form and tempo, and with different registration precisely given, as in de Grigny's and Clérambault's works which appeared shortly after Couperin's. In many of these pieces the thematic treatment is completely free, but some are built on a Gregorian plainsong chorale. Examples of the form: fugue (fughetta), duet, trio, solo with accompaniment, dialogue.

Examples of the registration: Fugue to be played on Reed stops; Krummhorn solo (Récits de chromhorne); dialogue between Trumpet and Krummhorn; Tierce (here Cornet Mixture) in the tenor; Plein jeu: Organo Pleno.

The first mass, more grandly and musically more richly conceived than the second, is constructed as follows:

Kyrie: plainsong of the first Kyrie in the tenor, fugue on Reed stops, Krummhorn solo, dialogue between Trumpet and Krummhorn, plainsong.

Gloria: Et in terra pax—plainsong; Benedicimus te—little fugue on the Krummhorn; Glorificamus te—duet on the Tierces; Domine Deus, rex coelestis—dialogue between the Trumpets, Bugles (clairons), or 4 trumpet stops, and Tierces of the Great Organ, and the Bourdon with the Larigot of the Positive; Domine Deus, agnus dei—trio for two sopranos on Krummhorn and bass on Tierce; Qui tollis—Tierce in tenor; Quoniam—dialogue on Vox Humana; Tu solus altissimus—dialogue for trio of Cornet and Tierce; Amen—dialogue for Organo Pleno (grands jeux).

Offertory: on Organo Pleno.

Sanctus: plainsong in canon; Cornet on solo (récit de cornet).

Benedictus: Krummhorn in the tenor.

Agnus: plainsong alternating in bass and tenor.

Deo gratias: little Organo Pleno (petit plein jeu).

These pieces are strikingly and completely different from the contemporary works written for the same ecclesiastical purpose in Germany. In France the customary court style of the harpsichordists also was dominant in the church, and its grace and charm, together with a fluidity and lightness which often hides behind richly ornamented solo parts, lent to this sacred music a cheerfulness and even playfulness which in the German tradition, born as it was of quite a different spirit, was for the first and only time to appear in Mozart's church sonatas.

Offertory on Organo Pleno (sur les grands jeux) from the first mass, duration 8 minutes. This is the only compound piece in either mass, and is in three sections: A has the following theme:

After the Organo Pleno opening comes a dialogue between Great and Positive with the same theme. B, in minor, with the motif:

Fugal beginning with further fugal insertions, first strictly in three parts, then in four. C, in major, a sort of gigue:

Fugal beginning in two parts on the positive, then the fugue continuing in four parts on the Great Organ, followed by a dialogue, as in A, and a final reprise.

Though they are so different in musical expression, all three themes are amazingly similar and surprisingly simply constructed, which gives the work its strong cohesion. A: fifth-octave, transition to dominant; B: Fifth-tonic and third, also moving to dominant; C: tonic-fifth, the latter already treated as the dominant.

The **Second mass,** for monastic use, also consists of 21 individual pieces, with similar construction and musical form as the sections of the first mass.

Publishers: Bärenreiter; Schott.

LOUIS MARCHAND

b. Lyon, February 2, 1669; d. Paris, February 17, 1732

Marchand was a musical prodigy, who at the age of 15 was engaged as an organist in Nevers, moving in 1693 to a post in Auxerre, and from 1708–1714 was court organist at the Chapelle Royale in Paris. His fame as a virtuoso and improviser was widespread, and in 1717 he went on the well known tour of Germany, without competing with Bach on the harpsichord. His only surviving compositions are harpsichord and organ works, bearing the mark of the virtuoso in their deft, elegant and sometimes rather shallow writing.

Marchand's works, collected in five organ books, show a modest versatility in form and character, as do those of his contemporaries, and indeed he sometimes extended the scope and joined several individual pieces together. All these compositions are solidly constructed.

Plein jeu (principal chorus) in six parts, with duets, trios and fugues; a **Quartet,** which should be played on three manuals and pedals to give all the parts their due—a difficult technical feat to perform, not used again until the end of the 19th century; **Tierces en taille** (Tierces in the tenor), **Récits** (Solos) etc. A **Basse de trompette** (Bass Trumpet) with a definite fanfare character sounds very lovely and makes dialogue effects by using a Cornet to vary the tone-color, with the accompanying manual and the Trumpet. The opening:

An arrangement of the Te deum in short single verses is very interesting, as is also the **Dialogue,** duration 9 minutes, composed in 1696. Its varied small movements, which in themselves form a dialogue, are joined together into a larger form. The opening is emphatically chordal:

the "Récit" (Solo) which follows and a dialogue inserted later both also use broken chords. As counterparts come the "Lentement" (lento) in minor and the "Légèrement" (leggero) in 6/4 time, to which are added a few bars of "Gravement" (grave). In all, this is a good attempt to avoid the dangers of writing too small-scale a piece for organ.

Publisher: Schott.

NICOLAS DE GRIGNY

b. St. Pierre le Vieil nr. Rheims, September 8, 1672;
d. Rheims, November 30, 1703

This composer was widely known as an organist, and already held such a post at St. Denis in Paris in 1693, moving to Rheims Cathedral in 1698. In his only book of compositions he demonstrates a stricter and more serious method of expression than do his French contemporaries, and gives an impression of being more loftily aristocratic and at the same time more spiritual.

First organ book, 1699. Contains a mass, and hymns for the principal feasts of the church year.

As with Couperin, pieces in the **Mass** with Gregorian cantus firmus (such as the first Kyrie in the tenor in five parts, a fugue on the Kyrie, "Et in terra pax" and the first "Sanctus") alternate with free compositions such as duets, trios, fughettas, tenor solos and dialogues between various voices and registers.

De Grigny wrote five-part movements "Dialogue à 2 tailles de cromorne et 2 dessus de cornet pour la communion" (Dialogue between 2 tenors on Krummhorn and 2 sopranos on Cornet for the Communion) which, as the title shows, are to be played on two manuals, while the pedals just play ground notes. This is most probably the inspiration for J. S. Bach's five-part Fantasy in C minor, because Bach knew and admired de Grigny's works. In France this fantasy "à la Grigny" is frequently played to this day.

The **Hymns** published with the mass—"Veni, creator", "Pange lingua", "Verbum supernum", "Ave maris stella" and "A solis ortus" are without exception four- or five-part arrangements of chant melodies, with the Gregorian cantus firmus mostly developed as a tenor part in the pedals. Further verses follow, generally fugues with themes taken from the cantus firmus, duets, dialogues, solos etc. referring to the theme. Here is an example of some of the themes of the "Verbum supernum":

Verse 1:

Verse 2, fugue:

Verse 3, solo:

Publishers: Bärenreiter; Schott.

LOUIS-NICOLAS CLÉRAMBAULT

b. Paris, December 19, 1676; d. ibid., October 26, 1749

This organist and harpsichordist worked at St. Sulpice and in his later years more and more at the royal court. He was also very active as a teacher. Apart from his organ works he was most successful with his cantatas, motets and trio sonatas and was clearly influenced by Couperin.

Suite in dorian mode in seven movements. "Grand plein jeu": a largely homophonic movement in four parts. "Fugue": in four parts with rich ornamentation.

"Duo": voices in canon. "Trio": with one solo part and *Vorimitation.* "Basse et dessus de trompette": Trumpet stop alternating in bass and soprano. "Récits" (Solos): dialogue between Krummhorn and Cornet. "Dialogue sur les grands jeux" (Dialogue on full organ): homophonic introduction, then short duet sections with change of manual.

The **Suite in hypodorian mode** is also in seven distinct movements: the "Plein jeu" (Principal chorus) in short spells of "lentement" (lento) and "gay". The duet and trio are quite like those movements in the *Suite in dorian mode,* while in the "Basse de cromorne" (Bass with Krummhorn) the reed sound remains confined to the bass part, and the upper voices are either imitative or just provide supporting chords when the bass is heard. "Flutes"—a new little piece for the Flute stops—sounds quite enchanting, especially with good registration to make the innumerable trills sound like a flight of birds. The last bars:

The "Récit de Nazard" (Solo with Nasard) in pastoral rhythm with a Solo Mixture stop in the fifth, is followed by the "Caprice sur les grands jeux" (Capriccio for Organo Pleno), which has a dancelike motif and, like several of Clérambault's works, lacks any serious reverence. Both suites are interesting compositions, with a fresh musical impetus.

Publishers: Bärenreiter; Schott.

PIERRE DU MAGE

b. Beauvais, November 23, 1674; d. Laon, October 2, 1751

Marchand's most famous pupil was organist in Saint-Quentin and at Laon Cathedral, but left this career to become a government official. His first organ book is the only one of his two Livres d'orgue *(Organ books) to survive, and in fact contains the only existing compositions by him of any kind. They belong stylistically within the framework marked out by his teacher and his teacher's contemporaries.*

This book, published in 1708, contains a **Suite in dorian mode.** But the church modes were not used any more at this time; this suite is in fact in D minor. As always when a sequence of major items is put together, the contrast between the individual pieces attracts special attention. After the "Plein jeu" (Principal chorus) in two parts, come the "Fugue" in four parts, the "Trio", "Tierce en taille" (Tierce in the tenor), "Basse de trompette" (Trumpet in the bass), "Récit" (solo), "Duo" marked "fort gai" and the final "Grand jeu" (Organo Pleno). In the last movement the first and last sections are in duple time with dotted rhythms and runs as in a French overture, while the middle section is in three time, and its various tone-colors on the Great organ, Positive and Swell create completely different effects. The pedals are rarely used independently and only in the "Tierce en taille" do they maintain an obbligato part.

Publishers: Bärenreiter; Schott.

JEAN-ADAM GUILAIN, whose biographical dates are wholly unknown, was probably called J. A. Guillaume Freinsberg. In 1706 he published organ settings for the Magnificat, collected into **4 Suites.** While he followed contemporary tradition in form and registration, it is remarkable that he deviated from it by not writing settings for the mass. Publisher: Schott—*Pièces d'orgues (Organ pieces),* ed. A. Guilmant.

JEAN-FRANÇOIS DANDRIEU (b. Paris, 1682; d. ibid., January 17, 1738) wrote a collection of settings for the Magnificat and the Offertory and variations on Noëls (Christmas carols). Surprisingly, these are written in church modes, beginning with D minor and ending with A major. This is a really practical book for an organist to use in church services. Publisher: Schott—*Premier livre de pièces d'orgue (First book of organ pieces),* ed. A. Guilmant and A. Pirro.

GEORG PHILIPP TELEMANN

b. Magdeburg, March 14, 1681; d. Hamburg, June 25, 1767

Telemann first studied jurisprudence and taught himself music. He took up his first post in 1704 as organist at the New Church (St. Matthew's) in Leipzig. After some years as music director in Sorau and Eisenach, in 1712 he became director of church music at St. Catherine's in Frankfurt-am-Main, and in 1721 music director of the five main churches in Hamburg, where he remained until his death. He wrote numerous cantatas and motets for use in church worship, passion music, masses and oratorios, but his chamber and orchestral works are even more extensive. His operas, serenades, secular cantatas and songs should also be mentioned.

Telemann's organ works occupy only a modest place within the scope of his entire instrumental output, and no conclusions about the quality of his other compositions can therefore be drawn from them.

The **Trio sonata in D major,** originally titled *Sonata au 2 Clavier con Pedal (Sonata for two manuals and pedals)* is Telemann's most important work for organ. In the four movements he combines the stylistic elements of late Baroque, such as contrapuntal elaboration, flowing movement and expressive chromatics with those of the emerging "style galant" in the rondolike finale. The impassioned "Grave" of the first movement is followed by a "Presto" with grand instrumental gestures which could just as well have come from a Baroque trumpet concerto:

The "Andante" employs the chromaticism already mentioned to intensify its expressive and often imitative lines, and thereby attains a rare intensity. In contrast, the light, bubbly "Scherzando" finale dances past in merry thirds with some surprise triplet effects.

The **20 small fugues** printed together in 1731 are attractive little four-part works which are easy to play and were intended by Telemann as teaching material. Here too he combines traditional polyphony, which rarely survives beyond the exposition of the fugue, with the homophonic style of his other instrumental music.

A collection of chorale preludes titled **48 fugierte und verändernde Choräle** (48 chorales with fugues and variations) has survived. It consists of 24 chorale tunes used twice each, first in three parts in Pachelbel's style with imitation at the beginning of each line of the chorale, and then in two parts like a bicinium. The chorale melody is written in large note-values, and its contrasting counterpoint is often rhythmic and lively. Some examples:

Ach Gott, vom Himmel sieh darein (Ah God, in mercy look from heaven) in the three-part version uses chromatic sequences when imitating the theme, in order to emphasize the imploring element in the text.

Christus, der uns selig macht (Christ who gives us blessing) is a bicinium, using a siciliano rhythm as counterpart, as often occurs in Telemann's Christmas and passion music:

Jesus meine Freude (Jesus my joy) reflects the spiritual content of the text in the illustrative motion and leaps of the accompaniment.

A final mention should be made of a cantabile version of **Nun komm, der Heiden Heiland** (Come, redeemer of our race) and two captivating trio settings of **Nun freut euch, lieben Christen gmein** (Rejoice, dear Christians together).

Publishers: Bärenreiter; Peters.

BOHUSLAV CERNOHORSKY

bapt. Nimburg, Bohemia, February 16, 1684; d. Graz, July 1, 1742

He was the son of an organist, and first studied theology. In 1703 he entered the Franciscan Order in Prague. It was during stays in Italy that he appeared as a musician, and on his return became choirmaster of St. James's monastery in Prague. Of this "father of Bohemian music," as he was often called in his native country, few works remain although he was composing throughout his life, because a fire in St. James's monastery in 1754 destroyed them. He was clearly inspired by the south German masters, among them Kerll, and became the starting point for a brief independent musical movement in Bohemia. Some fugues and one toccata in C major survive from his works for organ.

The **Toccata in C major** begins with imitative diatonic passage-work over an organ point on C, repeated on G and moving into a cadence with scales in the pedals. The last bars marked *grave* are strongly chromatic and homophonic with considerable retardation.

The **Fugues,** especially the two works in A minor and D major, present agreeable, flowing themes in their expositions and thoroughly develop them with a musical enthusiasm which tends to overshadow their noticeable harmonic polish.

The personality and compositions of this early Bohemian master also deserve a mention because of the wide influence of his pupils. The most important of those who wrote organ music were JOHANN ZACH (B. Celákovice nr. Brandeis, Bohemia, November 13, 1699; d. Ellwangen, May 24, 1773) and JOSEF SEGER (b. Repín nr. Melník, March 21, 1716; d. Prague, April 22, 1782), the latter having written toccatas, preludes, fantasias and fugues. Publishers: Orbis; Peters—*Orgelmusik aus drei Jahrhunderten (Organ music from three centuries),* Vol. 2, ed. T. Fedtke, *Alte tschechische Orgelmusik (Old Czech organ music),* ed. J. Smolka; Schott—*Antologia organi (Organ anthology),* Vol. 12, ed. S. Margittay.

JOHANN GOTTFRIED WALTHER

b. Erfurt, September 18, 1684; d. Weimar, March 23, 1748

Walther was a friend and pupil of J. S. Bach and like him worked for a time in Weimar. From 1707 he was city organist and music teacher to the princes and from 1721 court musician. He wrote chorale settings and concertos, of which the latter are the more valuable as compositions. His Musicalisches Lexicon (Musical dictionary) *published in 1732 is an important reference book.*

Toccata with fugue in C major. Begins with flowing scales,

followed by a chordal section which runs into the free recitative finale without interruption and in the same tempo. The fugue has two themes, the first of which

is stated and developed, after which the second more fluid theme is briefly developed and then immediately combined with the first. The close is rapid and surprising.

Organ concertos. Like J. S. Bach, Walther made transcripts of concertos for organ, mostly concerti grossi by composers such as Albinoni, Gentili and Torelli, which seemed to him significant. The resultant solemn, concertante works sound excellent on smaller organs as well.

Concerto in A minor after Torelli. Vivace in loose concerto grosso form, with frequent interchanges between tutti and solo. Adagio, actually more an interlude than an independent movement, and Allegro, again in concerto grosso form, with the following theme:

Walther's **Chorale settings** are exactly like the standard compositions of the second half of the 17th century in form and content. Their skillful technical construction and melodic tunes create a style akin to folk music.

Further works: Preludes and fugues.

Publishers: Bärenreiter; Breitkopf; Kistner; Peters—*Orgelmusik aus drei Jahrhunderten (Organ music from three centuries)* Vol. 2, ed. T. Fedtke, *Weihnachtliche Barockmusik (Baroque Christmas music)*, ed. T. Fedtke.

GEORGE FRIDERIC HANDEL

b. Halle, February 23, 1685; d. London, April 14, 1759

While still studying law, Handel was already cathedral organist in Halle, and was then engaged as violinist and harpsichordist in Hamburg. His further studies took him to Italy, where he visited Florence, Rome, Venice and Naples. In 1710 he went to London via Hanover. Apart from a few, his many operas are rarely given, but he is immortalized as a composer of oratorios, orchestral and chamber music and solo cantatas. He surpasses his exact contemporary J. S. Bach in his simple yet grandiose spans of melody, but did not reach the same spiritual depth.

Works for solo organ

Handel left very few works for solo organ, but his **Six fugues** composed in 1720 represent an important discussion of a form in which he showed his virtuoso mastery in the choral fugues of his oratorios. These are inventive pieces, each strongly characterized by its subject. The following example is the theme of **Fugue no. 5 in A minor,** published by Breitkopf and edited by D. Heilmann:

Works for organ and orchestra

Handel's **Organ concertos** are considered by many music-lovers as prototypes of the organ concerto. Principally because they are easy to play and require a small orchestra—mostly strings and two oboes—these attractive works are widely performed today, but they were already generally known and played in his lifetime and shortly after his death, especially in England.

Handel himself used to play them with the orchestra during the intermissions of his oratorio performances, which may have caused the popular, melodic qualities in his oratorios to pass into these concertos. They are all in four movements like chamber sonatas, rather than three like normal concertos. The composer obviously took a delight in writing this mellifluous music with its flowing, virtuoso groups of figures and runs. Slow, expressive themes are rarer here than melodic motifs. In form they follow the Italian concerto grosso by alternating tutti and solo. The organ part is only sometimes written out, and then usually in two parts. In the ad libitum sections the performer was expected to improvise. The figured bass accompaniment which is sometimes necessary has to be played by the organist if a second organ or harpsichord is not available to act as a continuo instrument.

Among his numerous organ concertos the six each in Op. 4 and Op. 7 are the most important. While Op. 4 originally bore the title "Concertos for harpsichord or organ", so allowing for performance on a pedalless positive organ, Op. 7 needs a two-manual organ with pedals. Further collections also contain concerti grossi by Handel revised by editors for organ and orchestra.

Op. 4 was published in London in 1738.

Organ concerto in G minor Op. 4/1, duration 16 minutes. Larghetto e staccato: shortly after the introduction of the main theme

come four bars marked "solo ad libitum"

to be ornamented by the organist. In the course of the movement new motifs appear and are adopted by the organ as well as the orchestra. The movement closes with some adagio bars modulating to D major.

The Allegro's main theme is in eighth-notes, but a second, calmly flowing idea joins in later. Extended virtuoso solo passages for the organ, mostly *piano,* are interrupted by the whole orchestra answering with its contrasting *forte.* This contrast also applies to the number of parts, as the solo has few and the tutti many. Adagio, for organ alone (organo ad libitum). The orchestra only joins in the final chord. Andante, with variations on its theme, first in harmonic variations, then with figuration which escalates to 32nd-note runs.

Organ concerto in B-flat major Op. 4/2, duration 12 minutes. A tempo ordinario, e staccato: a short, homophonic movement with dotted rhythms throughout, moving through a transitional bar marked *Adagio, e piano* to the Allegro. After the orchestral introduction, the organ takes up the theme and at once continues it in sixteenth-note runs.

There is a charming exchange and echo with a short motif:

and the whole movement is basically very playful. Adagio, e staccato. A six-bar interlude with organ figures over sparse chords in the strings.

Allegro, ma non presto. The terse, symmetrical theme is elaborated into a concentrated final movement,

characterized by changes of rhythm between sixteenth-note triplets and sixteenth-notes.

Organ concerto in G minor Op. 4/3, duration 10 minutes. This differs from the other organ concertos, in that in the first and third movements the tutti in strings and oboes is contrasted with a concertino by the violin and cello. In this pure concerto grosso method the little concertino even takes over the whole concerto function, while the organ simply accompanies.

After the somewhat strict and stiff Adagio opening comes a rhythmically pulsating Allegro in which, as in the fourth movement, the organ again dominates and represents the concertante element.

After the Adagio, again without organ solo, comes the Gavotte allegro in a measured dance step. The solo part is rich in figured ornamentation.

Organ concerto in F major Op. 4/4, duration 15 minutes. For a long time this was played more than any other organ concerto, probably because of its uncomplicated form and direct, agreeable, expressive spontaneity.

Allegro: theme:

The following motif, which sounds like tone painting, introduces the middle section of the piece, which is entirely dominated in the strings by the first four notes of the theme, while the organ plays figures on it.

Andante. Melodious movement with orchestra, consisting of introduction and finale connected by a weaving tune on the organ. Handel's original registration for this piece was "Open Diapason, Stopt Diapason and Flute."

Allegro. Fugal opening in the orchestra:

while the organ enters with new motifs. This cannot be called a fugue, because in its subsequent entries the theme is only hinted at and does not appear again in full until the final tutti.

The **Concerto in F major** Op. 4/5, duration 8 minutes, is an arrangement of four movements of the flute sonata in F major from Op. 11. The movements are Larghetto, Allegro, Alla siciliana and Presto, the last including two bars at the beginning and two at the end which do not appear in the flute sonata.

Organ concerto in B-flat major Op. 4/6, duration 12 minutes. This was first composed for the harpist Powell to play with orchestra and later arranged for organ. Instead of the oboes used elsewhere, two flutes join the strings. Andante allegro: A lucidly built concerto movement, its theme is equally intensively elaborated in both orchestra and organ, and its recapitulation is clear.

Larghetto. An orchestral framework with ostinato elements surround the intensely melodic unison solo on the organ. Allegro moderato. The theme

is developed in a terse form with frequent short changes between tutti and solo.

The other collection of six organ concertos—Op. 7—appeared posthumously in 1761.

Organ concerto in B-flat major Op. 7/1, duration 10 minutes. The Andante begins with an effective contrast between organ and orchestra. This movement is constructed like a chaconne.

Over the ostinato motif

the variations are played out in both orchestra and organ. The Andante again employs the ostinato from the first movement, now in triple time, as the basis for variations.

Largo e piano. A short movement, starting in chords over steadily moving quarter-note figures in the bass, repeated twice. The solo part is formed from the following motif:

Just after the Largo the marking "Fuga ex B" appears in the autograph, but only one page of the fugue has been written out. Sadly, this challenge to improvise a fugue is ignored in most performances.

Bourrée allegro. Even in this last movement the bass reminds us of the ostinato from the first movement, while the top part plays the following theme:

The glorious brilliance of this work, which makes it stand out from the others of the same kind, is due to the way it is composed—for instance with full chords on the organ in the first movement—and to the structural links between the first, second and last movements.

Organ concerto in B-flat major Op. 7/3, duration 11 minutes. Allegro. The entire movement obtains its motifs from bars 1, 2, 3 and 5 of the theme.

Spiritoso. A freely formed fugue:

Minuets I and II. Both are three-part song forms and should be performed as Minuet, Trio and Minuet da capo.

Organ concerto in G minor Op. 7/5. Allegro ma non troppo, e staccato:

Andante larghetto, e staccato. This has the following ostinato bass:

Minuet:

The Gavotte is another arrangement of the last movement of the Concerto in G minor Op. 4/3.

This collection also contains Op. 7/2 in **A major:** Overture, A tempo ordinario, Allegro; Op. 7/4 in **D minor:** Adagio, Allegro, Organo ad libitum, Allegro—identical to the Presto from the third Suite for harpsichord:

and Op. 7/6 in **B-flat major:** Pomposo, A tempo ordinario.

Handel's other organ concertos have no opus numbers and are generally known as concertos 13 to 16:

No.13, in **F major:** Larghetto, Allegro, Larghetto, Allegro. Also known as the "Cuckoo and nightingale" because of the birdsong figures in the first Allegro:

No.14, in **A major:** Largo e staccato, Organo ad libitum, Andante, Grave, Allegro. This is an arrangement of the concerto grosso Op. 6/11.

No.15, in **D minor:** Andante, Allegro. Published in 1797. The organist was supposed to improvise an Adagio and a Fugue between the two given movements.

No.16, in **F major:** Overture, Allegro ma non troppo, Adagio, Andante, Allegro, March. This is a rearrangement of a concerto grosso for two concertante wind bands, and the large forces—strings, two oboes, two bassoons, two horns—produce a superb sound. It is not certain whether the march should be played as well as the preceding Allegro or replace it as the finale.

Handel's London publisher, Walsh, commissioned an arranger to turn four other concerti grossi into organ concertos, and keyboard reductions also exist, from which W. Mohr has reconstructed the **Concerto No.17 in D minor.**

Publishers: Bärenreiter—Ops. 4 & 7, ed. K. Matthaei, and No.17, ed. W. Mohr; Peters—Nos. 13–16, ed. W. Mohr, and *Orgelmusik aus drei Jahrhunderten (Organ music from three centuries)*, Vol.2, ed. T. Fedtke; Schott—*Antologia organi (Organ anthology)* Vol.9, ed. S. Margittay.

JOHANN SEBASTIAN BACH

b. Eisenach, March 21, 1685; d. Leipzig, July 28, 1750

After his first short engagements in Weimar, Arnstadt and Mühlhausen he became chamber and court organist and later concert master in Weimar, music director in Köthen and, from 1723, cantor and music director at St. Thomas's in Leipzig. The significance of the man who has often been called the greatest musical genius ever cannot be even approximately sketched in such a small space. On the one hand he perfected polyphonic composition and figured bass music, and on the other it has recently become apparent that his music also pointed towards the future. His comprehensive organ works form the nucleus of organ music of all periods and the ultimate yardstick for both composers and players. But Bach was a prolific composer in almost all fields of music, as witness the compositions in the BWV, among them the four surviving volumes of cantatas for the church year, chamber and orchestral music, and oratorios. He achieved his greatest fame as an organ virtuoso, while composing was automatically expected of a church musician and court music director.*

*BWV = *Bach-Werke-Verzeichnis (Index of Bach's works)*, cf. W. Schmieder's *Thematisch-systematisches Verzeichnis der musikalischen Werke von Johann Sebastian Bach (Systematic thematic index of J. S. Bach's musical works)*, Leipzig 1950, 5th edition 1973. The Roman and Arabic numbers, e.g. II/7, denote the volume and number of the work in Peters' collected edition.

Works for organ solo

Free works

Preludes, toccatas, fantasias and passacaglia with fugues; fantasies, trios, pastorals, concertos; trio sonatas.

Prelude and fugue in C major BWV 547, II/7, duration 11 minutes. A very unified plan consisting of the theme:

and an approximate inversion in the pedals:

Developing only one idea gives the prelude an unusually coherent air, and as this work unfolds in one long breath it is not easy to listen to with concentration. Its goal is three seventh-chords before the cadence, C_7, B-flat$_7$ and G_7. In the peaceful fugue, in contrast to the prelude, the second part comes in after only one bar. The manuals alone carry the exposition and its repeat in inversion on the dominant, and shortly after, original and inversion are combined.

The harmonies build up to the pedal entry which states the theme in augmentation, and the piece ends over a pedal point.

Prelude and fugue in C major BWV 545, II/1, duration 6 minutes. Organo pleno. A brilliant outpouring of musical runs, controlled by a master's hand, beginning in the pedals and leading into a regular fugue. Bach had first intended the second movement of the C major trio sonata to be played as a middle section between this prelude and fugue. See example in the section on Bach's trio sonatas.

Prelude and fugue in C major BWV 531, IV/1, duration 6 minutes. A unified prelude on a simple thematic model opening as a pedal solo, mainly with broken chords. Fugue in 4/4 time and four parts.

Opening of the Prelude and fugue in C major BWV 545 from the Bach-Gesellschaft edition

Toccata, adagio and fugue in C major BWV 564, III/8, duration 14 minutes. The first section of the toccata consists of one of the most magnificent pedal passages in all organ literature, introduced by runs on the manuals. Then follows a kind of prelude based on the quoted theme and the motif as its thematic material. There is an interesting grand cadence formula on the minor subdominant. The Adagio—a decorated tune with sustained accompaniment in the left hand and the pedals which has the Italian sensuous sound of a slow Vivaldi movement—leads into a harmonically exciting Grave. Here transitional and often dissonant stacks of chords finally modulate into C major.

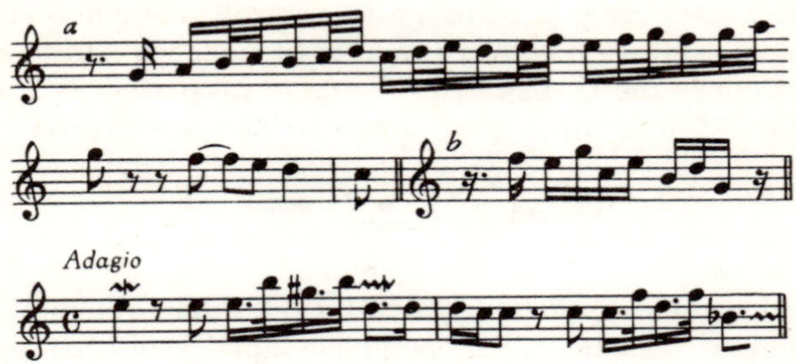

The swift fugue develops normally—in spite of which, or perhaps because of which, it is thrilling—until the last development, when the theme is heard in G major on the pedals.

Then the part-writing breaks up and the toccata style of the opening returns. The fugue is a work of great clarity and transparency, even for a listener unaccustomed to polyphonic composition.

Fantasia and fugue in C minor BWV 537, III/6, duration 8 minutes. This starts with a pedal point on C with the three upper parts entering fugally

until the new motif appears.

After modulating to the dominant the first ten bars are repeated in G major with the upper parts exchanging voices first soprano, alto, tenor; then tenor, soprano, alto. The motif is used extensively in the second section as though to punctuate the gentle repose of the whole piece with sighs. After this expressive prelude follows the fluent fugue in common time. After the exposition a second theme enters as a chromatically rising fourth and dominates the whole central section, only to disappear in the transition to the finale, leaving the field clear for the first theme until the conclusion is reached.

Prelude and fugue in C minor BWV 546, II/6 duration 12 minutes. The prelude can stand comparison with the masterpieces of Bach's Leipzig period—BWV 547 in C major, 548 in E minor, 544 in B minor and 552 in E flat major.

Section B, in small concerto grosso form, contains a fugato with sustained counterpoint and references in triplets to section A. The fugue may be contrapuntally simple, but its musical beauty cannot be so easily evaluated. Apart from those on E flat and F, the only entries are in the tonic and dominant.

Prelude and fugue in D major BWV 532, IV/3, duration 10 minutes. The prelude is a brilliant and magnificently designed piece in three sections. Examples here are a) scale runs and broken chords in D major, and b) the rhythm of a French

overture in F-sharp minor. The Alla breve is a preludelike middle section full of sequences, flowing into the final Adagio. The fugue states a theme which seems completely out of character for Bach.

The development, however, does not strictly adhere to the rules but imbues the theme with a uniquely brilliant life by varying the brightness and position of the keys and never letting its swift pace falter. The fugue runs with this thrilling impetus, as though on a steel spring, to its climax in a pedal solo, lending Bach's authority to this vital, imaginative piece of organ virtuosity.

Prelude and fugue in D minor BWV 539, III/4, duration 7 minutes. A simple prelude in 4/4 time on the manuals, without any great development of the opening theme, and a fugue based on the violin fugue in the 1st violin solo sonata in G minor with richly figured playful episodes between the individual thematic sections.

Toccata and fugue in D minor BWV 538, III/3, duration 14 minutes. This is wrongly called the "Dorian toccata," when the key is pure D minor. The toccata can also be described more accurately as a prelude, because the characteristics of that form are present and those of the toccata are not. The same applies to the Toccata in F major BWV 540. The original manuscript marking for the change of manual between Oberwerk and Positive survives. As there is no rest to allow either hand to change the stops for the pedals, one must conclude that the registration of Oberwerk and Positive were equally strong but distinct, so that the pedal registration could remain the same. The sixteenth-notes running through the entire prelude give this work a monumental grandeur if they are not played too quickly. The theme:

The fugue

has two sustained counterpoints:

Stretti already appear at the beginning of the development and soon after in the G minor counterpoint. This work is a real miracle of the composer's art: apart from the theme and counterpoints, very few "free" notes occur and those only fleetingly. The effect of the closing bars is achieved by the piling up of chords over the harmonic pedal on the dominant A.

Toccata in D minor BWV 565, IV/4, duration 9 minutes. This is Bach's only toccata which really deserves the name in the sense of the north German Baroque toccata. The rests in the first bar and the runs and arpeggios which follow,

the fugal section set apart by its meter, and the final resumption of the toccata elements in the last bars give this composition that expressive versatility which singles it out, even from among Bach's works, as a masterpiece molded by a strong and skillful hand. The theme of the fugue:

It is not because of its content that this toccata was and still is underestimated and even despised, but because for decades it was almost the only piece which was or could be played, and hearing the same work over and over again can irritate even a well-disposed listener.

Prelude and fugue in E flat major BWV 552, III/1. See pp. 85 under "Part Three of Clavierübung."

Prelude and fugue in E minor ("The Wedge Fugue") BWV 548, II/9, duration 14 minutes. Constructed like a concerto grosso in the clearest form with striking motifs. The themes: Section A

Section B

Section C

It is superfluous to describe how these three themes follow each other, and the resultant modulations, because all is readily grasped even at a first hearing.

The theme of the fugue seems to have been created by mirroring progressive intervals. After a conventional exposition the development is mixed with concerto grosso form, for Section B is presented in runs and turns of the highest virtuosity. Interestingly, the recapitulation of the fugue is identical to the exposition; this is unique among Bach's fugues and is presumably modelled on the recapitulations in the preludes, which intensify their unified form.

Prelude and fugue in E minor ("The Cathedral Fugue") BWV 533, III/10. A terse prelude in common time, full of pedal solos, and an equally short, lucid fugue, clearly constructed and easy to listen to, on a rather melancholy theme which enters three times.

Toccata and fugue in F major BWV 540, III/2, duration 15 minutes. It begins with a two-part canon in the upper voices over a pedal point on F, followed by a long monologue for pedals. Both are then repeated on C and lead into the main section with the following motif which divides into three short segments, the first

theme appearing in D minor, A minor and G minor. The double fugue is in four parts: the first theme is stated, then the second, and soon both ideas are combined, leading to a broad climax.

Prelude and fugue in F minor BWV 534, II/5, duration 9 minutes. Begins as a

trio with imitation in the upper parts and an ostinato motif for the pedals, repeated in the dominant with exchanged parts. The fugue is in five parts, and the suspense felt in the theme lends it a dramatic air:

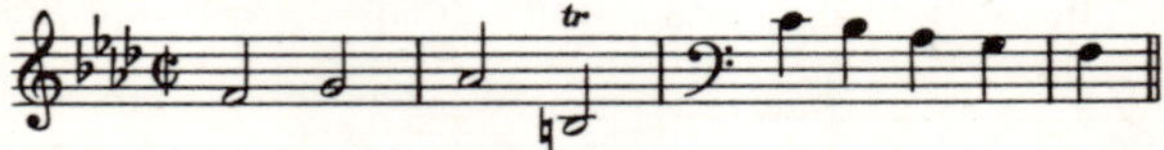

Prelude and fugue in G major BWV 541, II/2, duration 8 minutes. Vivace: brilliant runs of broken chords and scales, beginning in unison with a repeated motif in the pedals,

A dancelike fugue on the theme,

and towards the end a stretto which is easy to hear. In one copy the last movement of the E minor trio sonata BWV 528 has been inserted as a second movement between the prelude and the fugue.

Prelude and fugue in G major BWV 550, IV/2, duration 7 minutes. The prelude is strongly unified in its thematic material because it only uses the first four notes of the theme heard at the beginning:

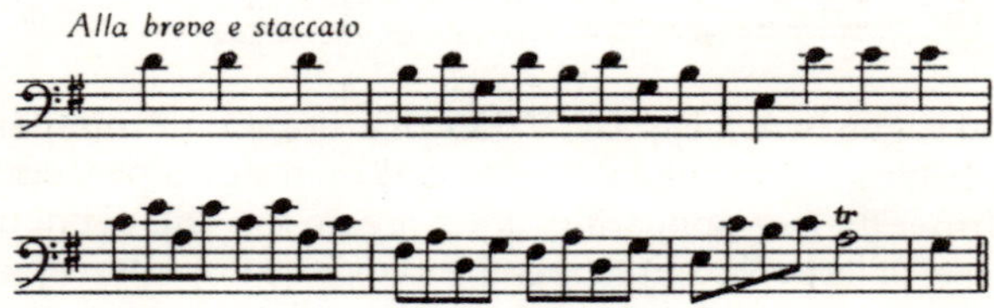

A bridge passage marked Grave leads into the dominant, in which the theme of the fugue begins:

Fantasia and fugue in G minor BWV 542, II/4, duration 13 minutes. The grandiose recitative lines of the fantasia sweep forward in a broad stream, not in parts, but often jumping from unison into polyphony and back. It is twice interrupted by a small, imitative, four-part phrase, first in D minor to A major and then in G minor to D major.

Next follows the most "modern" feature in all Bach's work: a spiralling modulation through many keys, starting with D major and creating a crescendo which continues on the manuals as the parts increase in number from two to five. Other deceptive cadences, harmonic anticipations and swift enharmonic changes of direction make this fantasia one of the most interesting and boldest of Bach's harmonic creations.

The fugue in four parts:

Soon after comes an episode motif

which has no connection with the theme but seizes rhythmically on the passagework of the interludes.

Prelude and fugue in G minor BWV 535, III/5, duration 7 minutes. Its runs and arpeggios make it sound like a toccata, and unlike other preludes it has no consistently unified thematic material. In bar 10 the fugue theme is already hinted at in the pedals, and eventually develops into a regular fugue with toccata features at the end.

Prelude and fugue in A major BWV 536, II/3, duration 7 minutes. The prelude is in 4/4 time, begins with broken chords and then flows peacefully to its close without any further themes appearing. If the organist is skillful enough it does not sound fast, in spite of its persistent sixteenth-notes. The fugue transports the listener into a pastoral idyll and exudes a spirit which anticipates Mozart.

In particular its three-part middle sections are of supernatural beauty.

Prelude and fugue in A minor BWV 543, II/8, duration 10 minutes. This is a particularly convincing example of a work with both sections born of the same idea: Prelude:

Fugue:

First come runs consisting of chord components and diatonic sequences and alternating between manuals and pedals. The fugue is very transparent, especially in the development, long stretches of which are only in three or even two parts. Towards the end the part-writing dissolves into runs as in the prelude, and thus both pieces finish in similar style as well as having closely related themes.

Prelude and fugue in B minor BWV 544, II/10, duration 12 minutes. Pro organo pleno: the theme appears in a wealth of arabesques which weave into garlands, an effect only achieved in a relatively slow tempo. A fugato B-section turns it into concerto grosso form; its theme contains the same diminished fifth leap as the theme in the A-section.

After completing the exposition, the fugue is developed at length on the manuals, and a repeated counterpoint figure in a new rhythm is added in the finale:

Passacaglia and fugue in C minor BWV 582, I/7, duration 14 minutes. Over an ostinato theme

Bach creates a musical texture rich in figures and melodic and harmonic phrases. See the example under "Passacaglia" in the Glossary. A clearly differentiated middle section written for manual alone, sounding like unison, obviously divides into three large groups of variations. Its effect is intensified by the fugue immediately following.

At first its course is more or less regular—there are just two inserts in the development, in E-flat and B-flat—but Bach brings it to a sudden end with a stroke of genius: a Neapolitan sixth-chord which occurs without warning a few bars before the close. The final cadence, like the exact center of the passacaglia, has the two pitch extremes of C in the pedals and C^3 in the manual and brings the work to an end in majestic splendor.

This passacaglia crowns the centuries-long development of that form because Bach was not only exceptionally endowed with imagination but also gifted in knitting together musical forms, so that he was able to join a fully-grown fugue on the same theme onto what is already a lengthy musical structure. As a result the whole composition gives the effect of greater suspense rather than greater length.

Fantasia in C minor BWV 562, IV/12, duration 5 minutes. In five parts throughout, based on the following theme

with two parts in each hand requiring different registration on the two manuals. In this way the inside parts emerge more clearly than if played on one manual, which would naturally produce a more imposing sound. The fugal exposition is in C minor and G minor, then briefly in B-flat major and E-flat major. Interludes and development follow and soon lead to a repriselike conclusion.

Fantasia in G major BWV 572, IV/11. In three movements: Très vitement (very fast): a unison introduction in 12/8 time with echo effects. Gravement (grave): five-part homophonic movement of dramatic grandeur. Lentement (lento): arpeggio figuration over an ostinato descending bass:

Trio in D minor BWV 583, IV/14. This is Bach's only independent trio. The first section is formed from one theme, imitated alternatingly by the two upper parts. The pedals sustain the theme and otherwise simply provide support. The second section contains new motifs, while the finale returns to the first theme.

Pastorale in F major BWV 590, I/8. Shepherds' music for Christmas with restrained imitation in the upper parts.

The pedals sustain a pedal point in the basic harmonies. Three other little movements are added to make a suite: a stately, chordal piece in C major, a solo for the right hand in C minor which can be made to sound like a shepherd's pipe, and a sparkling fugue leading back into the original F major.

Concerto in A minor BWV 593, VIII/2, duration 11 minutes. This is not an original work, but a transcription for organ of the Concerto for 2 violins Op. 3, No. 8 by Vivaldi. Bach was probably interested in arranging the typical violin figures for his very own instrument, but apart from that he revered Vivaldi and had learned form and structure from the latter's works. The three movements have the following themes: I (no marking)

Concerto in D minor BWV 596, duration 12 minutes, published separately by Peters. Another transposition from a Vivaldi work, this time the Concerto Op. 3, No. 11 for two violins, cello and string orchestra. His model here is a splendidly successful composition, even more so than the previous concerto, with its dynamic opening, an expressive fugue theme worthy of Bach, and a final Italianate, cantabile Largo, which Bach took up in the Adagio of his C major Toccata. The rushing finale with the entries chasing each other sounds more pedestrian on the organ, for nothing can replace a violinist's lightness of touch; but otherwise this work transfers to the organ without a hitch, with just one extra bar in the introduction. The themes are: Introduction

The **Six trio sonatas** BWV 525–530, I/1–6, for two manuals and pedals, were probably composed at the beginning of Bach's Leipzig period for the musical and technical education of his son Wilhelm Friedemann and other pupils. Though the sonatas are outwardly identical, each containing two quick outside movements and a slow middle one, they are very different in mood, and as they are consistently written in three parts they can effortlessly attain to any realm of expression. For technical reasons the pedals do not participate as much as the two upper parts in the development of the themes and in the filigree ornamentation. Marcel Dupré said that "They are a true synthesis of all symphonic forms used to this day," and in 1802 Nikolaus Forkel wrote enthusiastically, "One cannot say enough about their beauty." Because the individual forms are repeated in various ways, the themes and movement headings are given here:

1st sonata in E flat major, duration 14 minutes.
1st movement (no tempo marking):

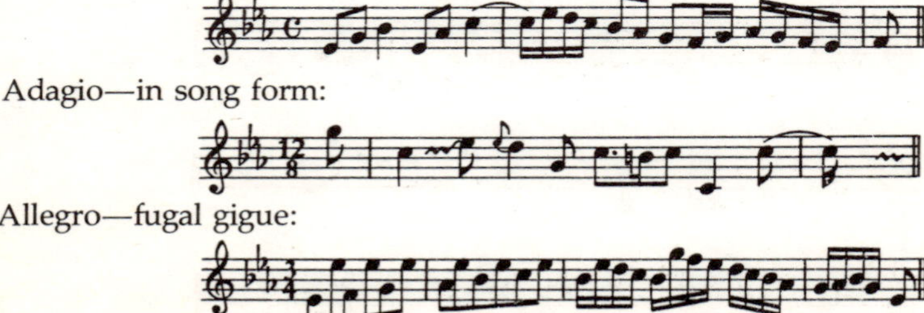

2nd sonata in C minor, duration 12 minutes.
Vivace—concerto form:

Largo:

Allegro—fugal, with stretto:

3rd sonata in D minor, duration 13 minutes.
Andante—da capo, with 2 themes:

Adagio—also used as the middle movement of the triple concerto in A minor:

Vivace—rondolike form:

4th sonata in E minor, duration 10 minutes.
Adagio-Vivace—fugal:

Andante:

Un poco allegro—fugal in all 3 parts:

5th sonata in C major, duration 15 minutes.
Allegro—rondolike form (ABABA):

Largo:

Allegro—with a second theme. The first theme:

The second theme:

6th sonata in G major, duration 14 minutes. Vivace—with exposition, 2 developments and recapitulation:

Largo in song form:

Allegro—with a second theme. The first theme:

The second theme:

Pieces from Bach's **Musical Offering** BWV 1079 of 1747 and the **Art of Fugue**

BWV 1080 of 1749/50 appear sporadically on the programs of organ concerts. We know that Bach did not indicate whether he wanted his last works to be played on one or several specific instruments, with the exception of the trio sonata from the *Musical Offering* for flute, violin and continuo. Fresh attempts are therefore always being made to perform these works in different guises, including on the organ. Although some parts, like the six-part ricercare from the *Musical Offering* or the four first fugues from the *Art of Fugue,* appear by theme and construction to have been written for keyboard, they are outweighed by those pieces which cannot be transposed for organ without distortion. Most call for strings and some for woodwind, and the most successful complete performances of both compositions are in fact those dependent on a string sound, with or without woodwind. For this reason it is superfluous to go into either of these late works of Bach's any further.

Further works: Toccata and fugue in C major BWV 566, also in an E major version; Prelude and fugue in C minor BWV 549; Prelude and fugue in A minor BWV 551; Prelude in G major BWV 568; Prelude in A minor BWV 569; Eight little preludes and fugues BWV 553–560, probably not by J. S. Bach. Fantasia with imitation in B minor BWV 563; Alla breve in D major BWV 589; Canzona in D minor BWV 588. Fugue in C minor BWV 574 on a theme by Legrenzi; Fugue in C minor BWV 575; Fugue in G minor ("The Little Fugue") BWV 578; Fugue in B minor BWV 579 on a theme by Corelli. Concertos in C major and G major BWV 595 and 592, after Johann Ernst of Saxony-Weimar; Concerto in C major BWV 594, after Vivaldi.

Chorale Settings

Little Organ Book; Part 3 of the *Clavierübung* (Organ Mass);
the Leipzig Chorales; the Schübler Chorales; Chorale Variations.

The **Little Organ Book** BWV 599–644, V is entitled "Little organ book, wherein is given direction to a beginning organist to perform a chorale in all ways and to become skillful in the use of the pedals, for in these chorales the pedals are treated in an obligato manner. To the honor of almighty God alone and for the instruction of my neighbor." It contains 46 organ chorales (the original plan was for 164) for the church year. Almost all these little gems of Bach's art are composed on one motif, and in many cases this motif symbolizes either the text of the chorale or some representative word from it. One can easily recognize the motif of joy: often ♩♫ ♩♫ or some quick phrase; sorrow: ♫ ♫ or chromatic scales, or some specific event depicted in the text, such as the Resurrection: rising fourth or fifth, the coming down to earth: a falling line, the Fall: descending intervals, and the wingbeat of angels: ascending and descending scales, which illustrate it visibly as well. The 17th-century doctrine of "figures" was to provide explanatory points of reference but also to leave scope for initiative in many respects. The symbolic content of numbers, and contrapuntal peculiarities like the treatment of canons also enter into this. The following examples refer to these motifs:

599 "Nun komm, der Heiden Heiland" (Come, redeemer of our race) in A minor, with cantus firmus somewhat ornamented in the soprano.

600 "Gottes Sohn ist kommen"—"Gott, durch deine Güte" (The Son of God is come—God, in thy goodness) in F major, with cantus firmus in canon in the soprano and bass. 601 "Herr Christ, der ein'ge Gottes-Sohn"—"Herr Gott, nun sei gepreiset" (Lord Christ, the only Son of God—Lord God, now be praised) in A major, with cantus firmus in the soprano.

602 "Lob sei dem allmächtigen Gott" (Praise to almighty God) in F major, with cantus firmus in the soprano.

603 Puer natus in Bethlehem" (A boy is born in Bethlehem) in G minor, with cantus firmus in the soprano.

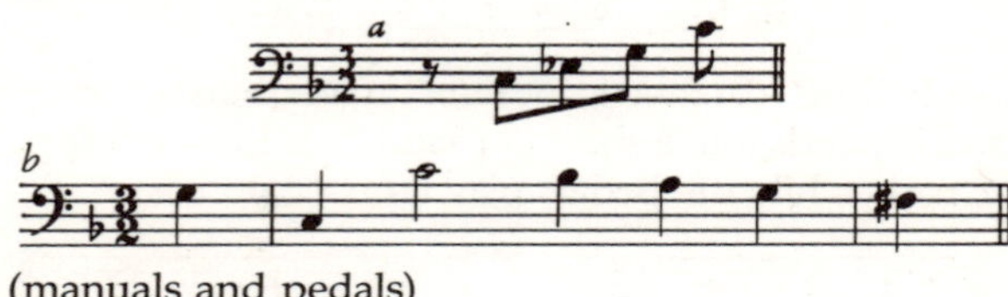

(manuals and pedals)

604 "Gelobet seist du, Jesu Christ" (Praise to thee, Jesus Christ) in G major, with cantus firmus ornamented in the soprano.

605 "Der Tag, der ist so freudenreich" (The day of exaltation) in G major, with cantus firmus in the soprano.

606 "Vom Himmel hoch, da komm ich her" (I come from heaven above) in D major, with cantus firmus in the soprano and the characteristic leaps of the "joy" theme in the pedals.

607 "Vom Himmel kam der Engel Schar" (From heaven came the angel host) in G minor, with cantus firmus in the soprano and ascending and descending lines in manuals and pedals to symbolize the beat of wings.

608 "In dulci jubilo" in A major, with cantus firmus in canon in soprano and tenor, and the alto and bass also in canon. This complicated double canon is both artistically highly skilful and musically entrancingly beautiful.

609 "Lobt Gott, ihr Christen, allzugleich" (Praise God, ye Christians together) in G major, with cantus firmus in the soprano and joyful runs.

610 "Jesu, meine Freude" (Jesu my joy) in C minor, marked Largo, with cantus firmus in the soprano.

611 "Christum wir sollen loben schon" (We should praise Christ) in D minor, marked Adagio, with cantus firmus in the alto and descending scales.

612 "Wir Christenleut" (We Christian people) in G minor, with cantus firmus in the soprano.

(manuals and pedals)

613 "Helft mir Gottes Güte preisen" (Help me praise God's goodness) in B minor, with cantus firmus in the soprano.

614 "Das alte Jahr vergangen ist" (The old year is past) in A minor, with ornamented cantus firmus in the soprano. The six chromatic semitones of the cantus firmus to the words "Wir danken dir, Herr Jesu Christ" (We thank thee, Lord Jesus Christ) appear 12 times in the lower parts.

615 "In dir ist Freude" (In thee is joy) in G major bursts out of the form of an organ chorale and expands into a short fantasy. Chorale motifs appear in canon in the three upper parts while the pedals play an ostinato bass.

616 "Mit Fried und Freud ich fahr dahin" (In peace and joy do I depart) in D minor, with cantus firmus in the soprano simplified as the "joy" motif in the pedals, cf. also BWV 629, 642 and 658.

617 "Herr Gott, nun schleuss den Himmel auf" (Lord God, now open the heavens) in A minor, with cantus firmus in the soprano.

618 "O Lamm Gottes, unschuldig" (O spotless Lamb of God) in F major, marked Adagio, with cantus firmus in canon at the fifth in tenor and alto and the "sorrow" motif:

619 "Christe, du Lamm Gottes" (Christ, thou Lamb of God) in F major, in five parts, with cantus firmus in canon at the twelfth in tenor and first soprano, and descending scales in second soprano, alto and bass.

620 "Christus, der uns selig macht" (Christ, who brings us salvation) in A minor, with cantus firmus in canon in soprano and bass.

621 "Da Jesus an dem Kreuze stund" (As Jesus hung on the cross) in E minor, with cantus firmus in the soprano. a) manual, b) pedals:

In example b the lines drawn between E and A, and between the two Bs form a cross and also a Greek Chi (X), the first letter of Christ's name.

622 "O Mensch, bewein dein Sünde gross" (O man, bewail thy grievous sin) in E-flat major, marked Adagio assai, and adagissimo at the end, has rich coloratura in the soprano over often surprising harmonies in the other parts.

623 "Wir danken dir, Herr Jesu Christ" (We thank thee, Lord Jesus Christ) in G major, with cantus firmus in the soprano. The rhythm 𝄾 ♫ ♪ is characteristic and also prominent in the pedal ostinato.

624 "Hilf Gott, dass mir's gelinge" (Help me God, that I may win) in G minor, with cantus firmus in canon in soprano and alto, and triplet runs in the left hand.

625 "Christ lag in Todesbanden" (Christ lay in the bonds of death) in D minor, with cantus firmus in the soprano and continuous movement.

626 "Jesus Christus, unser Heiland" (Jesus Christ our Saviour) in A minor, with cantus firmus in the soprano.

627 "Christ ist erstanden" (Christ is arisen) in D minor. Each of the three stanzas of the song is individually developed with cantus firmus always in the soprano.

Verse 1:

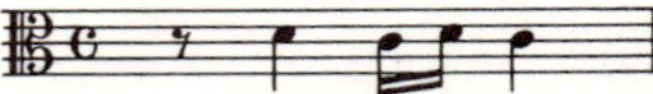

Verse 2:

Verse 3:

The last motif of a rising fourth within the scale occurs in many Easter chorales and symbolizes the Resurrection.

628 "Erstanden ist der heil'ge Christ" (Risen is the holy Christ) in D major, with cantus firmus in the soprano, Resurrection motif in the middle part, and also in the bass though with ostinato rhythm.

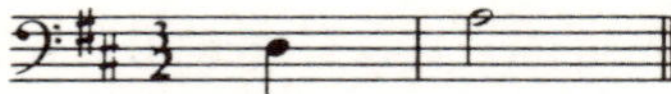

629 "Erschienen ist der herrliche Tag" (The glorious day has dawned) in dorian mode, with cantus firmus in canon in soprano and bass.

630 "Heut triumphieret Gottes Sohn" (Today is the triumph of God's Son) in G minor, with cantus firmus in the soprano, Resurrection motif in the middle parts and again an ostinato bass.

631 "Komm, Gott, Schöpfer, heiliger Geist" (Come God, creator, Holy Ghost)

in mixolydian mode, with cantus firmus in the soprano.

632 "Herr Jesu Christ, dich zu uns wend" (Lord Jesus Christ, turn to us) in F major, with cantus firmus in the soprano and imitation of the chorale in the bass.

633 "Liebster Jesu, wir sind hier" (Dearest Jesus, we are here) in A major, in five parts, with ornamented cantus firmus in canon in soprano and alto.

634 "Liebster Jesu, wir sind hier" (Dearest Jesus, we are here)—a variant of 633.

635 "Dies sind die heil'gen zehn Gebot" (These are God's ten commandments) in mixolydian mode, with cantus firmus in the soprano, and the bass and inside parts formed from the repeated notes of the opening.

636 "Vater unser im Himmelreich" (Our Father, who art in heaven) in D minor, with cantus firmus in the soprano.

637 "Durch Adams Fall ist ganz verderbt" (Through Adam's fall all is lost) in A minor, with cantus firmus in the soprano. The bass motif with falling intervals symbolizes Adam's fall:

638 "Es ist das Heil uns kommen her" (Our salvation is come upon us) in D major, with cantus firmus in the soprano and runs in the inside parts and pedals.

639 "Ich ruf zu dir, Herr Jesu Christ" (I call to thee, Lord Jesus Christ) in F minor, with ornamented cantus firmus in the soprano. This is a trio, the only one of its kind in the collection. There are repeated notes in the pedals, articulating the pleading and beseeching.

640 "In dich hab ich gehoffet, Herr" (In thee have I hoped, Lord) in E minor, with cantus firmus in the soprano.

641 "Wenn wir in höchsten Nöten sein" (When we were in deepest misery) in G major, with coloratura.

642 "Wer nur den lieben Gott lässt walten" (He who relies on God's compassion) in A minor, with cantus firmus in the soprano.

643 "Alle Menschen müssen sterben" (All men must die) in G major, with cantus firmus in the soprano.

644 "Ach wie nichtig, ach wie flüchtig" (Ah how weary, ah how fleeting) in G

minor, with cantus firmus in the soprano and ascending and descending runs in the middle parts to illustrate the fleetingness and mists referred to in the text. The following motif occurs in the pedals:

The *Little Organ Book* is published by Bärenreiter in a facsimile version with commentary, edited by H.-H. Löhlein.

Part 3 of the Clavierübung containing the **Chorales** BWV 669–689, VI &VII, the **Duets** BWV 802–805 plus the **Prelude and Fugue in E-flat major** BWV 552, III/1 which precedes and follows them, is often known simply as "Organ Mass" a handy description only adopted recently, perhaps because no one wants to offer the public "keyboard exercises," the literal meaning of *Clavierübung*. The edition of 1739 comprises settings of Luther's six Catechism Chorales, preceded by Kyrie and Gloria, also in the German hymn equivalents and four duets. Each chorale is composed twice, in a large version with pedals and also more briefly for manuals alone. "Allein Gott" (To God alone) is set three times. The Prelude and Fugue in E-flat major form an introduction and finale to the chorales, so that according to the first edition the order is as follows: Prelude in E-flat major; Kyrie, Christe, Kyrie; Gloria; the Ten Commandments; the Creed; the Lord's Prayer; Baptism; Penance; the Communion; four Duets; Fugue in E-flat major.

It is not clear why Bach placed the *Four duets* in a collection which he himself described as "consisting of various preludes on the catechism and other songs, for the organ". Possibly he wanted a specific number of pieces, and 27, being three to the power of three, is an obvious symbol of the Trinity. Alternatively he may have wished to produce a compendium of his organ compositions, like the organ books of French Baroque composers, which contain duets but are also practical handbooks for playing in church services.

Prelude in E-flat major BWV 552, duration 9 minutes. Organo pleno: this is brilliant, radiant festal music and its threefold nature, taken as a symbol of the Trinity, has given rise to numerous interpretations. It is written in concerto grosso form with three themes:

The key progression is A(E-flat)—B-flat(E-flat)—A(B-flat—C major(C minor)—A(A-flat)—B-flat(A-flat)—A(E-flat)—C(E-flat)—A(E-flat). C is treated fugally each time. The *piano* and *forte* markings are original.

Kyrie, Gott Vater (God the Father)—**Christe,** aller Welt Trost (comfort of all the world)—**Kyrie,** Gott Heiliger Geist (God the Holy Ghost) BWV 669–671. The three "great" settings in E-flat major belong closely together and evince a considerable and strongly contrapuntal density. It is interesting that Bach's working of the motifs is wholly confined to the first line of the cantus firmus, which is always divided into lines and appears in the soprano in the Kyrie, in the tenor in the Christe and in the bass in the five-part organo pleno of the second Kyrie, while the other parts employ head imitation. The preludes are reminiscent of the vocal polyphony of the Italian-style motet Bach also uses, for instance in the Creed of the B minor Mass. There as here, he is giving perfect musical expression to the very essence of his faith—the trinity of Father, Son and Holy Ghost. The three "little" settings each consist of one four-part movement with hints at the cantus firmus.

Allein Gott in der Höh sei Ehr (To God in heaven alone be honor) BWV 675–677 is set three times. The first is a three-part composition for the manuals in F major, with head imitation and cantus firmus line by line in the alto. There follows a trio in G major with the parts freely elaborating the choral opening. The lines of the chorale alternate between the upper voices, while the free one changes accordingly. The last line of the chorale also appears in the pedals. Cf. the Trio in A major BWV 664 from the *Leipzig Chorales.* The third setting is a three-part fughetta with the theme:

Dies sind die heil'gen zehn Gebot (These are God's ten commandments) BWV 678/679. The "great" version is in the myxolydian mode for two manuals and pedals with a densely interweaving quartet texture, in which two parts imitate and frequently take up the motif quoted here, two carry the cantus firmus in canon at the octave, divided into lines, and the bass is in the pedals. The severe, inexorable progress of the canon represents the strictness of the law.

The "little" version is a four-part fughetta, with a theme taken from the repeated notes at the beginning of the chorale:

The theme is heard ten times.

Wir glauben all an einen Gott (We all believe in one God) BWV 680/681. The three upper parts create a fugal movement on a theme containing the opening notes of the chorale.

The bass has this ostinato figure in the pedals:

The fughetta is in three parts, with the beginning of the cantus firmus changed somewhat melismatically and with the dotted rhythms of a French overture:

Diminished chords end its three-voiced texture shortly before the close.

Vater unser im Himmelreich (Our Father who art in heaven) BWV 682/683. Another quartet movement, in which two richly decorated voices are played on two manuals and accompanied on the pedals. The theme is taken from the head of the cantus firmus.

Two voices, again on the two manuals, present the cantus firmus line by line in canon at the octave. It is an almost insoluble problem for an organist to make two parts—cantus firmus and free voice—audible in each hand. This exceptionally dense and beautiful work acquires a certain swaying rhythm from juxtaposing and sometimes superimposing these rhythmical groups, so that the first, lombardic rhythm can be shifted in either direction, into a more sharply dotted rhythm or into triplet figures.

a

b

c

The "little" setting in D minor with cantus firmus in the soprano is a typical organ chorale: an open, four-part movement with the lower parts striding up and down the diatonic scale.

Christ unser Herr zum Jordan kam (Lord Christ of old to Jordan came) BWV 684/685. The cantus firmus appears line by line in the tenor in the pedals, in the bass and in the upper parts in sixteenth-note runs for the waves of the river Jordan, and eighth-notes which form a cross, or the Greek X for Christus, already mentioned under the *Little Organ Book.*

There is a "little" three-part setting in D minor with excerpts from the cantus firmus.

Aus tiefer Not schrei ich zu dir (Out of the deep call I to thee) BWV 686/687. Organo pleno: in six parts and phrygian mode. Cantus firmus line by line in the upper of the two pedal parts and extensive anticipation in the other five parts—four on the manuals, one on the pedals. This sorrowful, stern work contains only a few fleeting notes which do not belong to the theme.

There is a "little" version in F-sharp minor, with cantus firmus in the soprano and anticipation in the other three parts.

Jesus Christus, unser Heiland (Jesus Christ our savior) BWV 688/689. A trio with upper parts in canon and cantus firmus in the tenor.

There is a second setting as a four-part fugue, with the following theme from the chorale:

The **Four Duets** BWV 802–805 following are late works in the style of the two-part inventions, and therefore perfectly suited to the harpsichord; but as organ works they represent a culmination of the development of the bicinium, that rather dry form of choral prelude known since Scheidt's day, which composers liked to insert into a partita. In any case it is surprising to find in them works which far outstrip the inventions as to harmonic richness and melodic characterization. Duets 1 and 3, in E minor and G major respectively, are more like dances, while numbers 2 and 4, in F major and A minor, go off into persistent and often penetrating chromatics.
Theme of duet No.1:

Second theme of duet No.2:

Fugue in E-flat major BWV 552, duration 8 minutes. Like its related prelude, this is designed in three movements: the first is in five parts, its exposition extended by four entries.

In the second part, after the exposition on the dominant B-flat, the first theme joins in in 6/4 time.

In the third part, the first theme comes in in the pedals after the exposition, and appears in all four times, always together with the third theme. The passage-work in this third movement can be taken as a reference to the second theme, which does not itself occur again, and this would justify the term "triple fugue." Even if that term, as is always maintained, does not apply, this composition has such thematic significance, such structural and rhythmic variety, and above all such superb strength of musical expression that it stands at the head of all Bach's fugues. This is a unique, tremendous climax of the centuries-long development of this genre.

Eighteen Leipzig chorales BWV 651–668, VI & VII, more correctly known today as the *Organ chorales from the Leipzig autograph.* Between 1747 and 1749 Bach planned a collection of 17 chorales revised from his Weimar period, but the 18th and last chorale he dictated on his deathbed. These are classic models of the larger chorale prelude in their most developed forms.

651 "Komm, Heiliger Geist, Herre Gott" (Come, Holy Ghost, Lord God). *Fantasia, in organo pleno.* A three-part figured work built over the cantus firmus in the pedals with the chorale divided into lines. This is a thrilling work of great intensity.

652 uses the same chorale, for two manuals and pedals, in G major. The cantus firmus in the soprano is very ornate, with head imitation. The last line of the chorale, "Halleluia," is more elaborate and also moves continuously in every part.

653 "An Wasserflüssen Babylon" (By the waters of Babylon). A four-part piece with free parts reliant on the opening of the chorale and the cantus firmus in the tenor.

653b "An Wasserflüssen Babylon." Five-part original version of 653, from Bach's Weimar days. A four-part section, in itself a very lovely example of a pliant, harmonically delightful composition, is contrasted with the cantus firmus in the soprano. Tenor and bass lie in the pedals, giving a strong clarity and transparency to the tenor part. 654 "Schmücke dich, o liebe Seele" (Soul, array thyself with gladness). A more or less independent movement in three parts forms a dancelike background for the cantus firmus in the soprano, which is divided into lines, giving the work its pious, devout expression.

655 "Herr Jesu Christ, dich zu uns wend" (Lord Jesus Christ, turn to us). A trio in G major with imitative parts of virtuoso variety. Cantus firmus in the pedals at the end.

656 "O Lamm Gottes unschuldig" (O spotless lamb of God), in A major. This is a triptychon, for the music runs right through the three stanzas. Verse 1—three-part writing for manuals, with cantus firmus in the soprano. Verse 2—also in three parts, with cantus firmus in the alto. Verse 3—in four parts, with cantus firmus in the pedals and grand massed harmonies at the words **"else we would have to despair".**

657 "Nun danket alle Gott" (Now thank we all our God). Head imitation of each line, beginning nearly always in unison, with cantus firmus in the soprano in long note values.

658 "Von Gott will ich nicht lassen" (From God I will not part). Three parts, predominantly in the rhythm of joyful faith, surround the tenor cantus firmus.

659–661 "Nun komm, der Heiden Heiland" (Come, redeemer of our race). These are three related settings of this chorale: 659 has a richly ornamented cantus firmus in the soprano and equally richly imitative alto and tenor parts over calm paces in the bass.

660 for two basses and cantus firmus, is a three-part piece for soprano with cantus firmus, and two low parts which proceed in canon. This strange method has given rise to many different assumptions, but the right one seems to be the stressing of the verse about the equality of God the Father and God the Son, symbolized by the two parallel bass parts.

661, *In organo pleno,* has cantus firmus in the pedals and three upper parts:

Is this perhaps the last verse, in praise of the Trinity?

662–664 "Allein Gott in der Höh sei Ehr" (To God in heaven alone be honor). There are three settings of this chorale as well:

662, *Adagio,* revives the lombardic rhythm with its slurred notes.

Ornamented cantus firmus in the soprano. The restraint of this piece is directly contrasted with the two trios on the same chorale, BWV 664 and 676, perhaps once again setting a verse other than verse 1.

663, Quartet, with ornamented cantus firmus in the tenor, moving through the extremes of its range, and

head imitation in the pedals in clearly audible form.

664 Trio in which, apart from references to the chorale elaborated on in the theme, only the first two lines of the cantus firmus come in towards the end in the pedals.

665/666 "Jesus Christus, unser Heiland" (Jesus Christ our savior). The "great" version in E minor with its cantus firmus in the pedals is entitled "sub communione". The four sections of the text are precisely characterized, most strikingly the last two. "Durch das bitter Leiden sein" (Through his bitter anguish) is illustrated by sinuous chromatic passages

and "half er uns aus der Höllen Pein" (he delivered us from the pains of hell) by the Resurrection motif:

The "little" version in E minor is for manuals only, with cantus firmus in the soprano.

667 "Komm, Gott, Schöpfer, Heiliger Geist" (Come God, Creator, Holy Ghost). In organo pleno and mixolydian mode, this is an enlarged version of BWV 631 from the *Little Organ Book.* An additional chorale passage with eighth-note runs over the cantus firmus in the pedals has been appended.

668 "Vor deinen Thron tret ich hiermit" (Forthwith I come before Thy throne). This was Bach's last work, an enlarged version of the chorale BWV 641 from the *Little Organ Book,* which he dictated to his son-in-law Altnikol. We have here another perfected form, this time the so-called "Pachelbel chorale" type, with a well-developed head imitation of each line of the cantus firmus appearing in the other parts. Apart from the first line of the chorale, which is slightly embellished, there is no ornamentation of line or part, but only simple notes radiating peace and confidence. This work was published posthumously as the last piece in the unfinished *Art of Fugue.*

Schübler chorales BWV 645–650, VI & VII, first published 1746–50, total duration 21 minutes. These are entitled "Six chorales of various kinds to be played on an organ with two manuals and pedals . . ." All six works are transposed from cantata movements, though the original of 646 is unknown, and are all da capo arias with ritornellos. Since the melodies of the chorales are well known, only the free counterparts are quoted here.

645 "Wachet auf, ruft uns die Stimme" (Sleepers awake, the voice is calling) is a trio with cantus firmus in the tenor. On the words in the cantata "Zion hears the watchman singing."

646 "Wo soll ich fliehen hin" (Whither shall I fly) is a trio with cantus firmus in the alto.

647 "Wer nur den lieben Gott lässt walten" (He who relies on God's compassion) is a quartet, with cantus firmus in the tenor.

648 "Meine Seele erhebet den Herrn" (My soul doth magnify the Lord) is a quartet, with cantus firmus in the soprano.

649 "Ach bleib bei uns, Herr Jesu Christ" (Ah, stay with us, Lord Jesus Christ) is a trio, with cantus firmus in the soprano.

650 "Kommst du nun, Jesu, vom Himmel herunter" (If you now come down

from heaven, oh Jesus) is a trio, with cantus firmus in the alto to the melody "Praise to the Lord, the almighty, the king of creation."

Chorale variations

Some canonic variations on the Christmas carol "Vom Himmel hoch, da komm ich her" (I come from heaven above) BWV 769,V, duration 14 minutes.

Variation 1: canon at the octave between soprano and bass, with cantus firmus in the tenor.

Variation 2: canon at the 5th between soprano and alto, with cantus firmus in the tenor.

Variation 3: quartet of great beauty, with cantus firmus in the soprano, free, decorated line in the alto:

and canon at the 7th between tenor and bass.

Variation 4: canon at the octave in augmentation between soprano and bass, with cantus firmus in the tenor.

Variation 5: various canons on the inversion of the chorale cantus firmus at the 6th, 3rd, 2nd and 9th, with the theme in diminution to a final stretto, the different parts presenting the entire chorale compressed within the last three bars.

These variations, which Bach submitted with his application for membership to the Mizler Society in 1746, were published shortly afterwards. They are among his most artful, ingeniously constructed works, but as complete pieces of music among his most artistic. Listeners unaccustomed to polyphony are advised to listen to them more than once in order to grasp the amazing beauty of their musical architecture.

Partita "Sei gegrüsset, Jesu gütig" (We greet Thee, sweet Jesus) BWV 768,V, duration 24 minutes, divided as follows: chorale in four parts; 1st variation—duet with ornamented cantus firmus in the right hand; 2nd variation with the following motif:

3rd variation—duet, the chorale being surrounded by figuration in continuous motion; 4th variation in three parts; 5th variation:

6th variation with the following motif:

7th variation—trio with cantus firmus in the pedals; 8th variation—quartet with imitative upper parts and a pizzicatolike effect in the pedals; 9th variation—trio with cantus firmus in the tenor; 10th variation—chorale treatment with the cantus firmus line by line in the soprano and head imitation of the top part alternating with the chorale melody so that this is an entirely four-part movement; 11th variation—five-part chorale In Organo Pleno.

Partita "O Gott, du frommer Gott" (Oh God, Thou holy God) BWV 769,V, duration 15 minutes. Nine variations, clearly interpreting Johannes Heermann's text, which enters in the second variation, after the chorale. Clearest examples of this are verse 3 of variation 4, variation 7, verses 6 and 7 of variation 8 and the last variation "Wenn du die Toten wirst" (When Thou shalt [raise] the dead):

"Let Thy voice be heard":

"and lead him in beauteous glory":

Independent chorale settings

Allein Gott in der Höh (To God in heaven alone) in G major, BWV 717, VI/4, is in three parts, with cantus firmus in the soprano. The tenor and alto start by imitating a tune which exactly follows the melodic notes of the first line of the chorale.

Christ lag in Todesbanden (Christ lay in the bonds of death) BWV 695, VI/16, entitled "Fantasia", is in three parts with imitation and cantus firmus in the alto.

Ein feste Burg ist unser Gott (A mighty fortress is our God) BWV 720, VI/22, is marked for two manuals and pedals, but in some copies even for three manuals. Bach composed this for the dedication of the Mühlhausen organ in 1709 in the form of a free fantasia with figuration playing round the cantus firmus. The chorale appears in all parts, sometimes ornamented, sometimes in half-notes and whole-notes. A copy made by J. G. Walther and printed in Schweitzer's book on Bach contains very interesting registration markings, probably originating from Bach's dedication performance.

Herr Jesu Christ, dich zu uns wend (Lord Jesus Christ, turn to us) BWV 709, V/26, is a four-part piece, with decorated cantus firmus in the soprano and the following motif worked on in the lower parts. This makes the work sound like one of the chorales from the *Little Organ Book.*

Jesu, meine Freude (Jesus, my joy) BWV 713, VI/29. Marked *Fantasia,* in three parts, with cantus firmus alternating between all the parts. The free voices are formed from an ostinato theme and the elaboration on it. Instead of a development of the cantus firmus in the second half of the chorale, a more homophonic finale appears in three to four parts, marked dolce.

Nun freut euch, lieben Christen gmein (Rejoice now, dear Christians together) BWV 734, VII/44. This is in three parts, with passage-work in the top part, cantus firmus in the tenor and the bass in eighth-notes, resulting in a compelling and intense impetus.

Valet will ich dir geben (I will bid thee farewell) BWV 735, VII/50. Fantasia, with cantus firmus divided into lines in the pedals with head imitation in the other parts.

Wer nur den lieben Gott lässt walten (He who relies on God's compassion) BWV 690/691, V/53/52. The first movement is a short section, not all written in parts, with cantus firmus in the soprano mostly built on passage-work, while the second development is melismatic. The ornaments are typical of Bach's work as a youth.

Wo soll ich fliehen hin (Whither shall I fly) BWV 694, IX/25 is a trio with cantus firmus in the pedals and free parts in both manuals.

Further works: "Allein Gott in der Höh" (To God alone in heaven) BWV 716; "Ach Gott und Herr" (Ah God and Lord) BWV 714; "Christ lag in Todesbanden" (Christ lay in the bonds of death) BWV 718; "Gelobet seist du, Jesu Christ (Praised be Thou, Jesus Christ) BWV 723; "Herzlich tut mich verlangen" (From my heart I beseech) BWV 727; "In dich hab ich gehoffet, Herr" (In Thee have I trusted, Lord), Fughetta BWV 712; Magnificat, Fugue BWV 733; "Valet will ich dir geben" (I will bid thee farewell) BWV 736; "Vater unser im Himmelreich" (Our Father, who art in heaven) BWV 737; "Vom Himmel hoch" (From heaven above), Fughetta BWV 701; "Vom Himmel hoch" (From heaven above), Fugue BWV 700; "Wir glauben all an einen Gott" (We all believe in one God) BWV 740.

The Bach chorale settings recently found in manuscript at Yale University belong to his early works written between 1703 when he was at Arnstadt, and about 1708, which was his first year at Weimar.

Works for organ with orchestra

Concerto in D minor for organ and string orchestra BWV 1052, duration 25 minutes. In its harpsichord version this is well known as the "piano" concerto in D minor. Apart from the missing original version for violin, there exists one for organ, which avoids all the wealth of decoration and passage-work the harpsichord needs to amplify its volume of sound. Bach used this three-part work as a prelude for the church cantatas 146 "Wir müssen durch viel Trübsal" (We must pass through great tribulation) and 188 "Ich habe meine Zuversicht" (I have my confidence), and it makes a truly royal introit.

Allegro with the following theme:

Between the tutti passages containing this theme the organ spins out broad solos, accompanied by the strings. Listing the keys of the tutti entries will throw light on the harmonic progression of this work: D minor, A minor, F major, A minor, C major, G minor, B-flat major and G minor. Before the recapitulation in D minor the orchestral writing slowly disintegrates, leaving the organ to take wing into a free arpeggiated cadenza which concludes with a succession of seventh chords.

Adagio. Great solo on the organ, a solo part with accompaniment. In this work the advantages of the organ over the harpsichord must be generally acknowledged, as the solo part really rings out and carries. An ostinato bass figure alone opens and closes the work.

Allegro. Again in concerto grosso form. The organ begins after the grosso introduction with the theme:

The rhythmic grouping ♫ ♬ ♪ predominates over long stretches, to which it gives a springlike tension. More arpeggio chords and runs form interludes between the blocks of tutti writing. A cadenza gives the organist an opportunity to show off his skill and gifts of improvisation and is followed by a recapitulation of the introductory tutti. This concerto is one of Bach's few works in which the organ plays a concertante role with the other instruments, a scoring only found elsewhere in the symphonies of some cantatas. Most of the works here are concerto movements:

Sinfonia in D major, the introduction to the Ratswahl (Election) Cantata No. 29 "Wir danken dir, Gott, wir danken dir" (We thank Thee, God, we thank Thee) duration 5 minutes. The scoring for three trumpets, timpani, two oboes and strings produces a brilliant piece of music:

Two sinfonie in D minor come from Cantata No. 35 "Geist und Seele wird verwirret" (Soul and spirit bend before him), duration 12 minutes. They are scored for three oboes and strings.

Sinfonia in E major from Cantata No. 49 "Ich geh' und suche mit Verlangen" (I go and seek with longing), duration 9 minutes, is also known to us as the last movement of the harpsichord concerto in E major. Only one oboe d'amore here joins the strings.

Sinfonia in D major, prelude to Cantata No. 169 "Gott soll allein mein Herze haben" (God shall alone possess my heart), duration 12 minutes, appears in another key as the first movement of the above-mentioned harpsichord concerto in E major, and again three oboes and strings join the organ.

Publishers: Bärenreiter—*Neue Ausgabe sämtlicher Werke (New edition of collected works),* ed. K. Heller, H.-H. Löhlein, D. Kilian, H. Klotz and M. Tessmer); Bornemann; Breitkopf—*Sämtliche Orgelwerke (Collected organ works),* ed. H. Lohmann, from it also single editions of the *Little Organ Book,* the *Eight little preludes and fugues,* the Toccata in D minor BWV 565 and the Fantasia in G major BWV 572; Peters—*B-A-C-H Fugen der Familie Bach (B-A-C-H fugues by the Bach family),* ed. T. Fedtke; Schott—also a single edition of the Toccata in D minor BWV 565, ed. R Walter, the Concerto in D minor BWV 1052 and sinfonie, ed. W. Auler; Universal—*Lea Pocket Scores.*

The third composer of importance born in 1685 is DOMENICO SCARLATTI (b. Naples, October 26, 1685; d. Madrid, July 23, 1757). He studied with his father Alessandro, and while he did work in Rome he was mainly employed at the courts of Lisbon and Madrid. From his main output of over 500 harpsichord sonatas, five carry additions which identify them as compositions for the organ: the sonatas K*. 254/255 in C minor/C major, K. 287/288 in D major and K. 328 in G major. K. 328 suggests a change from Organo (Pleno) to Flauto (flute), and K. 287 bears the title "per organo da camera con due tastatura flautado e trombone" (for chamber organ with two manuals, flute and trombone), which indicates changing between open and reed stops. Publisher: Bärenreiter, ed. L. Hautus; Peters—*Orgelmusik aus drei Jahrhunderten (Organ music from three centuries)* Vol.2, ed. T. Fedtke.

In 1687 the Bolognese organist GIULIO CESARE ARESTI (1625–c.1704) published his *Sonate da organo di varii autori (Organ sonatas by various composers),* which contained 18 compositions, some by Aresti himself and others by CARLO FRANCESCO POLLAROLO (c.1653–1722), GIOVANNI BATTISTA BASSANI (c.1647–1716), LODOVICO MARIA GIUSTINI (1685–1743), GIOVANNI PAOLO COLONNA (1637–1695), BERNARDO PASQUINI (1637–1710) and, as the only non-Italian, J. K. KERLL, q.v. These lovely sonatas—which are actually canzone, capriccios, fugues or tocattas—give us a good general view of organ composition and playing at the end of the 17th century. Publishers: Merseburger—*Ten Sonatas,* ed. A Reichling;Peters—*Barockmusik Italiens. Zwölf Sonaten (Italian Baroque music. Twelve sonatas),* ed. T. Fedtke.

The master of the Dresden court opera, JOHANN ADOLF HASSE (bapt.

*K. refers to Ralph Kirkpatrick's Scarlatti catalogue, *Complete Keyboard Works,* New York 1972.

Bergedorf nr. Hamburg, March 25, 1699; d. Venice, December 16, 1783), whom Bach also admired, published six concertos for organ or harpsichord. Though they were arranged as chamber music as well, the keyboard versions contain very attractive music of no great technical difficulty. Publisher: Forberg, ed. M. Weyer.

DOMENICO ZIPOLI

b. Prato, October 16, 1688; d. Cordoba, January 2, 1726

At an early age Zipoli came to Rome, where he was organist at the Jesuit church. In 1717 he went to South America on a missionary expedition, and studied theology there while working as a church musician. In 1716 his collection Sonate d'intavolatura per org. e cimbalo (Sonatas in tablature for organ and harpsichord) *appeared, and is the only work by him to survive.*

Toccata in dorian mode. Some chordal opening bars form the introduction to the figure-work which, together with short motifs treated like improvisations, form the substance of this toccata, similar to Frescobaldi's compositions. Homophonic blocks of chords in the middle divide the passage-work of the first and second sections. His other, short organ works were collected in groups of four verses and a canzona, the verses resembling in character the versets of the Magnificat.

Group in C major. Verse 1: short cadence, like an intonation—tonic-subdominant-dominant-tonic—with diatonic runs and broken chords. Verse 2: three-part fughetta on the following theme:

Verse 3: four-part fughetta. Verse 4: imitative movement, beginning in the alto. Canzona: Fugal piece built on one theme with a free conclusion.

Further works: Similar groups in D minor, E minor, F major and G minor; music for the Elevation, Post-communion and Offertory; Pastorals.

Publisher: Müller, ed. L. F. Tagliavini.

LOUIS-CLAUDE DAQUIN

b. Paris, July 4, 1694; d. ibid., June 15, 1772

Daquin had a brilliant career. After playing for the king when only six years old, he became organist at St. Paul's, in 1739 at the Chapelle Royale and later at Notre Dame. He was famous as a virtuoso and improviser, and in addition to his organ works he left a collection of pieces for harpsichord.

Nouveau livre de Noëls (Variations on Christmas carols). Daquin elaborated on his originals in an engaging way, and turned these folk tunes into simple, devout, artless and joyful pieces of music. Apart from French tunes, he arranged a "Noël étranger" (Foreign carol) and a "Noël suisse" (Swiss carol), making 12 in all.

The variation technique is always the same; a relatively strict process depending on ornamentation predominates, as eighth-notes move through triplets to sixteenth-notes and 32nd-notes, without altering the character of the theme.

Like his older compatriots, Daquin writes out his registration: sur les jeux d'anches (reed stops), en dialogue, duo, trio, en musette—with a sustained bourdon note—sur les flutes and even a récit en taille (solo tenor). Cf. Couperin.

A spontaneous and childlike delight in the events of Christmas is expressed in these pieces.

Publishers: Schott, ed. A. Guilmant; Schola Cantorum, ed. N. Dufourcq.

MICHEL CORRETTE (b. Rouen, 1709; d. Paris, January 22, 1795) wrote very similar Christmas music and also published *Pièces d'orgue (Organ pieces)* in three volumes, and a keyboard tutor. Publisher: Schola Cantorum.

The **Pastorellen** for organ and strings by GREGOR JOSEPH WERNER (bapt. Ybbs-on-Danube, January 29, 1693; d. Eisenstadt, March 3, 1766) offer us Christmas music of quite another kind, in popular alpine style. Werner was Haydn's predecessor as music director to Prince Esterházy. These pieces have an earthy, Baroque cheerfulness but the sincerity of folk music in their quiet passages; the music is good, and easily absorbed by the less expert listener. Publisher: Bärenreiter, ed. E. F. Schmid.

The south German monk MARIANUS KÖNIGSPERGER (b. Roding, Upper Palatinate, December 4, 1708; d. Prüfening Monastery nr. Regensburg, October 9, 1769) also wrote a **Pastorella** and belongs to this group. Publisher: Coppenrath

JOHANN ERNST EBERLIN

b. Jettingen nr. Burgau, Swabia, March 27, 1702;
d. Salzburg, June 21, 1762

After his schooling in Salzburg, Eberlin resided there and in 1729 became court and cathedral organist, a post he held until his death. His extensive work includes church compositions, oratorios and operas.

Nine toccatas with fugues, published 1747. Without exception they have the character of preludes, with one basic idea developed in each. In the first toccata broken chords:

in the fifth an arioso melody with subdued accompaniment:

in the sixth syncopations:

in the seventh ostinato rhythmic figures:

Double fugues follow the second, fifth and seventh toccatas, and these are also similarly constructed: the first theme is treated in normal fugal style, as is also the case with the others, with a cadence at the end. Then the second theme enters, and after the exposition the two are joined and both worked on in the development. The fugue from the second toccata:

While these works of Eberlin's offer no artistic revelation, because of their benevolent, ingenuous and sincere nature they are beautiful examples of south German music style at the moment of transition to classicism.

Eberlin is the co-author of the 12 pieces entitled *Der Morgen und der Abend (The morning and the evening)* written (together with Leopold Mozart, Wolfgang Amadeus's father, who contributed seven of them) for the *Hornwerk* on the fortress of Hohensalzburg. At dawn and again at dusk a composition was played on this mechanical instrument, for instance in April a minuet, in August an aria and in December a lullaby.

Publishers: Coppenrath; Doblinger—*Der Morgen und der Abend (The morning and the evening)*, ed. F. Haselböck.

The Benedictine monk CARLMANN KOLB (bapt. Kösslarn, Lower Bavaria, January 29, 1703; d. Munich, January 15, 1765) also belongs to the group of south German Baroque organ composers. His *Certamen aonium* contains preludes, versets and cadenzas in the church modes. Individual pieces are inventive and effectively brief. The preludes in the phrygian and lydian modes are dramatically accented, mainly by the use of rests within the otherwise flowing phrases. Publisher: Coppenrath, ed. R. Walter.

The Franciscan monk GIOVANNI BATTISTA MARTINI (b. Bologna, April 24, 1706; d. ibid., August 3, 1784) was director of music at the basilica of St. Francis in his home town. He was equally famous as a composer, teacher and theoretician, so that entire generations of musicians sought his advice, including Mozart and J. C. Bach. He is survived both by his three-volume history of music and his instrumental and organ works, which he published under the title *Sonate d'intavolatura per l'organo e 'l cembalo (Sonatas in tablature for organ and harpsichord)*. The collection includes toccatas—short pieces, each with a single theme—versets, fugues and settings for parts of the liturgy, such as the Deo gratias, the Elevation and the Communion. The most interesting are the **Sonatas for the Offertory** or *sui flauti* (on the flutes), which all consist of a short introduction followed by a longer main movement. An example of the beginning of one of them:

His slow movements, such as largos or sicilianos, have all the expressive sweetness of Italian melodic invention combined with harmonic surprises. Publishers: Merseburger—*Geschichte des Orgelspiels und der Orgelkomposition (History of organ playing and composition)*, volume of examples, ed. G. Frotscher; Zanibon, ed. I. Fuser.

WILHELM FRIEDEMANN BACH (b. Weimar, November 22, 1710; d. Berlin, July 1, 1784) was J. S. Bach's eldest son, for whom he wrote the *Little Organ Book*. After working as an organist in Dresden and Halle he went to live in Berlin as a freelance musician. His chamber music and orchestral works show a sentimental tendency, but his organ music—fugues and chorales—is more traditional. Only the larger fugues for two manuals and pedals, and above all the triple fugue in F major, turn from the often dry mannerisms of Baroque music to a concertante virtuosity which covers up the contrapuntal basic material. Publishers: Breitkopf—Fugue in F major, ed. G. Ramin; Peters—*Orgelwerke (Organ works)*, ed. T. Fedtke.

An English composer of the same age, THOMAS ARNE (b. London, March 12, 1710; d. ibid., March 5, 1778) made a contribution to organ literature of some concertos for organ with string orchestra. Publisher: Faber.

JOHN STANLEY (b. London, January 17, 1713; d. ibid., May 19, 1786) was admired by Handel as a composer and player. He left 30 **Voluntaries** Op. 5–7 of 1748–54, which demonstrate all the musical expressiveness of the contemporary organ. They are cheerful, lighthearted and rarely serious. As a rule they start with a short, slow passage to be played with the Principal, followed by a quick movement to be played, according to the type of piece, either with the Cornet, the Trumpet or with both tone colors alternating and possibly interrupted by echo effects. The **Full voluntaries** are played in Organo Pleno and are fugal in form. Many of them, particularly the slow ones, display an affinity with Handel's works in successfully transferring orchestral characteristics onto the organ, producing the rhythms of the French overture and introductions marked largo e staccato. In 1775 he published six **Concertos** Op. 10, for keyboard—organ, harpsichord or fortepiano—and strings, of which No. 4 in C minor, duration 12 minutes, bears traces of the Baroque in all its three movements—Vivace, Andante affetuoso and Presto. The string complement is two violins and a bass. Publishers: Oxford University Press; Hinrichsen, ed. G. Philips; Schott—*Antologia organi (Organ anthology)* Vol.11, ed. S. Margittay.

JOHANN LUDWIG KREBS

b. Buttelstedt nr. Weimar, October 10, 1713;
d. Altenburg, January 1, 1780

After studying with J. S. Bach, Krebs worked as an organist in Zwickau, Zeitz and Altenburg. Like his teacher, he was a forceful player, and most of his music was composed for the organ, his vocal works and instrumental sonatas not being their equal in quality.

More significantly than any other composer, this highly-gifted pupil of Bach's continued in his master's monumental footsteps. His organ works are distinguished by the mature technique of their composition, and while they are naturally built on his teacher's art, in style they simultaneously point towards the precursors of Classicism.

Toccata and fugue in E major, duration 8 minutes. This is clearly derived from J. S. Bach's Toccata in F major or at least inspired by it. It is also a concert piece with a great pedal solo at the beginning and figure work running through it. The fugue presents a simple, melodic theme, which also appears inverted in the course of the development.

Prelude and double fugue in F minor, duration 11 minutes. The beginning of the prelude bears the hallmark of an aria, as its prominent melodic line in the right hand stands out above the accompanying figures in the other parts. After the intro-

ductory bars the melody changes into the left hand and, in altered form, into the pedals. After the first section a fugato on a similar theme joins in; both sections are then repeated in dominant C minor, with the fugato theme inverted, and the final bars are in F major. The double fugue first develops theme 1 and theme 2 separately, until in the last bars they appear four times in synthesis.

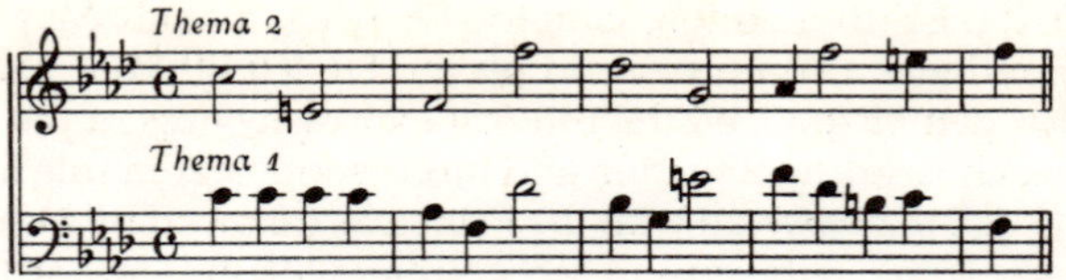

Krebs gave his collection of **Chorale arrangements** the title "Piano exercises, consisting of various preludes and variations on some hymns." A choral bicinium—only occasionally a three-part movement—and a four-part figured chorale with bold harmonic phrases follow each *Präambulum* (prelude).

The **eight chorales** for oboe or trumpet and organ are an early example of chorale music for two instruments. The orchestral instrument carries the cantus firmus while the organ plays the lower parts, which are often written in complicated three-part form.

The **Fantasia in F minor** for oboe and organ is an expressive duet and should also be mentioned.

Further works: Toccatas and preludes with fugues; Fugue on B-A-C-H.

Publishers: Heinrichshofen—*Eight chorales;* Peters—*Orgelwerke (Organ works),* ed. W. Zöllner, K. Tittel & K. Soldan; Breitkopf—Fantasia in F minor, ed. J. N. David; Schoot—*Antologia organi (Organ anthology)* Vol.11, ed. S. Margittay.

CARL PHILIPP EMANUEL BACH

b. Weimar, March 8, 1714; d. Hamburg, December 14, 1788

Philipp Emanuel studied both music with his father Johann Sebastian and jurisprudence at Leipzig and Frankfurt-an-der-Oder. For a long period he was a harpsichordist at the court of Frederick the Great in Berlin, and in 1768 succeeded his godfather Georg Philipp Telemann as director of church music in Hamburg. He was well known as a brilliant harpsichordist, and his compositions favor the piano. His tutor Versuch Über die wahre Art das Clavier zu spielen *(*An essay on the true manner of keyboard-playing*) still carries weight today. His other works are mainly chamber music, songs and sacred music.*

Sonata in G minor Wq*, 70/6, duration 13 minutes. I Allegro moderato. It is obvious from the first bars that this movement is homophonic, not in parts. Two and three-part episodes do indeed occur several times in the course of its development, but it remains orchestral in character like an early Classic symphony, the form of which was in fact influenced by C. P. E. Bach. A second theme can be detected in various motifs and brief phrases which also appear in the recapitulation, but its development is not yet that of a Classic sonata form.

*Wq stands for A. Wotquenne's *Catalogue des oeuvres de Carl Philipp Emanuel Bach (Catalogue of the works of C. P. E. Bach),* publ. in French and German, Leipzig, 1905; repr. Wiesbaden, 1972.

II Adagio. A simple melodious movement with a prominent solo part and accompaniment. The last bar contains a rest over a 6/4 chord to indicate a cadenza flourish.

III Allegro. After the opening few bars in two parts comes a transition to unison in arpeggios and scale runs, and new motifs are briefly introduced. The second section begins with the theme in B-flat major and the recapitulation returns to G minor.

This sonata is one of a collection of six (Wq 70) in A major, B-flat major, F major, A minor, D major and G minor. All are in three movements—two fast, with a slow middle one—but the fourth differs in that its last movement is a theme with variations.

Further works: Prelude in D major Wq 70/7, Fugues Wq 119, Fantasia and fugue in C minor Wq 119/7.

Publishers: Fitzsimmons, ed. J. Langlais; Peters—*Orgelwerke (Organ works)*, ed. T. Fedtke; Schott—*Antologia Organi (Organ anthology)*, Vol.12, ed. S. Margittay.

(Padre) ANTONIO SOLER

bapt. Olot, Catalonia, December 3, 1729;
d. Escorial, December 20, 1783.

He entered the choir school of Montserrat at the age of six and was later taught by a pupil of Juan Cabanilles. His first engagement was as music director of Lerida Cathedral, and in 1752 he entered the Escorial Monastery as monk, organist and choirmaster. In his first years there he also studied with Domenico Scarlatti in Madrid. He wrote sacred vocal music, music for the theatre and instrumental works, of which his piano sonatas are the best known today.

Six concertos for two obbligato organs were written for the studies of Prince Gabriel of Bourbon, and Soler played them with him on two chamber organs or possibly on the harpsichord or **hammerklavier.** All six are in two movements only, the first a Scarlatti-style sonata in two sections, the second a minuet with variations. The music for both instruments carries equal weight.

1st concerto in C major: Andante, minuet.

2nd concerto in A minor: The Andante movement opens with an elegiac theme:

later crowded out by other ideas. A bridge passage leads into the Allegro:

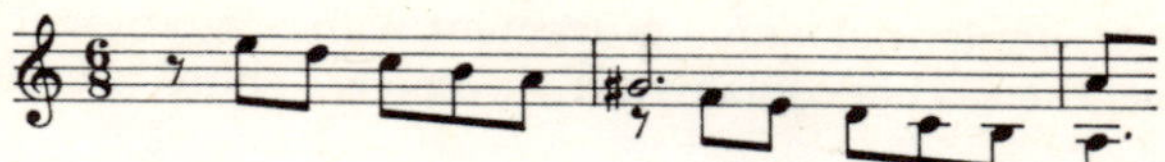

a vigorous concerto movement. The theme of the Tempo di minué has a Mozartian grace which continues in the pleasing A major variations.

3rd concerto in G major, Andantino, Minuet.

4th concerto in F major, Affetuoso andante non largo with the theme:

and Minuet with the opening:

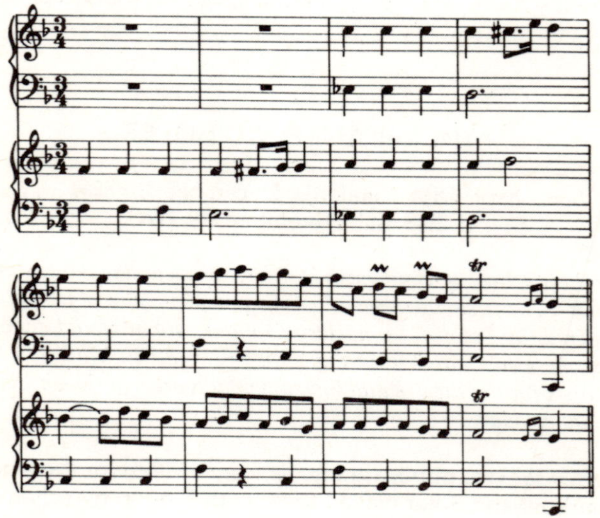

5th concerto in A major, Cantabile, Minuet.

6th concerto in D major, Allegro, Andante, Allegro, Andante, Minuet.

The **Sonata de clarines** (horizontal discant trumpets) for one player is a good example of freshness of musical expression even within this genre.

Publishers: Schott—6 concertos, ed. M. S. Kastner; Müller—*Spanische und portugiesische Sonaten des 18. Jahrhunderts (18th-century Spanish and Portuguese sonatas)*, ed. G. Doderer.

The Italian composer GIOVANNI BERNARDO LUCCHINETTI and the Spaniard JOSEF BLANCO followed Soler's example in writing works for two organs. Their exact dates are unknown, but they were active from approximately the middle of the 18th century. Lucchinetti composed a densely concertante two-part work, while Blanco's one-movement piece is designed with alternating solos for both organs, which only play together in the tutti passages. Publishers: Doblinger—Lucchinetti, *Concerto a due organi (Concerto for two organs)*, ed. R. Ewerhart; Schott—Blanco, *Concierto de dos organos (Concerto for two organs)*, ed. M. S. Kastner. Finally, mention should be made of published works for two organs by three contemporary Italians, SEVERO GIUSSANI, GAETANO PIAZZA and BONAVENTURA TERRENI, none of whose dates are known. Publisher: Breitkopf, ed. T. Fedtke.

FRANZ XAVER BRIXI

b. Prague, January 2, 1732; d. ibid., October 14, 1771

Brixi was one of the most prolific Classic composers in his field. He grew up in the Bohemian musical tradition, free of foreign influence, and wrote church music such as masses, vespers, litanies, cantatas and oratorios. His instrumental works are less numerous, consisting of five organ/harpsichord concertos. He was organist at St. Veit's Cathedral in Prague, and while working on folk music material he also participated in the great movement from Baroque polyphony to Classic simplicity of line. His works clearly show features associated with Haydn and Mozart.

Concerto in F major for organ and orchestra, duration 24 minutes. Scored for two horns, strings and continuo.

I Allegro moderato. The theme, which is firmly in the tonic key, is first stated by the orchestra and then by the solo instrument, and figures and passage work follow without any distinctive tunes. The grace of the little melodic turns and the attractive exchanges between orchestra and organ make this a very cheerful movement.

II Adagio. The simple, melodic tune is colorfully decorated with ornaments and rhythmic figures in quickening tempo, and the piece is composed like a song with an F major middle section and a final return to the B flat major of the theme.

III Allegro assai. This is the least complicated movement, like a merry dance, with the theme repeated.

It manages with few basic harmonies, and when appropriately executed is infectiously and thrillingly emphatic. Publisher: Artia (*Musica Antiqua Bohemica 26*).

JOSEPH HAYDN

b. Rohrau, Lower Austria, prob. March 31, 1732;
d. Vienna, May 31, 1809

Haydn, the oldest of the Viennese Classic composers, started as a chorister in Vienna and in 1761 entered the court of Prince Esterházy, whom he served for 30 years. In his last two decades he travelled to London and also stayed in Vienna. His extensive oeuvre of symphonies and chamber music indicates that a new age had dawned in which there was actually little place for the organ, but to which that instrument did in fact contribute some peripheral compositions.

Pieces for flute-clock, Hob*. XIX. These enchanting little works were originally intended for a tiny mechanical organ connected to a clock, with just one rank of pipes. As each hour struck one of the pieces would be played.

These are short pieces—minuets, marches and even a fugue—each built on one theme, and because of the limited number of pipes the range of notes is very small.

Twelve pieces of 1792, among them the minuet "Der Wachtelschlag" (The song of the quail):

Twelve pieces of 1793 and six pieces, among others, are played on the 1772 clock.

These are Haydn's settings of some of his own works, such as the finale of the Quartet Hob. III:69, the finale of the *Lerchenquartett (Lark quartet)*, from which a quotation follows, and the minuet from the *Clock Symphony.*

*Hob. refers to Anthony van Hoboken's *Joseph Haydn. Thematisch-bibliographisches Werkverzeichnis (Joseph Haydn. Thematic and bibliographic catalogue)*, Vol.1: "Instrumentalwerke" (Instrumental works), Mainz 1957.

In all, 32 pieces survive, though not all are authenticated as being Haydn's, some of which have been written out and can be heard on mechanical clocks still in operation.

Concerto for organ and orchestra in C major Hob. XVIII:1, 1756, duration 19 minutes. Scored for two oboes and strings. I Moderato. Laid out like a sonata with two themes. Theme 1:

Theme 2:

A lengthy orchestral introduction comprising both themes opens this movement and is followed by variations on the theme and on the bridge motifs, with arabesques for the organ.

II Largo. An artless, melodic movement with a simple theme beginning in the first violin and taken up by the organ. Five bars before the end comes a 6/4 chord, giving the soloist the opportunity to play a cadenza.

III Allegro molto. Main theme:

The secondary theme is formed of broken triplet figures on a descending G major chord. The effervescent charm of this movement comes from its interchange between sixteenth-notes and triplets. As in the first movement, the theme appears in minor towards the end.

Concerto for organ and orchestra in C-major Hob. XVIII:8, 1766, duration 12 minutes. Scored for two trumpets, timpani, and strings, without viola. This is a more modest piece than the previous one, both in forces and treatment. It is more concisely planned but still succeeds in conveying something of Haydn's magical way with a melodic line.

I Moderato with the theme:

which the strings present and the organ then takes up. The keys in the development are varied in character, but no new conclusions are reached and the organ plays in figures.

II Adagio with broken triads as the thematic figure:

III Finale allegro is sparkling and concertante, with a lively interchange between violins and solo.

A further **Concerto for organ and string instruments in C major** Hob. XVIII:10 has three movements: (Moderato), Adagio, Allegro.

Publishers: Bärenreiter—*Flötenuhrstücke (Flute-clock pieces)*, ed. E. F. Schmid; Breitkopf—Concerto Hob. XVIII:1, ed. M. Schneider; Henle—Concerto Hob. XVIII:10, ed. Horst Walter; Doblinger—Concerto Hob. XVIII:8, ed. H. C. Robbins Landon; Peters—*Orgelmusik aus drei Jahrhunderten (Organ music from three centuries)*, Vol.2, ed. T. Fedtke.

JOHANN CHRISTIAN KITTEL (bapt. Erfurt, February 18, 1732; d. ibid., April 17, 1809) was born in the same year as Haydn and was one of J. S. Bach's last pupils. The old school of composition mingles with the new galant style in his *Great preludes for organ,* so that the 16 often very short pieces offer us a colorful series of contrasting compositions. The dramatic D major prelude and the two in E-flat major and E major which entirely belong to Viennese Classicism should particularly be mentioned.

Publishers: Möseler, ed. W. Stockmeier; Schott—*Antologia organi (Organ anthology)*, Vol.11, ed. S. Margittay. CHRISTIAN GOTTHILF TAG (b. Beierfeld, Erzgebirge, April 2, 1735; d. Niederzwönitz, Saxony, July 19, 1811) was slightly younger. Beside chorale preludes we have his *Twelve short, easy organ preludes together with an organ symphony,* which are enchanting Rococo music, and the symphony, a splendidly bombastic piece for orchestrion. Publisher: Breitkopf, ed. D. Wieghorst.

JOHANN GEORG ALBRECHTSBERGER (b. Klosterneuburg nr. Vienna, February 3, 1736; d. Vienna, March 7, 1809) brings the south German tradition to a worthy close with his collection of versets—**Octo toni ecclesiastici per organo** (Eight church modes for organ). His fugues, some on such themes as "Christus ist erstanden" (Christ is risen), "Der Tag, der ist so freudenreich" (The day of exaltation) or B-A-C-H, show him as a brilliant contrapuntalist, who rightly occupied a central position in Viennese musical life for many years. Only his **Pastorale** indicates that he too was an exponent of the new age. Publishers: Doblinger, ed. O. Biba; Coppenrath—*Octo toni (Eight modes)*, ed. R. Walter.

WOLFGANG AMADEUS MOZART

b. Salzburg, January 27, 1756; d. Vienna, December 5, 1791

Mozart was in the service of the Archbishop of Salzburg for a time, but spent his last decade in Vienna as an independent composer and teacher. His organ works stand on the periphery of his complete oeuvre, which is not enumerated here; they should not be any the less respected for that reason.

Works for solo organ

Mozart's three works for solo organ are marked "for an organ in a clock," that is, for a mechanical instrument which produced the music by means of cylinders and small rows of pipes, like Haydn's flute-clocks. The editions for organ which determine how these pieces are played are arrangements from manuscript scores, only some of the original scores having survived.

Adagio, allegro and adagio in F minor K*. 594, duration 11 minutes. This is the memorial music for Field Marshal Laudon's mausoleum in Count Deym's art cabinet in Vienna. The Adagio is a very elegiac introduction to the work, and the middle section in F major is a small but complete sonata form—almost the only one in all organ music. Both themes are developed as tellingly as possible and the result is a theoretical and musical masterpiece. The first Adagio concludes the work with only minor alterations for the cadence. While the Adagio articulates the mourning for the famous general who died in 1790, the Allegro recalls his military deeds.

Fantasia in F minor K. 608, duration 11 minutes: Chordal Allegro in F minor, Fugue in F minor, Allegro, as above, in F-sharp minor, modulating to C minor, Andante in A-flat major, Allegro, as above, in A-flat major, Double fugue in F minor. As the three Allegro movements are based on the same thematic material this com-

*K. refers to the Köchel-Verzeichnis—Ludwig Ritter von Köchel's *Chronologisch-systematisches Verzeichnis sämtlicher Tonwerke Wolfgang Amadeus Mozarts (Systematic chronological catalogue of W. A. Mozart's compositions)*, Wiesbaden, 6th edition 1964.

position seems almost as concentric as a rondo.

All these individual sections are short, in contrast to the Andante and the double fugue; they are thematically so simple and penetrating that they can be immediately memorized. The fugue, only briefly developed, has as its theme the bottom part of the double theme from the second fugue, at the end of which the four

parts appear in stretto formation. This section demonstrates Mozart's great contrapuntal ability, is musically interesting and technically very complicated for the organist. The Andante is a peaceful middle section with several variations on the melodic theme and its accompanying music.

Andante in F major K. 616. Again in variation form, and of all three compositions the most suited to the typical chamber music character of a small organ.

The **Fugue in C minor** K. 426 was composed by Mozart for two pianos, but the expressive Baroque character of the theme fits it well for an organ setting:

Works for organ and orchestra

Church sonatas. This term defines short, one-movement pieces in concise sonata form composed by Mozart for the services in Salzburg Cathedral. A "Sonata all'Epistola" (Sonata for the Epistle) was played between the readings of Epistle and Gospel. The orchestral complement varies among the individual works: the early pieces are scored for two violins and bass while the later ones add oboes, horns, clarini and timpani which enhance the beauty of the sound. The organ treatment also varies: the early pieces make it a continuo instrument, first with an unfigured and then with a figured bass, but later the organ part is obbligato and in the last sonata, K. 336, reaches concertante dimensions, as shown in the example below. All the pieces are marked Allegro and exude an unearthly serenity. In spite of their brevity, due to the short time spans available for them within the liturgy, they are concise in form and sometimes even contain a very small development section.

The theme of **Sonata in C major** K. 336, written in Salzburg in March 1780, first appears in the strings and is then taken up by the organ. A concertante exchange between strings and organ follows. In the recapitulation comes the then customary 6/4 chord in the strings, to invite a cadenza from the solo instrument.

Sonata in D major K. 144:

Publishers: Bärenreiter—*Neue Mozart-Ausgabe (New Mozart edition)* Ser.IX, group 27, Vol.2, ed. W. Plath, score—also the excellently-developed Fugue in G minor K. 401, of which the last eight bars had to be supplied; Bärenreiter—performing editions of K. 594, 608, and 616, ed. F. Brinkmann; Doblinger—K. 594, 608 and 616, arr. M. Henking; Bärenreiter—*Neue Mozart-Ausgabe,* Ser. 1, group 16: "Church sonatas", ed. M. E. Dounias; Leduc—Fugue in C minor K. 426, ed. M. Dupré; Schott—*Antologia organi (Organ anthology),* Vol.12, ed. S. Margittay; Peters—*Orgelmusik aus drei Jahrhunderten (Organ music from three centuries),* Vol.2, ed. T. Fedtke.

G. J. Vogler and J. H. Knecht were contemporaries of Mozart's who also wrote for the organ:

Abbé GEORG JOSEPH VOGLER (b. Pleichach, nr. Würzburg, June 15, 1749; d. Darmstadt, May 6, 1814) is known for the "System of Simplification" by which he hoped to build cheaper and less complicated organs, and for his improvised concerts with naturalistic tone painting of orchestral proportions. A contemporary reported on his playing: "The thunderstorm (from the piece 'Walk by the Rhine interrupted by a storm') really amazed me. Vogler actually played three or four pedals at the same time with his feet and let the wind of the Trumpet and other roaring bass stops bluster on for a long time without harmonies, rhythm or any playing on the manuals." And about Vogler's "Siege of Jericho": ". . . at the collapse of the walls he pressed as many keys as he could reach with both arms and had all the manual stops out." His surviving organ works certainly give no idea of his performing style.

There are 112 **Preludes,** dating from 1808, a collection of very small pieces in almost all the keys, and another collection of preludes containing 32 longer works, among them the E-flat major prelude, remarkable for its surprising changes of dynamics and tempo. Publishers: Pustet—Preludes in E-flat major and B minor, ed. E. Kraus; Forberg—112 Preludes, ed. J. Dorfmüller.

JUSTIN HEINRICH KNECHT (b. Biberach on the Riss, September 30, 1752; d. ibid., December 1, 1817) left in writing what Vogler improvised—a scene with an organ thunderstorm. **Shepherd's delight interrupted by a thunderstorm** was published in 1794 and has been reprinted in facsimile by Bärenreiter with a thorough preface, edited by H. W. Höhnen. The whole action is indicated by the list of contents and the preface contains registration suggestions for the thunder. Whether this represents a decline in organ music or an impetus towards new horizons is for each player or listener to decide. One may mention in passing that the "Shepherd's delight" and Knecht's symphony **Tongemälde der Natur** (Tonal portrait of nature) may be considered forerunners of Beethoven's *Pastoral Symphony,* since their programs are exactly the same.

The "**Flute Concerto**" (because of the flute stops used) by CHRISTIAN HEINRICH RINCK (b. Elgersburg, Thuringia, February 18, 1770; d. Darmstadt, August 7, 1846) might be considered a continuation of Vogler's and Knecht's works. The galant style here reaches its climax in melodic upper parts over Alberti basses, solo voices contrasting with tutti effects and free cadenzas for concertante display by the soloist result in a concert piece of virtuoso calibre. Herewith an extract from the Adagio:

Publisher: Forberg, ed. M. Weyer.

A brief glance reveals that the organ works of LUDWIG VAN BEETHOVEN (b. Bonn, December 16, 1770; d. Vienna, March 26, 1827) are of two kinds: a short **D major fugue** Op. 137 and **Two preludes** in all major keys Op. 39 are characteristic of the organist of the Minoriten church in Bonn, while the **Suite for a mechanical organ** was intended, like Mozart's organ pieces, for Count Deym's automaton. The Adagio of the three-movement suite is surprising because of its length and its development of two themes with exuberant melodies, which sound marvellous when played with resonant flute stops. The Scherzo and Allegro on the other hand have the musical clock character of Haydn's compositions. Publisher: Hinrichsen, ed. L. Altman; Peters—*Orgelmusik aus drei Jahrhunderten (Organ music from three centuries)*, Vol.2, ed. T. Fedtke.

The Viennese court organist and famous teacher of musical theory SIMON SECHTER (b. Friedberg, Bohemia, October 11, 1788; d. Vienna, September 10, 1867) was a more traditional composer. He published **Fugues** in pure style, among them a **Pastoral fugue** which is an interesting blend of Baroque form and Classic character piece, and the surprising **Six variations or contrapuntal movements on the Austrian folk song "Gott erhalte Franz den Kaiser"** (God save Francis the Emperor), which uses Haydn's well known tune (also used in his *Emperor Quartet* and later to become the German national anthem) in the manner of the (old) art form, like a spiritual return to the tradition of Scheidt's song variations. Publisher: Doblinger, ed. O. Biba.

FELIX MENDELSSOHN BARTHOLDY

b. Hamburg, February 3, 1809; d. Leipzig, November 4, 1847

After many journeys—to England, Scotland, Italy and France—he took the post of conductor in Düsseldorf in 1833 and in 1835 moved to the Gewandhaus Orchestra in Leipzig, while making guest appearances in Berlin and other cities. He was also co-founder of the Leipzig conservatory. Mendelssohn left symphonic works and the important oratorios Elijah *and* St. Paul. *His organ works result from his preoccupation with Bach and with Protestant church music, and he gained lasting historical recognition for his performance of the* St. Matthew Passion *in 1829—the first since the composer's death—and for his indefatigable commitment to Bach.*

For many years Mendelssohn's organ works were tolerated but ridiculed as relics, by an age hostile to the organ. Just one of the sonatas, the sixth, was performed now and then, not because of its value as a composition, however, but because it featured the beloved "Our Father" chorale. More recently this picture has changed, and a study of his organ works, comprising three preludes and six sonatas, has revealed that they form a link between the Baroque and the Romantic, and point the way forward.

Three preludes and fugues Op. 37, 1837:

Prelude and fugue in C minor, duration 7 minutes. The prelude with its prominent melody in the top part springs to life with energetic octaves followed by descending lines and broken chords. This theme returns in the second and third parts, while the pedals mostly just provide the bass notes. After the "grand" gestures of the prelude—in the musical sense, too—the fugue's 12/8 meter gives it a more intimate character, in spite of the fact that its thematic construction clearly depends on Baroque examples, including Bach. The development continues in a classic equilibrium skillfully enhanced with harmonic devices, and flows into the short, more symphonically planned finale.

Prelude and fugue in G major, duration 10 minutes. The prelude's marking, Andante con moto and *mezzopiano,* indicates a sort of song without words, a calm floating motion of sounds and lines, almost without aim or end. In contrast the fugue is strict in its development of the theme and Baroque in its striding intervals with their references to the notes B-A-C-H.

Prelude and fugue in D minor, duration 8 minutes. A recitative opening structured with supporting chords prepares for the main theme, which is at once answered fugally in the dominant. An exposition in all four parts follows and a development-style middle section starts in F major. A skillful succession of eighth-notes, eighth-note triplets and sixteenth-notes intensifies the motion until the runs become unaccompanied and lead into the recapitulation. The fugue is regular in formation, but the theme and its treatment lack fascination.

Six sonatas Op. 65, 1844:

Sonata 1 in F minor, duration 18 minutes. Allegro moderato e serioso. A polyphonic concert piece with homophonic chords in the introductory bars. Only later does the thematic material emerge to serve as framework for the chorale lines "Was mein Gott will, das gescheh allzeit" (What my God wills, may that ever be). The chorale sections sound dynamically detached on another manual.—Adagio. Melodic movement with echo effects.—Andante/Recitative. Again an exchange, on the one hand between manuals with differing timbres and on the other between unison and a mixture of polyphonic and homophonic bars. Then comes a transition to the Allegro assai vivace, a virtuoso final movement in runs, broken chords and arpeggios.

Sonata 2 in C minor, duration 11 minutes. Out of the muted Grave of the introductory bars arises the intensely melodic Adagio for solo voice with accompaniment. The singing line moves most effectively from soprano to tenor; next has both accompanying parts above it, and then returns to the soprano. In the same way the Allegro maestoso e vivace, a martial piece wholly atypical of Mendelssohn, serves as preparation and guide into the short concluding fugue.

Sonata 3 in A major, duration 10 minutes. A very orchestral piece both in form and feeling, radiant with the idiosyncratic spirit of its creator. It has only two movements, the first by far the better both in quality and length, while the second can only be described as an appendix. In Con moto maestoso Mendelssohn offers an artistic musical framework to embrace the exquisite detailed working which follows.

Out of the unison opening a fugato in minor develops two themes, to which is added the chorale melody "Aus tiefer Not schrei ich zu dir" (Out of the deep call I to Thee) in the pedals. The tempo is not rigidly maintained, but steadily grows in vivacity and excitement as the volume increases until, after a soaring pedal solo, the framework music of the opening (see the previous example) returns to complete the picture. The Andante tranquillo is a song full of yearning and an echo of what went before.

Sonata 4 in B-flat major, duration 14 minutes. Allegro con brio, a flamboyantly melodious movement in chivalrous tone, with two sections. Andante religioso. Behind this description, later used for a number of sentimental little pieces, there lies a simple, homophonic movement with occasional solo interpolations which one can well imagine played with Clarinet stops or the Vox Humana. An Allegretto provides a broad sweeping melody over background music in the lower parts. Here too the tune moves into the tenor, returns to the top part and ends in a two-part epilogue. The Allegro maestoso e vivace is a fugue expanded into a concertante movement and ends the sonata in the splendor of B-flat major.

Sonata 5 in D-major, duration 8 minutes. This is the shortest of the six, beginning with a chorale movement and leading into an Andante con moto which does not refer to it melodically and has a pizzicato effect in the pedals.

This piece is reminiscent of many of Mendelssohn's scherzos, even though its tempo is more measured. After the B minor of the slow movement comes a quick finale, Allegro maestoso, in D major. Once again a few markedly melodic bars enclose a middle section with a quiet melody in the top part.

Sonata 6 in D minor, duration 14 minutes. This is a set of variations on the chorale "Vater unser im Himmelreich" (Our Father, who art in heaven). After the melody has been stated these variations follow: 1. Cantus firmus in the soprano, in three parts. 2. Chordal cantus firmus in the soprano, with independent runs in the pedals. 3. Cantus firmus in the tenor, in four parts. 4. Passage work with cantus firmus divided between the pedals and the manuals. 5. Fugue, with a theme taken from the opening of the chorale. The finale is a spiritual Andante with no thematic relation to the chorale. One can place this chorale sonata without reservation beside similar great works from the distant and recent past; in fact it is more expressive than many others and is supple and fluid, in spite of a certain routine formality which can occasionally be glimpsed.

Publishers: Breitkopf—Sonatas; Peters—Sonatas and Preludes; Bornemann; Universal—*Lea Pocket Scores.*

ROBERT SCHUMANN

b. Zwickau, June 8, 1810; d. Endenich nr. Bonn, July 29, 1856

He was the leading exponent of Romanticism in German music. He studied in Leipzig where he founded the "Neue Zeitschrift für Musik" (New musical journal), then in 1844 went to Dresden and in 1850 to Düsseldorf as music director. Schumann mainly wrote piano music and songs, and his organ works are not very original as he was influenced by his predecessors. His orchestral compositions include four symphonies and a piano concerto, and he also wrote choral and chamber works.

Six canons Op. 56, composed for pedal piano in 1845. The first "Étude" (Study), as Schumann called them, consists of a trio with the two upper parts in canon at the octave and therefore easily audible. It is more difficult to hear how the other pieces are constructed, because either the canon is in the right hand, with the left hand and the pedals playing the accompaniment, or the part carrying the canon has changing accompanying notes set very close to it, which is the case in the well known canon in B minor. Even without following the canon closely—and this is not the main object—a listener will enjoy these unusual pieces.

The **Four sketches** Op. 58 of 1845 are artful, almost humorous miniatures, all in three movements—Minuet, Trio, Minuet. The third in F minor and the fourth in D-flat major sound like scherzos.

Six fugues on B-A-C-H Op. 60, 1845. A very important treatment of the B-A-C-H theme so often chosen, and here imbued with the spirit of Romanticism.

For the **1st Fugue,** Langsam (slow), Schumann uses another relatively conventional form of the theme and a masterly composing technique learned from the old contrapuntalists.

2nd Fugue, Lebhaft (lively), with toccatalike sections, free and stately, again built on the B-A-C-H theme.

3rd Fugue, Mit sanften Stimmen (in soft voices), a peaceful five-part movement.

4th Fugue, Mässig, doch nicht zu langsam (moderate, but not too slow). The theme is joined by a retrograde statement of the B-A-C-H theme and is then treated in stretto.

5th Fugue, Lebhaft (lively), is like a scherzo, and is contrasted with another simple B-A-C-H line in quarter-notes.

6th Fugue, Mässig, nach und nach schneller (moderate, gradually growing faster) is a double fugue. The second theme is stated and then appears in inversion. At the end the two themes merge to great effect and close with chords.

This last fugue interestingly combines symphonic form and epic breadth with fugal development of the themes.

Publishers: Bornemann—all works, ed. M. Dupré; Breitkopf—Fugues, ed. W. Dallman; Oxford University Press—Sketches; Peters—Fugues.

FRANZ LISZT

b. Raiding, Burgenland, October 22, 1811;
d. Bayreuth, July 31, 1886

Success came early to this child prodigy, who travelled to Vienna and Paris and became one of the greatest virtuosos of the century. Later he taught in Weimar, Rome and Budapest, and among his wide circle of pupils were von Bülow, Cornelius, Weingartner and Sauer. He mainly wrote for orchestra and piano.

Fantasia on the chorale "Ad nos, ad salutarem undam" 1855, duration 30 minutes. This is an enormous, (over) long tone painting on a tune which, once heard, can remain indelibly stamped on the listener's memory. Cuts are made in almost all performances because the Fantasia has a wealth of lovely individual effects all too easily lost in an unabridged rendering. The fugue at the end draws its theme from a version of the chorale adapted in military fashion:

Prelude and fugue on B-A-C-H, 1855, duration 13 minutes. This work is full of romantic extravagance and elegant virtuosity, but is still clearly developed and lucidly constructed. As a composition it is typical of Liszt's piano works, which makes performance on the organ musically and technically difficult. After a varied prelude entirely dominated by the theme, a fugal fantasia rather than a fugue appears, because the theme never appears again in its entirety after the four-part exposition:

instead the structure dissolves into passage-work, runs and trills and ends with a hymn. The harmonies of the *pianissimo* chords before the five last cadence bars clearly demonstrate how many successors this master has had, down to the present day.

Variations on the continuo bass "Weinen, Klagen, Sorgen, Zagen" (Weeping, wailing, mourning, fearing) by J. S. Bach, 1863, duration 18 minutes. This is a tightly-knit working of the theme with contrasting variations, sometimes set in parts, sometimes in chords. At the end comes the chorale "Was Gott tut, das ist wohlgetan" (What God does, it is well done).

Further works: Évocation à la Chapelle Sixtine (Evocation of the Sistine Chapel), Funeral ode, Mass, Requiem.

Publishers: Bornemann; Musica—*Orgelwerke (Organ works)*, ed. S. Margittay; Peters.

At about the turn of the 18th century the organ was claimed by a movement which, beginning with Mozart, had shortly before begun to strike up new sounds on the piano—music for four hands. In the organ's case four feet came into play too, an activity which was by no means easy and often became quite comical. As the modern house organ was not yet known, this domestic-sounding music was played in church. The pleasure derived by two people from making music together on a normally solo instrument must have disposed the players to be indulgent about the musical quality of these works.

FRANZ SCHUBERT (b. Liechtenthal nr. Vienna, January 31, 1797; d. Vienna, November 19, 1828) wrote only one piece for organ, the Fugue in E minor for four hands Op.post. 152, D.* 952, 1828. This is a melodious occasional piece written for an excursion to Heiligenkreuz Abbey near Vienna, to try out its famous organ. The theme:

For a similar occasion Schubert's friend FRANZ LACHNER (b. Rain, Upper Bavaria, April 2, 1803; d. Munich, January 20, 1890) wrote his **Introduction and fugue in D minor.**

Publishers: Doblinger, ed. O. Biba; Peters—*Orgelmusik aus drei Jahrhunderten (Organ music from three centuries)*, Vol.2, ed. T. Fedtke.

A collection of four more fugues by GOTTFRIED PREYER (1807–1901), DAVID HERMANN ENGEL (1816–77), ERNST FRIEDRICH GAEBLER (1807–93) and CHRISTIAN GOTTLOB HÖPNER (1799–1859) are published by Forberg, edited by K. Lueders.

ADOLF FRIEDRICH HESSE (b. Breslau, August 30, 1809; d. ibid., August 5, 1863) composed two more extensive fantasias for four hands. The **Fantasia in C minor** begins with a serious Adagio, followed by an Andante grazioso and a concluding Fugato in 6/8 time. The movements of the **Fantasia in D minor** are: Andante, Allegretto (song form), Allegro vivace, Poco moderato (fugue). Publishers: Forberg, Leuckart. Of Hesse's organ works for two hands mention should be made above all of his **Introduction, theme and variations in A major,** a brilliant, convincingly structured virtuoso piece, and the two **Fantasias** in E minor

*D. refers to Otto Erich Deutsch's *Franz Schubert. Thematisches Verzeichnis seiner Werke in chronologischer Folge (Thematic catalogue of his works in chronological order)*, Kassel 1978.

and F minor. Publisher: Möseler, ed. W. Stockmeier.

This music reaches its climax in the **Sonata in D minor** Op. 30 by GUSTAV MERKEL (b. Oberoderwitz, Saxony, November 12, 1827; d. Dresden, October 30, 1885). The three movements are based on verses from the Psalms: the rather ponderous Allegro moderato is a setting of verses 6–8 and 10 from Psalm 42 "As the hart panteth after the water brooks," and the Adagio of verses from Psalm 23 "The Lord is my shepherd." The music, especially in the tenor melody, underlines the confident faith inherent in the words.

The end of Psalm 42, which is the same as verse 6, is set to the Allegro con fuoco—Fugue, and though the fugue starts with some wild and stormy bars it ends in the same recitative manner as the first movement. It has a strong impetus and heightened tension. Publishers: Forberg; Leuckart.

A **Fantasia, prayer and fugue** survives from the works of JOHANN HEINRICH LÖFFLER (b. Oberwind, Thuringia, March 1, 1833; d. Pössneck, Thuringia, April 15, 1903). This is late Romantic music, with a highly chromatic Prayer, and a beautiful, freewheeling Fugue. Publisher: Leuckart. CHARLES HENRI VALENTIN ALKAN (b. Paris, November 30, 1813; d. ibid., March 29, 1888) created a remarkable curiosity in his **Bombardo-Carillon** for four feet only. The name indicates the stops to use. It is gentler and more musical than the martial title and the anticipated low notes lead one to expect. This might be called "domestic music for lovers." Publisher: Forberg, ed. H. J. Busch.

CÉSAR FRANCK

b. Liège, December 10, 1822; d. Paris, November 8, 1890

He was the greatest organ composer of the 19th century. At the age of 13 he came to Paris to study with Anton Reicha and others at the Conservatoire. There, after several other posts, he was appointed organist at St. Clothild's in 1859 and in 1872 became professor at the Conservatoire. Franck marks the start of the revival of French organ composition, and also of French organ playing, with which the names of Widor, Guilmant, Dupré and Messiaen are associated. Only towards the end of his life did he write the masterpieces among his numerous works—the three chorales, the symphonies, the symphonic variations, chamber music and operas. As his important works were not confined to church music, his influence was felt in almost all fields of French music in the last third of the 19th century.

Fantasia in C major Op. 16, 1860. This is in three movements: a peaceful introduction, a solo middle section to be played with the Trumpet stop, transitional bars and an Adagio finale in simple song form.

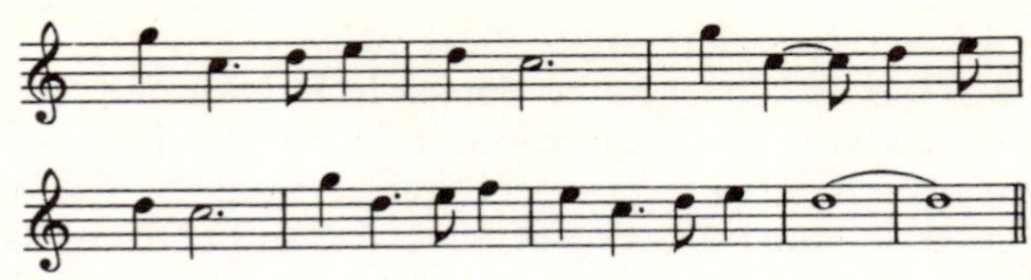

Grande pièce symphonique (Great symphonic piece) in F-sharp minor Op. 17, 1863, duration 18 minutes. This is really a "great" symphonic piece, as extensive as Franck's chorales but without achieving their concision. Though it is clearly divided into several movements it still has an organic and imaginative effect, and heralds his later mastery of symphonic form.

The beginning, Andante serioso, is markedly full of contrast with its interchange of high and low notes. The first eighth-note motif is emphasized by its

accompanying chords in syncopated quarter-notes. A melodious phrase ends the introductory section and leads to a diminished chord which opens the Allegro non troppo e maestoso, with the following main theme:

This striking quotation is forcefully elaborated, appearing in different voices. The intervals between the first three notes are particularly used in the thematic development, but this movement brings in another melodious and stately contrasting theme, and even the second motif from the introduction quoted earlier is heard again. Andante, a peaceful movement with a cantabile melody over accompanying chords leads into the Allegro, which offers little motifs over accompanying figures until a *cantando* theme emerges, first in the bass, then answered in the soprano. After a brief develpment a shortened form of the Andante returns. The introduction to the final movement combines most of the themes and motifs used so far, especially those from the first section, the Allegro non troppo and the Andante. Then the main theme previously quoted appears, soaring in the upper voices over full, effective chords and scales in the bass. The impetus thus obtained is weakened by a somewhat undistinguished and long, drawn-out fugato, which enters again superfluously and brings the work to an end.

Prelude, fugue and variation in B minor Op. 18, c. 1862. The prelude in Andante cantabile consists of a lullaby tune with simple accompanying figures:

The middle section consists of a bridge passage and a simple, uncomplicated fugue, until the theme of the prelude is taken up again. The Variation has filigree, virtuoso figures in the accompaniment.

This is an enchantingly graceful work in Rococo style, which is much too seldom performed.

Pièce hèroique in B minor, 1878, duration 9 minutes. This imaginative piece combines three themes, or rather tunes, without any formal consistency but as though they were the inspiration of an improvising performer, either controlling the melodic lines or letting them flutter away. The resulting formal sequence in this work is free, but musically convincing. The first part of the theme

mainly appears in the bass, and is soon answered by the soprano with an inconsequential tune based on a falling and rising fifth. Finally the third component enters—a stately chorale air which also provides the climax in the final bars:

Three chorals, 1890. Franck uses the term "choral" to describe an original choralelike melody which forms the basic theme of any composition, and therefore it has nothing to do with either the Gregorian chorale or the German hymn. Sometimes it only attains its full stature as the work progresses.

Choral No. 1 in E major, duration 12 minutes. After a peaceful, restrained opening, played with basic stops and having few melodic references to the chorale, the latter appears in the soprano, harmonized, on the Vox Humana.

The Trumpet melody which then enters is like many found in Franck's works. On his organ he had a Trumpet stop in the Swell, and wrote a number of pieces for its use, so as to give it a proper chance to be heard. Later bars of broad chords alternate with faster, imitative ones, and the melody is broken into individual motifs then worked on in various voices. The Maestoso finale presents the chorale in its full breadth.

The **Choral No. 2** in B minor, duration 14 minutes, is constructed like a chaconne, for the theme is an ostinato, beginning in the bass. First it alternates between bass and soprano and then appears in new, free parts. The first section—

and later the finale as well—ends with a short mystical polyphonic phrase:

Fantasia bars lead into a fugato with the chorale theme, and the resulting counterpoint is then linked with the shorter sections which follow, to make a densely woven texture. After the ostinato in E-flat and F-sharp minor comes a final

fortissimo chorale in the upper part and the peaceful finish with the Vox Humana already mentioned.

Choral No. 3 in A minor, duration 14 minutes, is very simple and lucidly formed. In the first section the restless, fluctuating movement of the top part and the broadly proclaimed seventh chords in arpeggios alternate with the chorale theme

quoted here. As in the first chorale the Trumpet solo then enters in the Adagio, with further dynamically intensified imitations which flow into the finale. This last section is based like the first on the motif and the chorale, which are both skillfully combined and towards the end reach a hymnlike climax.

These three chorals, composed in the last year of Franck's life, are of equal stature. They represent the climax of his organ works and demonstrate his superb composition technique, his unerring instinct for contrasting tone colors on the organ and abundant powers of expression and direct communication with the listener. The registration given is the composer's.

Of his earlier works, collected in the edition of the *Six pieces,* mention should be made of the **Pastorale** in E major Op. 19, 1863, the comical middle section of which is obviously related to Schumann's Canon Op. 54; the serious **Prière** (Prayer) in C-sharp minor Op. 20, c. 1860, and the **Final** in B-flat major Op. 21, c. 1862. Out of the interval of a fourth, like a bugle call, a piece develops which belongs entirely to the virtuoso repertory and can properly be called a hit.

In 1878 Franck published the striking **Fantasia in A major** and the little **Cantabile.** They appeared in the same year as the *Heroic piece* under the title *Three concert pieces for organ.*

Publishers: Bärenreiter—*Ausgewählte Orgelwerke (Selected organ works);* Bornemann; Durand; Peters—*Complete works.*

AUGUST GOTTFRIED RITTER (b. Erfurt, August 25, 1811; d. Magdeburg, August 26, 1885) wrote **Sonatas,** of which Op. 19 in E minor and Op. 24 in A minor are outstandingly rich in musical invention and organistic in character. Publisher: Forberg.

The Frenchman LOUIS JAMES ALFRED LEFÉBURE-WÉLY (b. Paris, November 13, 1817; d. ibid., December 31, 1869) wrote in a more pianistic salon style. His **Pastoral scene, March** or **Exit** introduce a merry, worldly, even turbulently comic element into church. Publishers: Forberg, ed. H. J. Busch; and *Pariser Orgelmeister des 19. Jahrhunderts (19th-century Parisian masters of the organ),* ed. K. Lueders.

The Belgian NICOLAS JACQUES LEMMENS (b. Zoerle-Parwijs, January 3, 1823; d. Linterpoort Castle nr. Mecheln, January 30, 1881) had a strong influence on the French school of organ composition via his pupils Guilmant and Widor. In his **Three sonatas—Pontificale, O Filii** and **Pascale**—he wrote organ music of high quality, and many of the movements can be compared with works by his great predecessors, for instance the finale of the first—Fanfare, Fugue—and that of the third—Finale Alleluia. Publisher: Forberg, ed. K. Lueders.

ANTON BRUCKNER (b. Ansfelden, Upper Austria, September 4, 1824; d. Vienna, October 11, 1896), the great symphonist, belongs to this period. There is little to report on his organ compositions because he was a thrilling improviser and wrote down virtually nothing. Only some preludes and a fugue—six pieces in all—have survived, and they are early works, not important within his total oeuvre. Publishers: Böhm; Universal.

JOHANNES BRAHMS

b. Hamburg, May 7, 1833; d. Vienna, April 3, 1897

Known above all for his symphonies and Lieder, Brahms came via Detmold to Vienna, where he made his home. His organ works rely on their Baroque precursors and stylistically do not speak the same language as his symphonic works.

Chorale prelude and fugue in A minor WoO* 7, 1856, on the chorale "O Traurigkeit, o Herzeleid" (Oh sorrow, oh agony of heart). The prelude is in the form of a simple organ chorale, with cantus firmus in the soprano and triplet movements in the accompaniment. The fugue is another chorale setting, in that the actual fugue in the soprano, alto and tenor on the theme from the opening of the chorale is joined by the chorale melody in the pedals, divided into lines and in long note values, as in the fugal finales of Reger's chorale fantasias.

Fugue in A-flat minor WoO 8, 1856. This is a very densely contrapuntal piece. With the exception of a few incidental bars the theme appears throughout in its original form and inverted, insistently punctuated with rests and expanded. It is remarkable that the contrapuntal construction does not impose itself on the listener as the skeleton of the work, but only creates a foundation on which its rare wealth of exquisite sound can grow.

Prelude and fugue in A minor WoO 9, 1856. This is in two parts, with a fugal opening which soon dissolves into free figuration. In the fourth bar of the pedals the head of the fugue theme can already be heard. The fugue starts regularly in four parts, which enter in order from soprano to bass, but then renounces contrapuntal devices except for augmentation in the pedals. Harmonies and figuration grow towards the close.

Prelude and fugue in G minor WoO 10, 1857. This contains equally rich figuration in the toccatalike prelude, with two appearances of the striking motif. The fugue theme contains a characteristic jump of a sixth.

Eleven chorale preludes Op.post. 122, 1896. All Brahms's chorale settings are collected under this title. Although, with the exception of the final echo effect mentioned below, he only worked with conventional forms and particularly those

*WoO refers to works without opus number (Werke ohne Opuszahl). c.f. Margit L. McCorkle, *Johannes Brahms. Thematisch-bibliographisches Werkverzeichnis (Johannes Brahms. Thematic and bibliographic catalogue of his works)*, Munich 1984.

known to J. S. Bach, Brahms still created masterpieces representing a late, almost unearthly, echo of the Baroque age. Head imitation, cantus firmus in the pedals—No.1 "Mein Jesu, der du mich" (My Jesus, Thou who . . .) in E minor. Cantus firmus in the soprano—No.4 "Herzlich tut mich erfreuen" (With all my heart do I rejoice) in D major and No.7 "O Gott, du frommer Gott" (Oh God, Thou holy God) in A minor.

Organ chorale style with cantus firmus in the soprano—No.2 "Herzliebster Jesu" (Most beloved Jesus) in G minor; No.3 "O Welt, ich muss dich lassen" (Oh world, I must leave thee) I, in F major; No.6 "O wie selig seid ihr doch" (O how blessed are you yet) in D minor; No.8 "Es ist ein Ros entsprungen" (A rose has flowered) in F major; and No.9 "Herzlich tut mich verlangen" (I desire with my whole heart) I, in A minor. Trio—No.5 "Schmücke dich, o liebe Seele" (Soul, array thyself with gladness) in E major.

Noteworthy: No.10 "Herzlich tut mich verlangen" II, in A minor, has a broad, sweeping theme as a counterpart to the chorale in the bass, rather like Bach's Schübler settings, and No.11 "O Welt, ich muss dich lassen" II, in F major, where the end of each line is repeated twice and should be played as a double echo.

Publishers: Breitkopf; Peters.

JULIUS REUBKE

b. Hausneindorf, Harz, March 23, 1834; d. Pillnitz, June 3, 1858

He was a highly talented pupil of Liszt's, and in addition to his organ sonata wrote one for piano, which shows his debt to his teacher more clearly than does the organ work.

Sonata in C minor, the 94th Psalm, duration 24 minutes. This is a freely constructed work, though it is formally divided into three movements, and the main idea runs through it all.

After the introductory bars marked Grave with their towering *fortissimo* chords comes a Larghetto which recalls the characteristic intervals between the first four notes of the theme. This is a setting of the first two verses of the psalm: "O Lord God, to whom vengeance belongeth; O God, to whom vengeance belongeth, shew thyself. Lift up thyself, thou judge of the earth: render a reward to the proud." There follows a gradual transition to the Allegro con fuoco with the theme elaborated in the manuals over runs in the pedals, or in the pedals with arpeggios and octave figures in the manuals, to the words of verses 3–7: "Lord, how long shall the wicked, how long shall the wicked triumph? . . . They slay the widow and the stranger, and murder the fatherless. Yet they say, The Lord shall not see, neither shall the God of Jacob regard it."

This first section gives way to an Adagio which in general uses the same thematic material, and offers expressive lines for the words [of verse 19]: "In the multitude of my thoughts within me thy comforts delight my soul." Thereupon Reubke moves into the final so-called Fugue, to which this term only applies for the first bars. It is contrapuntal in character, and the part writing soon gives way to freely imaginative elaboration. This form continues to the end, though rhythmic or melodic elements of the main idea are constantly being used. This finale is a setting of the last two verses: "But the Lord is my defense; and my God is the rock of my refuge.

And he shall bring upon them their own iniquity, and shall cut them off in their own wickedness; yea, the Lord our God shall cut them off."

The sonata is a markedly orchestral organ work, a symphonic poem making good use of the organ's shimmering tone colors, which are all too prominent next to its "regular" sounds. It is worthy of attention, and bears the mark of its short-lived creator's genius.

Publisher: Peters

ALBERT BECKER (b. Quedlinburg, June 13, 1834; d. Berlin, January 10, 1899) was born in the same year as Reubke and achieved fame as the director of the Berlin cathedral choir. In his **Fantasia and fugue** Op. 52 original invention combines with effective formal principles to produce a great and successful organ work. Publisher: Breitkopf.

CAMILLE SAINT-SAËNS (b. Paris, October 9, 1835; d. Algiers, December 16, 1921) is known in the organ world above all for his **Symphony in C minor** Op. 78, 1886. It belongs among his best works and features the organ as the crowning glory of the symphony orchestra's sound, which it enhances in grandiose manner, especially in the *forte* passages. A second work with orchestra, **Cypress and laurel,** is equally effective. Here the first section is reserved for the organ, while the orchestra only joins in gradually, beginning *pianissimo.* For organ solo he wrote preludes and fugues, fantasias and three rhapsodies. The first movement, Con moto, of his **Fantasia in E-flat major,** 1857, paints an exquisite musical picture by using the colors of three manuals, simultaneously and in quick succession. A bubbling second section provides contrast. Publishers: Billaudot; Durand.

ALEXANDRE GUILMANT

b. Boulogne-sur-mer, March 12, 1837;
d. Meudon, nr. Paris, March 29, 1911

After studying with his father and with Lemmens in Brussels, Guilmant became organist of Holy Trinity Church in Paris in 1871, and succeeded Widor as Professor at the Conservatoire, where he taught Dupré, Vierne and Nadia Boulanger. Most of his works were written for the organ, and many are only of passing interest on account of his late Romantic, post-Lisztian style. He gained great merit for his collected editions of the works of numerous old masters, especially French composers. He also succeeded in making the organ an almost popular instrument by clever choice of programs for his concerts. Guilmant was co-founder of the Paris Schola Cantorum.

The **Eight sonatas** are Guilmant's principal organ works, and they outshine his other compositions. It is historically noteworthy that they were written during a period when very few composers knew how to write for the organ at all. The sonatas are in several movements without demonstrating a stricter form common to all or some of them. A lightness in form and expression characterizes their musical presentation, which is markedly inspired by pianistic technique and clearly distinct from the cumbersome counterpoint of comparable contemporary compositions. Guilmant handles his light, airy melodies in the same manner.

The **First sonata** in D minor Op. 42, duration 28 minutes, was composed in 1874 as a symphony for organ and full orchestra, and only later rewritten for organ solo, without any alteration in the notes. The first movement begins with a slow introduction in sharply dotted rhythms, followed by an Allegro with a 25-bar theme in the pedals. The second movement is a Pastorale with a beautiful melody, and the third a vigorous Finale in continuous sixteenth-notes which marks the start of the French style of toccata.

In contrast, the **Seventh sonata** in F major Op. 89 is a six-movement piece divided as follows: I Entrée, tempo di marcia, maestoso, like processional music with interludes in couplets. II Lento assai, marked "Dreams", a series of floating sounds. III Intermezzo, with flowing passage work for both hands and some quieter bars scattered among it. IV Grand chorus, tempo di minuetto, with a fugal opening, broad, sweeping scales and series of heavy staccato notes. V Cantabile, the slow, expressive section of the work. VI Finale, an Allegro movement like a ceremonial farewell, loosely put together, appealing and inviting applause.

Among his other works are the **Noëls** (Carols) Op. 60, 1886 and the 18 **Pièces d'orgue dans différents styles** (Pieces for organ in different styles), 1860–75, of which the most important is the **Concert piece,** consisting of Prelude, Theme, Variations and Finale.

Publishers: Schott; Forberg.

JOSEPH RHEINBERGER

b. Vaduz, March 17, 1839; d. Munich, November 25, 1901

At the age of 12 he moved to Munich, where he studied at the music school and privately with Franz Lachner. He worked as an organist, from 1859 taught piano and theory at the music school, where he later also became professor of organ, and in 1877 was appointed court director of music. He conducted the oratorio society and the royal choir. Acknowledged as a pedagogue, he was much in demand as a teacher and taught a whole generation the sound rudiments of comprehensive theoretical knowledge. He mainly composed for organ and piano, less for orchestra, while his vocal works include sacred and secular choral music, masses, some operas, Singspiele and Lieder.

For a long period Rheinberger's organ music lay almost forgotten, because like Mendelssohn's it was difficult to classify, and so also disappeared from the program of organ recitals and from the church organist's repertory. Just as Mendelssohn stood alone in his love of the organ at the beginning of the 19th century, Rheinberger was fighting for a lost cause at its end. In his youth he had already protested firmly against the innovations of the rising high Romanticism and composed traditional music, his form influenced by Mendelssohn and his contrapuntal technique based on Bach. His works were played more often in his lifetime, however, than at the beginning of the 20th century, when Reger and his chorale fantasias came on the scene. Nowadays Rheinberger's organ music is not just of historical interest; he was a master of form and succeeded in creating a personal style without any real original inventiveness.

Works for solo organ

In his 20 **Organ sonatas** Rheinberger largely contrasts the fugue with its introductory prelude or closing fantasia. In the middle there are usually one or two slow movements, called intermezzo, romance, cantilena, canzona or idyll, marked Andante and mostly contemporary in style, while the fugues reflect their Baroque predecessors. The most original are the prelude fantasias, many of the toccata final movements, and the passacaglias. Rheinberger twice uses Gregorian melodies as cantus firmus—in the third sonata the 8th Gregorian psalm tone, and in the fourth the 9th, or tonus peregrinus.

The **Second sonata in A-flat major** Op. 65, called the *Fantasy Sonata,* duration 19 minutes, has a pretty first movement marked Grave—Allegro, with great sweeping arcs of melody, an Adagio espressivo and, as its finale, a Fugue thematically connected to the first movement with a short reference to the Adagio.

Third sonata in G major Op. 88, the *Pastoral Sonata,* duration 12 minutes. The pastoral character is expressed in the 12/8 meter of the prelude and the 6/8 of the fugue. The prelude starts by quoting the first half of the 8th psalm tone which is developed in canon. The movement is mostly written in three parts, giving it great lightness and transparency. Notes from the cantus firmus later appear in the top part as well.

The Intermezzo is a simple movement, beginning in E-flat major and ending in D major, the dominant of the following fugue. The theme is symmetrically conceived and contains definitely pastoral touches, while the fugue opens more in chamber music style.

A second idea in eighth-notes—which also forms the coda—joins in, the 8th psalm tone soon returns, first as a chorale and then in unison against runs, and the whole builds to a climax. The sonata does not end like that, however, but with a short epilogue featuring the second idea. This is a very unified, concise work, suggesting Classic form.

Fourth sonata in A minor Op. 98, duration 17 minutes. In it Rheinberger quotes the 9th psalm tone, the tonus peregrinus, which is used in the liturgy for the Magnificat and in this form found its way into many chorale preludes. In the first movement, which can be described as a prelude, the Gregorian quotations are sometimes chordal, sometimes heard over wavelike triplets enmeshed in orchestral phrases. The Andante Intermezzo introduces various solo effects in beautifully written melodies. A Fuga cromatica with a rare chromatic theme encompassing an entire octave forms the finale. The writhing sound weaves its way through every part and all manuals, until the composer returns briefly to the theme of the prelude and allows the tonus peregrinus to appear again in Organo Pleno.

The **Sixth sonata in E-flat minor** Op. 119 consists of Prelude, Intermezzo, Marcia religiosa and Fugue.

The **Seventh sonata in F minor** Op. 127 consists of Prelude, Andante and Finale

(Introduction and Fugue).

Of the movements of the **Eighth sonata in E minor** Op. 132, duration 23 minutes, the last, a Passacaglia, is particularly worth mentioning. Above the ostinato Rheinberger builds an impressive structure of variations, some with figuration, others being character variations. They flow by in a broad stream, touch on a soft and peaceful middle section and reach the climax at the close by restating the introductory motif from the first movement.

The **Ninth sonata in B-flat minor** Op. 142 begins with a Prelude—Grave, Allegro moderato—followed by a Romance (Andantino). As in the seventh sonata, the final movement consists of a Fantasia and a Fugue, the Fantasia further extended with strong distinctions between Adagio molto and Allegro moderato and between *fortissimo* and *pianissimo,* so that a seething, emotional torrent of sound surges to and fro before finally flowing into the B-flat major fugue, marked Con moto.

The **11th sonata in D minor** Op. 148 has four movements, making it an extensive work, more like a symphony in scope. It lasts over 20 minutes. The first movement, marked Agitato, can be called a fantasia and the second, Cantilena, is marked Adagio. The example below gives its opening bars in the right hand and the pedals.

It looks at first sight very Baroque, reminiscent of Bach's C major toccata or the slow movement of his F minor harpsichord concerto. But the outward appearance is deceptive, for 19th-century sentiment prevails in the sound, insinuates itself into the harmonic weavings of the eighth-note passages and creates a melancholy mood at the start and finish of the delicate lines. The third movement, Intermezzo, serves as a bridge to the Fugue, which begins by being very correct and restrained, but later reveals its origins by supporting the theme with arpeggio chords in a very unfugal way and by dragging it down into an orchestral maelstrom which then builds to a brilliant climax. Unfortunately the final effect is somewhat weakened by the composer's habit, mentioned earlier, of reintroducing a second musical idea at the end.

The **13th sonata in E-flat major** Op. 161 is also in four movements—Fantasia, Canzone, Intermezzo, Fugue; the **12th sonata in D-flat major** Op. 154 in three movements—Fantasia, Pastorale, Introduction and fugue, and the **15th sonata in D major** Op. 168 also in three movements—Fantasia, Adagio, Introduction and ricercare.

From among Rheinberger's large series of works the **14th sonata in C major** Op. 165 stands out. Though it only has three movements, it is of comparable size to the 11th sonata and lasts in all about 20 minutes. The Maestoso prelude includes a fugato and has the grandiose features of a symphonic movement, while the Idyll really lives up to its title: in the solo passages of the middle section one can imagine the sentimental sound of a French horn carrying over hill and dale. The toccata returns to the character of the first movement. It has a second theme and lively swift eighth-notes run through it and carry it forward. The piece builds to a thrilling climax in the last bars.

The **16th sonata in G-sharp minor** Op. 175 contains a movement entitled "Skandinavisch", and the **19th sonata in G minor** Op. 193 one called "Provençalisch", referring to the folk tunes quoted in them.

The last, the **20th sonata in F major** Op. 196, was written in the late 1890s and is entitled "For a peace celebration" but without saying whether the composer had any particular political event in mind. It is in four movements, lasts 26 minutes and brings the series to a dignified conclusion. The Prelude is somewhat like a hymn and has two contrasting ideas which flow in a broad stream of sound.

The Intermezzo is a more intimate adagio with a melodic theme but also with an undulating motion recalling the first movement. Clearly towards the end of writing his sonatas Rheinberger was transferring an explicitly pianistic style to the organ, which naturally does the organ no harm but demands an appropriately skillful interpretation. The Pastorale develops its Shawmlike theme in variations, while the finale, which is musically somewhat lighter than the previous movements, ends in grandiose chords.

Further works: Trios, fughettas, meditations, monologue and character pieces.

Works for organ and orchestra

Rheinberger wrote two concertos for organ and orchestra. The **Concerto for organ in F major** Op. 137, duration 25 minutes, is scored for three horns and strings. It dates from 1884 and is the first example of a genuine organ concerto since the end of the 18th century. Rheinberger not only gives the organ a solo, virtuoso role, but makes it contribute woodwindlike support and harmonies to the orchestra. As the only brass instruments, the horns give the overall sound a typically romantic atmosphere. After the Maestoso and the Andante, the interesting third movement contrasts the theme in the orchestra with the chords, runs and arpeggios on the organ and still combines them into a concentrated piece of music.

The later and more important **Concerto in G Minor** Op. 177 was completed in 1894 and lasts 23 minutes. Orchestra: two horns, two trumpets, timpani, strings.

Two main ideas are revealed in the introduction to the Grave, of which the second already changes into the parallel E-flat major in the opening section. This theme keeps the upper hand, particularly in the second section of the movement which modulates to G major and brings the piece to a close. The melodious Andante is a duet for solo instrument and strings, interrupted by a more emotional middle section strikingly announced by the brass. The third movement Con moto is symphonic in character and in the solo passages offers the organ the best opportunities to show itself off. Its two-theme layout comes to a climax in a maestoso motif:

Publishers: Forbert—also the concertos; Hinrichsen; Novello.

CHARLES-MARIE WIDOR

b. Lyon, February 21, 1844; d. Paris, March 12, 1937

He studied organ and theory in Brussels with Lemmens and Fétis and was then appointed organist at St. Sulpice in Paris, where he stayed from 1870 to 1934, and also organ professor at the Conservatoire, succeeding César Franck. His students included Dupré and Albert Schweitzer. Widor's extensive oeuvre includes symphonies and concertos for orchestra and compositions for choir, chamber groups and the theater. His organ works occupy a place of pride.

Symphony in D major Op. 13/2. Praeludium circulare. This is a short movement with only one speed and only one motif/theme which is scarcely developed at all.

The Pastorale has the following theme:

a pastoral motif which alternates later with a choralelike melody and a fugato, all in the characteristic 12/8 time.

The Andante has a melodic theme elaborated into a song form, with a few brief, contrasting agitato phrases scattered about in the development.

The Salve regina is in two sections: an Allegro in flowing motion alternates with a short, imitative Tranquillamente assai. Towards the end comes the cantus firmus with Trumpet stop in the pedals.

After a blossoming unison line the Adagio states the theme,

the only motif in the whole movement and frequently interruped by the yearning opening line.

The Finale is an Allegro with motifs connected by chords and a continuous impetus occasionally halted by incidental quarter-notes.

The **Fifth symphony in F minor** from Op. 42 is well known for its last movement, the exciting **Toccata in F major** as beloved today as Bach's toccata in D minor and rightly so, because it is a virtuoso piece without the usual empty tinkling sound.

The **Symphonie gothique** (Gothic symphony) Op. 70, 1895, duration 28 minutes, is built on the musical model of the Gregorian "Puer natus" from the Christmas liturgy. This cantus firmus clearly dominates the fourth and last movement, which begins Moderato with the following theme:

which is quoted in the lower part and then treated in canon in the two outside parts. A contrasting Allegro in 12/8 time is then inserted before the Moderato returns, followed by a fugal Andante, whose motifs are also formed from the Gregorian cantus firmus.

The symphony ends with a toccata section marked Allegro, which begins *piano* with a shimmering filigree movement using the characteristic fifth from the opening of the cantus firmus, and then broadens out increasingly in sound and in density of line until the theme bursts forward again on the pedals in an organ tutti. The finale is dynamically restrained. Also in the third movement, the Allegro in 6/8 time, the main theme of the symphony can be heard, not in the giguelike top part, but alluded to in the pedals, especially on B-flat and G. The short first Moderato movement with its motif always beginning on the upbeat, and the second, Andante sostenuto, are both attractive self-contained individual pieces.

The **Symphonie romane** (Roman symphony) Op. 73, 1900, duration 30 minutes, also has a musical source—the Gregorian "Haec dies" for Easter:

The cantus firmus is unfolded right at the start of the first movement. In the truly solo passages Widor suggested different versions suitable for the freely-moving Gregorian chorale, which can be used ad lib., as for example for , , and for . When the cantus firmus appears in the middle of a polyphonic phrase it must of course be played in strict time.

The motif runs like an "idée fixe" through the entire symphony, through the first movement and the Chorale as well as the Finale, where the eighth-note runs rise out of it. Only in the third movement, the Cantilena, is the motif hidden.

Further works: Symphonies from Op. 13, four symphonies from Op. 42, and the Latin Suite.

Publishers: Hamelle; Schott.

EUGÈNE GIGOUT (b. Nancy, March 23, 1844; d. Paris, December 9, 1925), an exact contemporary of Widor's, wrote a number of pieces for organ, mostly for use in church services. The loveliest of them are among the **Ten pieces,** for instance the allegro Toccata and the charmingly elegant Scherzo. Publisher: Leduc.

At a time when there was a dearth of organ compositions, the organist of the Viennese court orchestra and harmony professor ROBERT FUCHS (b. Frauenthal, February 15, 1847; d. Vienna, February 19, 1927) composed two **Fantasias** in C major and E minor which are well written for organ in a clear and never overloaded style and simply expressed. Publisher: Coppenrath.

HEINRICH REIMANN (b. Rengersdorf, nr. Glatz, March 14, 1850; d. Berlin, May 24, 1906) is considered a forerunner and inspirer of Max Reger, on account of his **Fantasia** Op. 25 on the chorale "Wie schön leuchtet der Morgenstern" (How brightly shines the morning star). In the somewhat symphonically enriched chorale partita this work does not deny its origins, but in its fugue which combines theme and chorale melody it is an immediate herald of Reger. Reimann's great **Toccata** in E minor Op. 23 combines Baroque seriousness and mobility with suggestions for crescendo and decrescendo, as in French toccatas. Publisher: Forberg.

EDWARD ELGAR (b. Broadheath, Worcester, June 2, 1857; d. Worcester, February 23, 1934) made an English contribution to the new Romanticism in his great **Sonata in G major** Op. 28, a four-movement work with an orchestral sound. Strongest is the Allegretto second movement with its impressionistic, shimmery motion. Publisher: Breitkopf.

LUDWIG THUILLE (b. Bozen, November 30, 1861; d. Munich, February 5, 1907) was well known in Munich as a teacher of composition, and wrote a **Sonata in A minor** which sounds very like Elgar's G major work, in that it contains an orchestral, high-Romantic Prelude and Andante, followed by a skillfully constructed fugue. Publisher: Forberg.

A pupil of Gigout's, LÉON BOËLLMANN (b. Ensisheim, Alsace, September 25, 1862; d. Paris, October 11, 1897) was well known as a virtuoso organist. Outstanding among his compositions are his **Gothic suite, Heures mystiques** (Mystic hours) and **Twelve pieces,** among them a **Prelude,** an **Elegy** and an especially noteworthy **Intermezzo.** Publishers: Leduc; Forberg.

MARCO ENRICO BOSSI

b. Salò, Lake Garda, April 25, 1861;
d. on board ship between New York and Le Havre, February 20, 1925

The son of an organist, Bossi studied in Bologna and Milan and in 1881 obtained his first post as music director of Como cathedral. Later he taught composition and was director of the conservatories at Naples, Bologna, Venice and Rome. He also toured as a concert organist, wrote operas, orchestral and choral works, and chamber and organ music. His organ compositions rank among the best known of his works today.

Concert piece in C minor Op. 130. Having originally written it for organ, string orchestra, brass and timpani, Bossi wrote a second version for solo organ and dedicated it to Karl Straube. The introductory theme runs like an "idée fixe" through the entire work, whether in the powerful opening *forte,* in the Quasi Recitativo of the middle section which is developed like a chorale, or in the Meno allegro of the finale, where the theme slips past in short note values and often in little haphazard pieces. The orchestral version may well have sounded more grandiose, but the tone colors created on a medium-sized organ make the solo version just as effective.

Like his Concert piece, all Bossi's other organ works are "character pieces" and appropriately titled as such, with the exception of the **Sonata in F minor,** Op. 71, in which the composer apparently intended to abandon the established stylistic course of the 19th century for new forms of expression. In this departure he concentrated on music intended for the organ as a concert instrument rather than for religious or liturgical performance.

The **Two characteristic pieces** contain the famous **Prayer,** subtitled "Fatemi la grazia" (Grant me the favor)

and the **March of the bards.**

From the collection **Op. 132** the **Funeral procession** and particularly the **Country scene** are worth mentioning. Further works: Character pieces Op. 92, 94 & 104, Theme and variations in C-sharp minor Op. 115, Heroic piece Op. 128, Symphonic study Op. 78, Symphonic fantasia for organ and orchestra Op. 147.

Publisher: Peters.

FRIEDRICH KLOSE

b. Karlsruhe, November 29, 1862;
d. Ruvigliano nr. Lugano, December 24, 1942

Klose studied in Karlsruhe and Geneva, and with Bruckner in Vienna. He taught in Basle and Munich, and wrote a mass, the music drama Ilsebill, *the oratorio* Der Sonne Geist (Spirit of the sun) *and songs.*

Prelude and fugue in C minor, 1907, duration 18 minutes. Scored for four trumpets and four trombones.

Klose modeled the nucleus of the fugue's theme and the similar opening of the

prelude on an improvisation Bruckner played in the city church of Bayreuth, where the two met to honor Wagner. A chorale melody joins this theme and together with passage work makes a movement of orchestral style. This is followed by a fugue, the theme of which is developed in the manuals, as the pedals do not have the requisite range and it is technically difficult to play. The tune of the prelude then appears as the second theme and is combined with the first. As before, the movement which

had started as part writing blossoms into a symphony with crescendos building to the entry of the brass with the chorale, i.e. the choralelike theme of the prelude. One can catch references to the fugue's theme in the organ part. Klose's only organ work is on a high artistic level and strongly constructed, even though the influence of his teacher Bruckner can be heard.

Publisher: Peters.

CHARLES-ARNAUD TOURNEMIRE

b. Bordeaux, January 22, 1870;
d. Arcachon, November 4, 1939

He studied with Widor and Franck, became organist at Sainte Clothilde's in Paris and made many concert tours. Later he conducted a chamber music class at the Conservatoire. Apart from his organ works he wrote symphonies, choral works, an opera and chamber music.

Five improvisations, 1930. Fortunately these are not composed improvisations, but genuine ones, written out by Maurice Duruflé from a live recording. Like his predecessor as organist at Sainte Clothilde's, César Franck, Tournemire was a genius at improvisation. The five works collected here have wonderfully flowing lines which surpass his melodic inventiveness, because he only improvised on Gregorian liturgical themes. They show a light touch in fusing the individual sections into a greater whole. Many groups of notes recur, often at great speed, but this is no disadvantage in an improvisation.

Besides the **Little rhapsody** and the soaring **Cantilena** the other three pieces are obviously improvisations on specific Gregorian tunes, i.e. **Ave maris stella, Victimae paschali** and **Te deum.** The last begins at once by quoting the chorale, of which the call in the first three notes is particularly used again in sequence form, in contrast with the quiet parts.

The **Sacred symphony** Op. 71, 1936, duration 23 minutes, on the other hand, is another large scale symphonic work inspired by the experience of seeing Amiens Cathedral. In the composer's own words it is to be "an exaltation of the beauty of ogival lines and a synthesis in sound of our cathedrals," and the work completely achieves and realizes this conception.

Suite evocatrice Op. 74, 1938. Tournemire wants to awaken a recollection of the great Baroque French masters, above all François Couperin, into whose spiritual sphere he steps from his usual symphonic world, and gives the individual movements names we recognize from the time of the harpsichordists. This is a charming idea and compellingly beautifully executed.

I Grave, in Mixture style, with ornaments written out, and chordal.

II Tierce in the tenor and Krummhorn solo. Over a mostly sustained bass the solo tenor describes a freely soaring line with Cornet stop, while the Krummhorn appears as solo in the second section.

III Echo flute, a very pretty, short fantasia for a Flute stop:

IV Jeu Doux (soft stops) and Vox Humana. Here the various voices sound together on one manual, therefore either all with the Vox Humana or all with the soft stops.

V Caprice, the longest movement of the suite. This looks at first technically very ponderous and calls for the composer's exact fingering to be followed. It starts with a regular fugato in three parts, followed by waves of arpeggios. There are some lovely duets and chords leading into the Largo, which is an extended cadenza.

The **Triple choral** was written in 1910.
'Orgue mystique contains five pieces for each Sunday in the church year.
Further works: Choral symphony, Symphonic fantasia.
Publishers: Bärenreiter; Bornemann; Durand; Schott.

LOUIS VIERNE

b. Poitiers, October 8, 1870;
d. Paris, June 2, 1937

This composer and famous organist was nearly blind. He studied with César Franck and Widor and was organist at Notre Dame from 1900 until his death. From 1911 he taught organ at the Schola Cantorum, where Dupré was among his pupils. He wrote organ works, including six symphonies, and composed for orchestra and chorus as well.

Third symphony Op. 28, 1912, duration 31 minutes. The description "symphony" already points to the orchestral wealth of sound which the composer dreamt of, and actually had at his disposal in the organ of Notre Dame, but the structure is also symphonic.

I Allegro maestoso. A regular sonata movement with two themes in the exposition, a development and a recapitulation:

II Cantilena. A slow movement, marked Andantino moderato, has a melodious tune developed over accompanying chords which give it colorful support; after a monologue middle section a flowing counterpart joins in.

III Intermezzo in scherzo style, in three parts, A, B, A.

IV Adagio, quasi largo, has two themes, of which the second one appears only in the middle section.

V Finale. A magnificent, soaring, floating movement in moto perpetuo, with repeated sixteenth-note figures and a theme which changes little. Two episodes with a new motif are soon swamped by the elemental force of the tempestuous, raging movement. There is an ecstatic finish, with the theme in F-sharp major in pedals and manuals.

This is a virtuoso piece of the highest craftsmanship.

The **First symphony** Op. 14, 1899, has the following movements: Prelude, Fugue, Pastoral, Allegro vivace, Andante, Finale.

Fantasia pieces Op. 51, 52, 53 and 55. This is a collection of short compositions with partly programmatic titles to indicate their contents, such as "Marche nuptiale" (Nuptial march), "Clair de lune" (Moonlight), "Sur le Rhin" (On the Rhine), "Naiades" (Naiads), etc. Vierne removed pieces like "Fantomes" (Phantoms) from religious use by adding explicitly "Only for recitals", but it is surprising that those not so marked might still be appropriate for church services, if only as postludes. The names themselves, like "Clair de lune", indicate a spiritual affinity to French musical impressionism, very clearly heard in the music. From this collection comes the **Westminster carillon.** The famous four note chime of Big Ben, heard from countless clocks throughout the world, is the unmistakable basis of this piece, in which Vierne transposes onto the organ and makes audible the vibrating overtones which occur when the clock chimes. Since this piece was acoustically destined for the vast spaces of the cathedral, it should only be played in large halls and on appropriate instruments.

Further works: Triptych Op. 58; Symphonies; Masses; Freestyle pieces.

Publishers: Durand; Lemoine.

MAX REGER

b. Brand, Fichtelgebirge, March 19, 1873;
d. Leipzig, May 11, 1916

Reger first studied in Weiden and later with Hugo Riemann in Leipzig. His early compositions were written on his return to Weiden. He then took up posts teaching composition and conducting in Munich, Leipzig and Meiningen, but finally abandoned them for freelance composing and performing. His musical inspirations are Brahms and Liszt, but his compositional technique derives also from the Baroque period. He has often been misunderstood and misjudged because of his highly expressive style, with verdicts such as "too densely structured and too chromatic." Though he was a Catholic, his compositions for organ, numerous and artistically very important, were still able to give a forceful impetus to Protestant church music. He also wrote choral works including a setting of the 100th Psalm, orchestral music such as variations on Hiller and Mozart, and wide-ranging chamber music. As a Classical composer at the start of the modern era he wrote for the most diverse genres, but for a long time he was only properly respected for his organ music, because the rest was largely unknown.

Free Works

In the **Three pieces Op.** 7 of 1892 the influence of J. S. Bach can be detected, especially in the first one, the **Prelude and fugue in C major.** The **Fantasia** is a setting of the Gregorian Te deum, which Reger was to develop again in his *Twelve pieces* Op. 59, and the last piece is a four-part double fugue.

The **Suite in E minor** Op. 16, 1894/95, duration 45 minutes, bearing the inscription "Den Manen Joh. Seb. Bachs" (To the spirit of J. S. Bach), is both the first of Reger's truly original compositions and also a great success. It is in fact so long that one would hardly play it in its entirety, and later on the composer wrote a more tightly organized fugue, but in its overall conception Reger's strong technical power and inventive talent can be seen and compared with those of his later works.

I Introduction. Grave. Opens with a discord, followed by short bars of alternating chords and recitative. The following Fugue is a rich, protracted tableau, with the theme and its development reappearing in inversion, together with a recurrence of the theme in its original form.

A second theme is then stated and worked on, and finally the two ideas are combined. Unlike many of Reger's fugues, this one ends *pianissimo.*

II Adagio assai. A melismatic solo top part with figuration in the accompaniment. In the middle section the composer achieves a thrillingly grandiose intensity by using the chorale quotations "Out of the deep call I to Thee" and "When I one day must depart." The recapitulation ends the movement on a note of consolation.

III Intermezzo. This consists of Un poco allegro which darts by like a ghost and is repeated after the Andantino Trio.

IV Passacaglia (Andante). In three parts, the customary unison opening of ostinato and slow escalation, a restrained middle section in E major and a finale returning to E minor with mounting speed and dynamics culminating in Organo Pleno.

The **First sonata in F-sharp minor** Op. 33, 1899, duration 19 minutes, consists of Fantasia (Allegro energico), Intermezzo (Sostenuto) and Passacaglia (Andante con moto).

The **Fantasia and fugue on B-A-C-H** Op. 46, 1900, duration 20 minutes, is often performed and demonstrates Reger's deep reverence for Bach's genius. It has two apparently contradictory peculiarities: the powerful **concision** of the recurring short theme, and a massive diversity resulting from the series of different phrases which keep appearing to challenge the theme. When one hears an above average interpretation of this difficult work or possibly reads the score, the musical unity of Reger's conception becomes apparent.

The beginning, marked sempre quasi improvisatione, presents the theme like a fanfare in the top part, while the pedals play a phrase which frequently recurs thereafter.

After several such openings the theme appears in counterpoint with the motif quoted here.

Rising and falling runs and groups of chords join in, but the B-A-C-H theme is always incisively present. The theme changes into:

and is inverted. Forcefully escalating runs all through the manuals prepare for the end of the fantasy, which is followed by the fugue, marked attacca. Its peaceful, flowing theme is audibly based on B-A-C-H, while the contrasting second theme consists of eighth-note runs, but closer examination reveals its origins in the main theme:

For clarity's sake the two themes are quoted here where they first appear simultaneously:

After some bold "forced rides" with the two themes together, the first in sixths and the second in thirds, the opening phrases of the fantasia are heard again, this time carried away by the speed of the second fugue theme.

The **Symphonic fantasia and fugue in D minor** Op. 57, 1901, duration 20 minutes, is called the *Inferno Fantasia* after Dante's *Inferno,* and is mentioned here because of its curious situation. It is not popular among organists when building a program, and few listeners have been privileged to hear it even once. The symphonic element Reger was trying to express is swallowed up in chromatics, demonstrating the main problem of Reger's composition technique—his love of one modulation after another and one chromatically altered chord after another, so that in one instance six different keys march through a single bar, only to return to their point of departure. The music of the B-A-C-H fantasia, always controlled by the theme, here spreads out into a free improvisation and presents a virtually impenetrable pageant of chords related by thirds and chromatically altered. The inner conflict and massive spiritual agitation are partly smothered by the chromatic vagaries—which for Reger are always a genuine way of expressing spiritual unrest—and limited by the monumental supporting chords accompanying the flow of melody. The following phrase can be regarded as a basic motif, but only to a limited degree as the foundation of the composition. Technically the inconsistent and uncompromising key changes of the fantasia point towards the future.

In the fugue all tensions are released. Its structure is lucidly audible and as music it is a thrilling piece. The theme is followed later by a second one to form a double fugue.

Toccata in D minor and fugue in D major from the **Twelve pieces** Op. 59, 1901. This work is frequently performed because of its soaring toccata with runs and chords—an ancient recipe for a stately keyboard piece which Reger manages to blend together in successful new and varied ways. The fugue forms a calming close to the toccata:

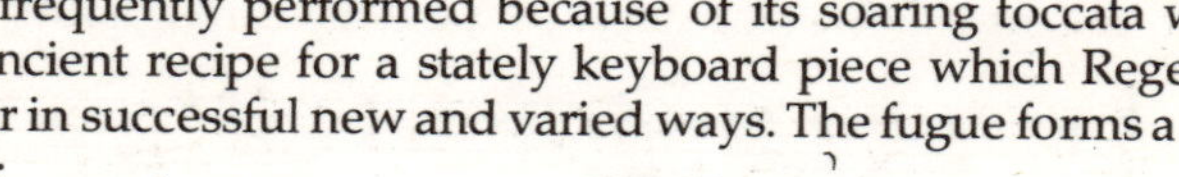

Con moto

The **Gloria in excelsis** from Op. 59 is a short, compelling piece. From its tempestuous chorale opening

emerge some *pianissimo* bars leading into the fugato, marked più mosso, which closes with the Gregorian melody, while a second little fugato continues the development, until the short final section crowns the whole with a fourfold repeat of the Gloria motif. The last piece in this collection is an equally concentrated **Te deum,** beginning with a unison quotation from the cantus firmus which the other parts then take up in quick succession, until out of a return to unison the finale develops in broad crescendo with the other parts joining in.

Second sonata in D minor Op. 60, 1901, duration 20 minutes. I Improvisation. The unfettered sweep of this movement is repeatedly brought up short by the introductory motif | ♩. ♬ ♩ |. Quieter passages having fewer runs and turns alternate with this Allegro con brio section, and eventually introduce a melodic theme.

II Invocation. A darkly-veiled and mystical Grave with its middle section marked "sehr bewegt" (con moto).

III Introduction and fugue with the following fugue theme:

Of the **Monologues** Op. 63, 1901/02, the **Introduction and passacaglia in F minor,** duration 14 minutes, is worthy of note. The Introduction begins and ends with an ornamental figure:

and in between the short sections develop like fantasias in attractive and varied colors.

The Passacaglia is based on a conventionally arranged eight-bar theme in half-notes and quarter-notes. From the calm first entry of the top part the speed and part writing escalate, but as in many of these works the crescendo does not grow steadily, but is held back by a peaceful, soft variation, only to unleash the closing music all the more tempestuously.

Of the **Twelve pieces** Op. 65, 1902, two pairs can be singled out: first, the **Prelude in D minor and fugue in D major,** of which the prelude is in striking contrast to the toccatas as it flows peacefully and evenly throughout:

The fugue has a relaxed and jaunty theme. Second, the **Toccata in E minor and fugue in E major,** where the roles are again reversed, as the lively toccata is partnered by an Andante con moto fugue.

The **Prelude and fugue in E minor** from the **Ten pieces** Op. 69, 1903, is an uncomplicated work with a merrily flowing and swinging 12/8 tune taken mainly from the scale of E minor. The fugue is in three clearly audible parts and only towards the end becomes polyphonic and therefore denser.

The **Toccata and fugue in D major,** also from Op. 69, by contrast is a lordly and fiery work. The toccata, marked con spirito, begins with a long, stately pedal solo, followed without a break by the other sections, which develop in short flourishes or arpeggios. The four-part fugue has this rather merry theme, which Reger uses in inversion and stretto, and through which a chain of broken staccato chords flashes playfully.

Allegro possibile

The strongly chromatic **Prelude and fugue in A minor** also belongs to Op. 69.

In the **Variations and fugue on an original theme in F-sharp minor** Op. 73, 1903, duration 30 minutes, an Introduction starting with the following theme precedes the variations:

After playfully changing about in all kinds of nuances, Reger's original Andante theme appears:

The variations burst the bounds of all that has gone before. The figurative, melodic and harmonic ideas used here show that Reger was one of the truly great masters of the art of writing variations. He abandoned tonality and achieved cluster effects which anticipate the organ music of the 1960s. This is an extremely difficult work to play and reaches its climax in the fugue, where the individual motifs of the theme—up-beat and bars 2 and 3—are also worked on in the interludes. In this way Reger weaves a dense musical texture based exclusively on the theme and creates a very concentrated composition.

In the **Twelve pieces** Op. 80, 1904, there is a **Toccata and fugue in A minor,** a very short but very typical work, which combines many of Reger's best stylistic features. While in the toccata lively dynamic changes break up the texture and frequent alterations in tempo divide it clearly, the fugue runs its course in a steady, fast time:

The attractive possibility of creating a double echo in the second and third bars of the theme gives the piece, in spite of its strict tempo and the linearity it sustains to the very end, an untrammelled cheerfulness rarely found in the fugues of this master of counterpoint.

The other pieces which make up Op. 69 (e.g. No. 4, **Musical moment** and No. 5, **Capriccio**) and Op. 80 (Nos. 6 and 10, **Intermezzo,** No. 7, **Scherzo,** No. 9 **Moto perpetuo** etc.) are little gems which ought to be played more often.

The **Four preludes and fugues** Op. 85, 1904, in C-sharp minor, G major, F major and E minor may be considered intimate chamber music, in spite of occasional intentional dynamic outbursts. They are so far removed from all the storms and torrents of the toccatas and introductions, and contrast so markedly with the great fugues—even with those which give intensity to the choral fantasias—that as organ music they open up for us a view of the great and marvellous world of Reger's chamber works.

Introduction, passacaglia and fugue in E minor Op. 127, 1913, duration 27 minutes, is a work with hidden spiritual dimensions which one can only follow with mental and physical effort. It was commissioned for the dedication of the organ in the Breslau Centenary Hall in 1913. The interpreter is faced with even greater problems than with the B-A-C-H work, while the listener embarks on an onerous journey, though the final destination is a composition full of unsuspected and imaginative ideas. With 45 printed pages its physical proportions are huge and the spiritual ones no less so; it is an erratic block and not easily accessible. The structure does not appear in the least complicated: Introduction—Grave, Passacaglia with 26 variations, Fugue 1 with extensive development, Fugue 2 without development, combination of both themes.

The typical concise introduction consists of chords, runs and dynamic fluctuations and ends in F-sharp major, being the dominant of the passacaglia opening in B. The following ostinato now enters:

The variations built on this divide into three groups: 12 which gradually grow in motion, tempo and density of part writing, with the theme in the soprano in the last two; 4 marked "tranquillo", to be played *pianissimo,* without any real center of repose, and 10 which also work to a climax, this time to the conclusion of the passacaglia. The first theme of the fugue has an orchestral feeling (Mozart variations!) and is marked Moderato, sempre leggiero.

It is richly developed and acquires the following interlude motif:

together with a triplet figure marked sempre grazioso e leggiero. The long, struggling climb towards the great climax is actually indicating the end of the movement, but surprisingly a second theme emerges from the last chord, starting in quarter-notes in contrast to the first one. This episode is shortlived, however, and transitional bars lead into a synthesis of both themes repeated four times like an exposition.

Fantasia and fugue in D minor Op. 135b, 1916, duration 15 minutes. Leggiero falling cascades open:

and return shortly before the end. There follow Adagio bars based on a melody, alternating precisely with Quasi-vivace sections which sparkle with life and dissolve into arpeggios, runs and mounting chords. At the end, after tempestuous runs, the unison opening of the fantasia appears in the bass, in double its former note values.

In the double fugue only the first theme is developed, and its somewhat

unemphatic rhythm—perhaps the work's only shortcoming—makes it difficult to follow it through the course of this first section, but it does form a perfect contrast to the second theme which, after the close of the first section on the dominant E major, begins in A minor.

The second theme is immediately introduced with a similar counterpart. The first fusing of the two is in D minor with the first theme in the bass, and the second theme beginning in F minor in the soprano. After that the movement is continuously intensified, and the tempo slows down almost automatically to Adagissimo, definitely the right description as it is a written-out ritardando.

Because of its brevity (when compared to similar pieces) the D minor fantasia is by far the most concise of Reger's free works. It gives a unified impression, and the fugal sections are easy to grasp as a whole and are as tersely worked as possible.

Introduction and passacaglia in D minor, duration 6 minutes. This is a well known work, with no opus number. It consists of a short, 15-bar chordal introduction and a passacaglia which grows in a simple, uninterrupted line.

It should be noted that Reger's performing and dynamic markings are only intended to result in a lively and, as Karl Straube said, "spiritually moving" performance, despite the extreme exaggerations to be found. Taking his markings literally would only make his work harder to understand.

Chorale settings

Fantasia on the chorale "Ein feste Burg ist unser Gott" (A mighty fortress is our God) Op. 27, 1898, duration 12 minutes. The four verses of Luther's hymn are set in their entirety. After an introductory fanfare in the pedals, the first verse opens with the tune in the tenor and two parts playing round it in fast motion. Between these trio sections, all in D major, lines of the chorale set homophonically in B-flat major enter and create a colorful contrast.

The second verse "With force of arms we nothing can" opens quietly. The tune, still in the tenor but now with three other parts, is again interrupted by the B-flat lines of the chorale, which now carries right through, so that while the first two stanzas are being worked on the complete chorale can be heard in B-flat as well.

The third verse is a striking tone painting. The opening "And were this world all devils o'er" is a real witches' cauldron of up to nine parts plus harmonies. The cantus firmus in the upper pedals is almost concealed, but in the next line emerges in octaves in the soprano in all its unmistakable grandeur with the words "We lay it not to heart so sore." From here to the end of the verse, "The prince of this world . . . a word shall quickly slay him," the music falls and grows slower, softer and deeper. For the "slay" Reger employs a genuinely Bach-inspired motif:

The beginning of the last stanza—"God's word, for all their craft and force"—is presented with rigid density. At the words "And though they take our life, goods, honor, children, wife" the first line of the chorale with its reference to "A mighty fortress is our God" rings out in each part, one after the other, like a wonderful consolation for the oppressed. The texture grows increasingly dense as the music moves to the grandiose final line "The city of God remaineth!" Now comes another *pianissimo* and a modulation to F major, to illustrate with almost eerie thrill the collapse of the universe before the omnipotence and greatness of God. The work closes with a repeat of the last line.

The second work of this genre, the **Fantasia on the chorale "Freu dich sehr, o**

meine Seele" (Rejoice greatly, O my soul) Op. 30, 1898, duration 20 minutes, cannot be compared to "Ein feste Burg". The Introduzione certainly has fire and impetus, and Reger skillfully connects this opening section with the following verses in variation form by means of a short fugato theme, which later reappears at random. In this work, too, the content of the individual stanzas is illustrated, as for instance with melisma at the words "By day and night have I called," with a *fortissimo* surge on "The world, the devil, sin and hell," and by dying away on "Whether my eyes already fail," but unlike other works this does not establish a genuinely fundamental feature to weld it into a whole. Nevertheless it is an interesting example of illustrating a chorale.

Fantasia on the chorale "Wie schön leucht uns der Morgenstern" (How brightly shines the morning star) Op. 40/1, 1899, duration 17 minutes. The introduction which includes clear leaps of a fourth marked "pesante" (heavy) gradually prepares the listener for the chorale, and its dynamics also show what is to follow.

Verses 1 and 2 of the chorale state the cantus firmus clearly with free music moving around it. At the third stanza "Pour deep within my heart" an Adagio con espressione begins, and the chorale melody is decorated with ornamentation and flourishes. The first half of the following verse "From God my light of joy has come" is *forte* with the cantus firmus in the pedals; the repeat is *piano* fading to *pppp*, so that the second half of the chorale enters *forte* with even greater incisive power, its cantus firmus in the pedals and quick runs above it. The words here are "Yea, yea, he will give heavenly life." There is a soft transition into the fugue:

After the exposition of the theme and a very brief hint of development the cantus firmus of the fifth and last verse enters, first in the pedals and then in the upper part, with powerful intensity.

The second chorale fantasy from Op. 40, **Straf mich nicht in deinem Zorn** (Chastise me not in Thy wrath), duration 15 minutes, develops the six verses of the song one after the other in the form of a partita but with flowing transition passages. The individual variations are sharply defined and contrasted, and the mood is set by a few bars marked Grave.

The Fantasia on the chorale "Alle Menschen müssen sterben" (All men must die) Op. 52/1, 1900, duration 17 minutes, also consists of a series of variations on several stanzas, preceded by an Introduzione. The chorale melody is constantly present, and throughout the work, starting in the introduction, falling sevenths and other intervals continually recur to remind one of Bach's chorale from the *Little Organ Book* "Through Adam's fall". There is also a textual relationship, because here the words speak of man's mortality, while Bach's work tells how sin and death came into the world through Adam's fall. Making this connection with Bach serves to point out how his deep spirituality had shed its intense light on Reger.

Fantasia on the chorale "Wachet auf, ruft uns die Stimme" (Sleepers, awake, the voice is calling) Op. 52/2, duration 20 minutes. The introduction marked Grave has a psychological aspect to it: the listener expects to hear something of the famous chorale melody in whatever form, but no—instead, heavy, muffled chords hover above and next to each other.

Reger is portraying a graveyard silent with the peace of death and expectation of the Day of Judgment. Runs and chords dart twice, like flashes of lightning, into that peace, as a premonition of what is to come. At last, "äusserst zart" (extremely tenderly) like an angel's voice, the chorale melody is heard.

The dead are gradually awakened and the insistent E, D-sharp, E in the pedals which soon follows depicts the slow stirring of those who are lying in their graves. At the words "The hour is midnight" the tune sounds very restrained, and from "Arise, the bridegroom comes" it starts to shine ever more brightly. This first section, consisting of introduction and first verse, is probably the hardest to listen to, for Reger's chromaticism creates an elusive fluidity and avoids establishing any definite keys. Tempo and figuration are noticeably heightened in verse 2, following without a break with the words "Zion hears the watchman singing, her heart leaps for joy," marked Quasi allegro vivace and featuring triplet figures. Then the cantus firmus appears for the first time to brilliant fast chains of thirds and sixths running up and down in both hands on the words "Her friend descends from heaven in glory." The crescendo rises, then abruptly ceases, to give way to an Adagio con espressione with solo part and accompaniment, to the words "Now come, Thou worthy crown . . . and celebrate the holy feast." From this point in the text with its mention of the Eucharist the superbly soaring solo voice becomes a mystical accompaniment portraying the Sacrament and its transfiguration.

Before setting the first line of the third and last verse, Reger introduces a fugue whose theme is an inversion of the rising broken triads from the opening of the chorale.

All the problems of fugue writing seem to have vanished in this thrilling piece, strikingly constructed and yet filled through and through with musical impetus.

How many hundreds of well-written but expressionless fugues from all the centuries of organ music would we not happily trade for one such composition! After some 60 bars the fugue theme is joined by the cantus firmus to the words "Glory be sung to Thee", first in the pedals and then in the left hand. The last lines appear in the soprano, always combined with heads of the theme or hints of it, and only at "Alleluia for ever and ever" does the motion slacken and this great work ends in broad, full chords. This is a unique musical peak, both among chorale fantasias and among Reger's own compositions.

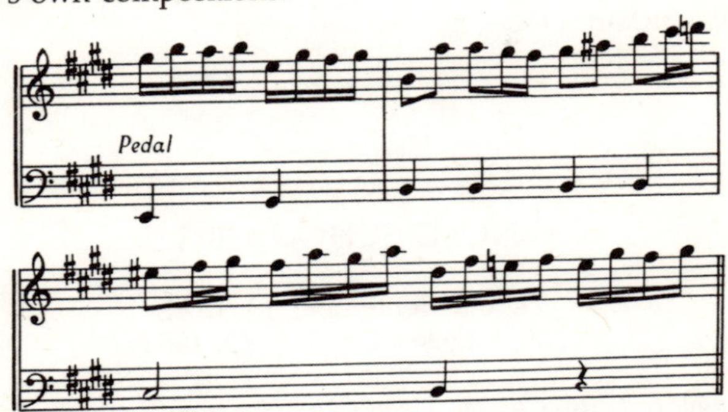

Fantasia on the chorale "Halleluja! Gott zu loben, bleibe meine Seelenfreud" (Alleluia! May my soul's delight ever be to praise God) Op. 52/3, duration 17 minutes. Karl Straube, a friend and sponsor of Reger's wrote that this work was "*technically* his best creation in this musical field." Here the composer has devised a series of variations which clearly and specifically delineate the separate verses of the chorale. In fact there is not so much to clarify in this simple paean of praise as there was in "Wachet auf," with its metaphorical verses.

The first verse is developed in the pedals after some restless introductory bars. The second, which speaks of the transitory nature of earthly power, gives a falling motif to the pedals, very like the one in "Ein feste Burg" quoted in the example on page 146, while the cantus firmus lies in the tenor. After short developments of verses 3, 4, 5 and 6 the fugue enters with the following theme:

In the course of its development the words of the last verse are accompanied by the cantus firmus in the pedals and soprano, together with the fugue theme.

The **52 easy preludes . . . to the most popular Protestant chorales** Op. 67, 1903, are without exception chorale arrangements of Protestant hymns in traditional style. There are pure renderings with figuration of the cantus firmus, which in "Warum sollt ich mich denn grämen" (Why should I then grieve) appears in the soprano, in "Von Gott will ich nicht lassen" (I will not part from God) in the bass, and in "Alles ist an Gottes Segen" (All relies on God's blessing) in the tenor. "Ein feste Burg" (A Mighty Fortress) features striking head imitation, and "Valet will ich dir geben" (I will bid thee farewell) and "Vater unser im Himmelreich" (Our Father, who art in heaven) contain echo effects.

Further chorale preludes are collected in Op. 79b of 1901–03 and Op. 135a of 1914. One prelude without an opus number is **Komm, süsser Tod,** which is melismatic and strongly chromatic. Of the independent works the **Nine pieces** Op. 129 of 1913, the **Seven organ pieces** Op. 145 of 1915–16, the **Suite in G minor** Op. 92, 1905 and the **Fantasia and fugue in C minor** Op. 29 should be mentioned. A **Romance in G major** for violin and organ has also been published in an arrangement by D. Hellmann.

Publishers: Breitkopf—collected organ works within the Collected Edition, ed. H. Klotz; Bote; Leuckart; Peters; Schott; Universal.

ARNOLD SCHÖNBERG

b. Vienna, September 13, 1874;
d. Los Angeles, CA, July 13, 1951

He was the founder of 12-tone music. He moved twice from Vienna to Berlin, where he taught, and in 1934 went to the United States to live in Boston and Los Angeles. Organ music lies outside the mainstream of his work, among which the best known examples are Verklärte Nacht (Transfigured night), Pierrot Lunaire, *a chamber symphony, chamber music and the unfinished opera* Moses and Aaron.

Variations on a recitative Op. 40, 1941, duration 16 minutes. This work consists of 10 variations which blend into each other and are followed by a fugue. The theme is varied basically by splitting the recitative into tiny motifs and phrases. Its opening appears in original form or in inversion, with a stress on the interval of a second, in variations 1, 4, 6, 8 and 10 which vary greatly among themselves. The motif from bars 6 and 7 also undergoes varied treatment in the sixth variation, marked Agitato, and the motif from bar 5 in the eighth.

In the fugue the notes from bars 1 to 4 inclusive are used for the theme. The first *comes* is already an inversion, while a partially repeated counterpoint is identical to the theme of the first variation. The treatment is tightly fugal but often interrupted by interludes with motifs developed out of the fifth bar of the theme. The head of the theme appears reversed in the pedals at the end.

Publisher: Gray.

FRANZ SCHMIDT

b. Bratislava, December 22, 1874;
d. Perchtoldsdorf nr. Vienna, February 11, 1939

Schmidt started as a cellist and taught as such at the Vienna conservatory, where in 1914 he became professor of piano and eventually of counterpoint and composition as well. From 1925 to 1927 he was director of the Vienna Musical Academy, and from 1927 to 1931 head of the College for Music and the Performing Arts. His style is symphonic and strongly influenced by the Romantics, especially Bruckner who taught him briefly. His main works comprise four symphonies, two operas, an oratorio Das Buch mit sieben Siegeln (The book of the seven seals) *and chamber music.*

Fantasia and fugue in D major, 1924, is an extended work in which the composer's contrapuntal gifts are fully displayed. The first line of the chorale theme, which appears at the end in its entirety in the pedals, forms the stately opening, and

after some short, slow bars each line enters in turn, harmonized in the soprano over pedal runs. Short fugal sections lead into the fugue which starts in D minor but soon

modulates violently and states the whole theme in A minor and E major, just its head in C-sharp minor and the whole again in A major. Another fantasia section follows, in the course of which the chorale theme rings out in the upper manual part and finally, in F-sharp major, is divided in turn between manuals and pedals. The fugue theme joins in, followed by a further development with small changes and inversions of the theme. After renewed modulations the piece ends with the chorale theme in two parts on the pedals, a fifth apart.

Prelude and fugue in E-flat major. "Lebhaft und schwungvoll" (Vivace con brio). The elaboration of the main idea is interrupted by a fugal section marked "ruhiger" (calmer) and by an interlude easily identified by its constant use of dotted rhythms.

Once a "langsam" (slow) version of the theme has also been heard, an obvious recapitulation occurs, followed by a transitional section which starts slowly and then adopts the pace of a toccata as it leads into the fugue. Of the fugue's two themes the first is in E-flat major and its development includes the theme from the prelude, while the second in G-sharp minor is heard in a three-part section before they are combined. More hints of the prelude theme are heard at the end. Strangely enough, neither of these important works enjoys particular popularity among either players or audience, possibly because their complexity of form and harmony present problems for performers and listeners alike.

On the other hand the **Toccata in C major,** 1924, is frequently performed, and its rather relentless driving motion is transparently easy to follow. The theme domi-

nates the entire work, apart from a legato line in quarter-notes which joins it later but never asserts itself thematically. After the recapitulation the tempo mounts to the final appearance of the theme in slow, double note values.

Further works: Introduction and fugue in F major; Prelude and fugue in E major; Toccata and fugue in A-flat major, 1935; Four little preludes and fugues.

Publishers: Österreichischer Bundesverlag; Weinberger.

SIGFRID KARG-ELERT

b. Oberndorf-am-Neckar, November 21, 1877;
d. Leipzig, April 9, 1933

At first he taught himself music, but later attended the Leipzig conservatory. His first post was as piano teacher in Magdeburg, from where he returned to Leipzig in 1907 as lecturer in theory, composition and piano. In 1919, three years after Reger's death, Karg-Elert succeeded him as professor of composition while applying unsuccessfully for positions as a church musician. He was famous as a composer and organ virtuoso and for years arranged music on the kunstharmonium [a two-manual reed organ] for the morning service on Leipzig radio. In 1930 there was a four-day Karg-Elert festival in London, and in 1932 he toured in the United States. He wrote a large number of works for organ, and his chamber and orchestral music is also worthy of note. As a late Romantic he was forgotten amid the precipitate musical developments of the Twenties, but there is hope that his works may soon be revived.

Free works

The **Six sketches** Op. 10, 1903, bear an affinity to Robert Schumann not only in name, for they are late Romantic character pieces with titles like "Ausfahrt" (Excursion), "Nachtgesang" (Nocturne), "Waldeinsamkeit" (Woodland solitude) or "Spätsonne" (Late sun). In the further **Sketchbook** Op. 102 which he wrote 10 years later we can see the development of his harmonic style to a preference for diminished, augmented seventh and ninth chords and for layers of impressionist effects, for instance in the "Savoyard" or the "Klösterliche Melodie" (Monastic tune). "Tempo di valse" (Waltz-time) sounds almost sacrilegious on the organ and resembles a study for the later "Valse mignonne" (Dainty waltz). In the Brahmsian "Ritornello", the Regeresque "Crucifixus etiam pro nobis" and the Scriabin-like "Poema esaltato" (Poem of exaltation) he showed his great colleagues what he had learned. The Reger piece especially proves that Karg-Elert could outdo his master in chromatic modulation.

Impressionist tone painting such as is rarely heard on the organ entirely pervades the **Seven pastels from Lake Constance** Op. 96, 1919. Here Karg-Elert portrays his impressions in broad, colorful "pictures", calling them "Die Seele des Sees" (The soul of the lake) or, even more evocatively, "Der gespiegelte Mond" The Mirrored Moon. Admittedly one needs large instruments with 8-foot stops to breathe life into this world of musical enchantment, but what organist who has grown up in the strict school of Baroque driving force will not be secretly happy to put on his music stand a piece entitled "Ruhig und unentschieden" (Calm and indecisive)?

The **Valse mignonne** (Dainty waltz) Op. 142/2 is both genuine and good drawing room music reminiscent of Gershwin. The central section is the "languendo" (languishing) waltz, which gives an idea of the composer's intentions:

This focal point is flanked by two other waltz tunes, introduced and followed by hovering, shimmering chords. Whether this is meant to mock the spirit of the age or exercise the fingers of an expert, it surprisingly still sounds superb on the organ. Though it is light and carelessly thrown off like a fleeting thought, it is still technically demanding.

The **Passacaglia and fugue on B-A-C-H** Op. 150 was composed in 1932 for his American concert tour and is Karg-Elert's most important free work for organ. In length and spiritual dimensions it is comparable to Reger's B-A-C-H. The opening:

Though at the end of his life the composer returned to the old passacaglia form, his conception of it is freer than that of his predecessors. The division into three sections impresses by its clear delineation, controlled harmonies and lively rhythms. The parts exist independently of each other like self-reliant individuals, and the earlier chromatic alteration is noticeably weaker than before, but there are unmistakable atonal sounds. The B-A-C-H theme also appears in F-sharp minor and in retrograde. The theme of the fugue had been planned to be combined with the B-A-C-H theme, as in Reger's work:

and the flow of this musicianly and captivating piece is clearly divided into a long, musical interlude and contrasting contrapuntal sections.

Chorale arrangements

Karg-Elert's many works based on chorales are very varied in type and size. There are simple preludes for part-time organists and technically demanding and difficult fantasias for concert performers. The chorales are mostly treated figuratively, but place clear emphasis on harmonic values. The mood of a chorale is often depicted by its actual name—Pastoral, March or Saraband—and elaboration of the melody decreases as the tone coloring and harmonies assume greater importance. One might therefore refer to them as chorale impressions, as Frotscher does.

The **66 chorale improvisations** Op. 65 present a multiplicity of forms. Improvisation does not exist, only carefully thought-out preludes in characteristic miniature forms. Examples are the saraband "Freu dich sehr" (Rejoice greatly), the canzonas "O Welt, ich muss dich lassen" (O world, I must leave you) and "Wer nur den lieben Gott" (He who relies on God's compassion), the marches "O Ewigkeit" (O eternity) and "Nun danket alle Gott" (Now thank we all our God), pastorals, etc. Some are long extended fantasias, as for instance "Komm, Heiliger Geist, Herre Gott" (Come Holy Ghost, Lord God) and "Wachet auf" (Sleepers, awake). This last piece gains a surprising vividness through its "misterioso" middle section marked *piano subito.*

The **20 preludes and postludes** Op. 78 are similar compositions, mostly clear and concise in character. "Vom Himmel hoch" (From the high heavens) contains parts for a singer and violin.

The grand chorale fantasia form is used by Karg-Elert in his **Three symphonic chorales** Op. 87. The first, **Ach bleib mit deiner Gnade** (Ah, continue in Thy mercy), duration 8 minutes, is technically the easiest and the most immediately comprehensible of the group. It is a partita with changing meter, changing harmonic illumination and contrasting modes of expression. The violent climax at the words "Ah continue with Thy protection... that the enemy may not defy us" is swift and chromatic, with dotted rhythms.

In contrast the second, **Jesu, meine Freude** (Jesus my joy), duration 16 minutes, is a great organ symphony in three movements.

I Introduction—Inferno (hell), mounts swiftly to a cry which illustrates the first quotation from the text: "Ah how long will my heart be anxious," and only thereafter does "Jesus my joy" ring out. Karg-Elert often elucidates his ideas by such evocative phrases as "schattenhaft dahin huschend" (slipping along like a shadow) or "vivacissimo misterioso" and gives instructions for registration. The end is triumphal.

II Canzona. A melismatic movement based on the chorale melody. The lower parts are chromatic and the freely soaring upper part is linear. Transition to

III Fugue with chorale. Here too, as in his work on B-A-C-H, Karg-Elert combines theme and chorale melody, but he is always ready to surprise us, as with the peaceful entry of "Good night, pride and pomp" in the middle of the vigorous exposition, and the *accelerando* transition to the closing "grandioso".

The third chorale, **Nun ruhen alle Wälder** (Now all the woods are sleeping) returns to the variation form. In the second half the addition of violin and singer causes a skillful escalation at a point where the textual basis of the work comes to the fore, even though only in two verses.

Further works: 3 impressions Op. 72; 3 symphonic canzonas Op. 85; 10 characteristic pieces Op. 86; *Kathedralfenster (Cathedral window(s))* Op. 106; Music for organ Op. 145.

Publishers: Breitkopf; Forberg; Hinrichsen; Novello.

From the group of Reger's pupils comes JOSEPH HAAS (b. Maihingen, Bavarian Swabia, March 19, 1879; d. Munich, March 30, 1960). Compared to his choral works, his oratorios such as **Die heilige Elisabeth** (St. Elizabeth) and his operas, his organ music output is quite small. Haas did not continue with Reger's chromaticism but carefully returned to a linear type of music of a miniature kind: **Variations on an original theme** Op. 31, 1911 and **Three preludes and fugues** Op. 11. His two **Church sonatas** Op. 62, 1926, in F major and D minor enrich the chamber music written for organ and violin with substantial and beautiful sounding works. Publishers: Coppenrath; Schott; Schwann.

The starting point for the works of JOSEPH JONGEN (b. Liège, December 14, 1873; d. Sart-lez-Spa, July 12, 1953) is César Franck's harmonic style, which he expands into the realm of impressionism. Apart from his works for solo organ, the **Symphony concertante for organ and orchestra** is worth a mention. KARL HASSE (b. Dohna nr. Dresden, March 20, 1883; d. Cologne, July 31, 1960) wrote **Chorale preludes** and a **Suite** Op. 10 in a rather simplified post-Reger style without the latter's dense harmonic tangles. Publisher: Merseburger.

The American CHARLES IVES (b. Danbury, CT, October 20, 1874; d. New York, NY, May 19, 1954) is little known as an organ composer. He wrote the serious **Prelude "Adeste fideles"** (O come, all ye faithful) and the ironically amusing **Variations on a National Hymn—America** in 1891 on the tune to which "God Save the Queen" is sung in Britain and which is remembered in Germany as the "Emperor's hymn"—"Heil dir im Siegerkranz" (Hail to the garlanded victor). Publisher: Gray.

One would not automatically rank ZOLTÁN KODÁLY (b. Kecskemet, December 16, 1882; d. Budapest, March 6, 1967) among composers of organ music, though that instrument does feature in his choral and sacred works. In 1942 he wrote a **Stille Messe** (Silent mass) for organ, containing all the parts of the mass from the introit to the "Ite missa est" in a restrained manner which favors musical sounds more than structure. Publisher: Boosey & Hawkes.

MARCEL DUPRÉ

b. Rouen, May 3, 1886;
d. Meudon nr. Paris, May 30, 1971

At the early age of 12 he was the organist at a church in his home town. Later he studied with Guilmant, Vierne and Widor and in 1926 became a professor at the Paris Conservatoire. In 1934 he succeeded Widor at St. Sulpice. From 1954 to 1956 he was the director of the Conservatoire and at that time was made a member of the Académie Française. He can be described as France's Karl Straube, for like that great cantor of St. Thomas's who founded a whole school of music, Dupré succeeded in restoring France to its role as a country in which the organ and its music flourished, albeit with the help of other musicians and the support of his teachers as far back as César Franck. We also must thank him for instructing a large number of organists who all became famous, and for laying the foundations of a scheme for teaching organ playing and improvisation. Dupré wrote a great quantity of important works for organ which constitute the majority of his compositions. His style is based on counterpoint, which he succeeded in combining with rich harmonies. His greatest success was as an improviser, especially of contrapuntal forms such as canons, fugues and ricercares.

Prelude and fugue in B major, the first piece from Op. 7—**Three preludes and fugues, 1912.** This work is well constructed on passage work: out of the accompaniment of the prelude, which has a not particularly original theme, a complicated fugue theme develops quite naturally. One only realizes just how difficult it is if one tries to play it on the pedals.

Prelude and fugue in F minor Op. 7/II. This is a cantabile piece in a rather elegiac, restrained mood. Once again continuous staccato sixteenth-notes accompany a melody which roams through all the parts. The fugue is a sophisticated composition with a harmonically colorful E minor Section.

Prelude and fugue in G minor Op. 7/III. This is the most musicianly of these three early, but very important, preludes with fugues. A manual section, whirring

like a spinning wheel, encloses short motifs which are at first in one part only, but later the number increases until there are eight, up to four of which are given to the pedals:

The fugue

is regular and shows Dupré's skill at its best, yet it is transparently simple and captivatingly convincing.

Variations on an old Noël Op. 20, 1922, duration 12 minutes. The tune on which these variations are based is as simple and popular as the models used by the Classical French arrangers of carols, such as Daquin, q.v. Dupré is here deliberately adhering to this tradition.

The variations are technically very diverse and effectively contrasted: I has the theme in the tenor and the soprano, II changes the figuration, III is a canon at the octave, IV marked "vif" (vivace) has the cantus firmus in the pedals with staccato runs, V varies the theme in the pedals, VI is a canon at the fourth and fifth, VII has appoggiatura figures, VIII is a canon at the second, IX is a free variation with contrasting legato and staccato, X is a fugato, with cantus firmus in the pedals, the soprano and again in the pedals, followed by a farewell Presto, with cantus firmus in the pedals against chords which change between the two hands.

This set of variations is certainly Dupré's best free work for organ.

Suite bretonne (Breton suite) Op. 21, 1924. The three character pieces which make up this suite are primarily suitable for concert performances, like those 19th-century organ pieces which were especially popular in France. Their importance extends beyond their impressionism, for Dupré effortlessly mingles "strange" notes with their more characteristic features. The *Berceuse (Lullaby)*, marked Lento, has an underlying elegiac feeling, the *Fileuse (Spinning girl)* turns her wheel in a whirring moto perpetuo, and in *Les cloches de Perros-Guirec (The bells of Perros-Guirec)* the bells ring out together and in single strokes by means of a sophisticated composition technique and a precise interchange between the exactly balanced manuals. In the last two pieces the stiff tone of the organ allows no modulation, creating a spellbinding effect on the audience.

Symphonie-Passion (Passion symphony) Op. 23, 1924, duration 28 minutes. The program of this work is the life of Christ.

I *Le monde dans l'attente du Sauveur* (The World Awaiting its Savior). The first section is dominated by a sense of instability, almost of barbarity, created by the use of five-time and seven-time bars which frequently alternate. Only at the marking "Plus lent" (più lento) do peace and an undistorted tune appear as the soprano plays the Gregorian chant "Jesu redemptor omnium" (Jesus, redeemer of all). After this middle section the third returns to the manner of the first.

II *Nativité* (The Nativity). This is a tone painting with clear sounds of shepherd's pipes and a march—either of the shepherds or the kings. A Gregorian cantus firmus "Adeste fideles" (O come, all ye faithful) is heard as well.

III *The Crucifixion.* This begins with a persistent ostinato figure, and out of the

pianissimo a great crescendo grows to a terrible clangor and reaches the maximum volume of sound, only to ebb swiftly away as the "Stabat mater dolorosa" rings out.

IV *The Resurrection.* This is a rushing toccata with figure work running through it and incorporating the theme of the "Adoro te devote":

This *Passion Symphony* is a brilliant example of effective and strongly formal program music in good taste.

Le chemin de la Croix (The Way of the Cross) Op. 29, 1931–32, duration 81 minutes. Another program piece, this time embracing the 14 Stations of the Cross. Dupré chooses for each station an appropriately descriptive melodic or rhythmic motif or else creates a general basic mood. Some of the stations musically are in several sections and depict the course of a whole event.

At the first station—"Jesus is condemned to death"—the piercing figure ♪♪ ♩ creates the feeling of irrevocable fate; at the second—"Jesus takes up His Cross"—one feels its weight in the stumbling rhythm ♫. ♫. The three times the Lord falls to the ground are illustrated with descending runs of tied notes ♩♩ ♩♩ ♩♩ in a manner reminiscent of J. S. Bach.

The intimate scenes, such as "Jesus meets His mother" or "Jesus comforts the women of Jerusalem", contrast sharply with the above. The nails which fix Him to the cross can be heard as clearly as the earthquake, the darkness and the terror of the people at Christ's death.

At the entombment we hear the same motif as at "Jesus comforts the women of Jerusalem", which indicates how deeply the composer understood and immersed himself in his subject.

Le tombeau de Titelouze (The tomb of Titelouze) Op. 38, 1942–43. This memorial to the early French master of the organ contains 16 three-to five-part chorales on liturgical chants. They are all very simple, with the cantus firmus appearing in all the parts, sometimes in canon.

Three hymns Op. 58, 1963. The first, **Matines** (Matins) is broken into individual sections which either elaborate on the theme

or play around it, continually offering new rhythmic ideas by means of changes in meter and tempo.

Vespers, on the other hand, has a very peaceful basic tempo and is unified by its persistent and slightly syncopated accompaniment.

The third piece, **Laudes** (Lauds), starts peacefully but increases in tempo to its toccata finale which closes like a hymn.

All three compositions have strong tone colors, and thanks to the composer's instructions on registration they can be effectively executed.

Concerto in E minor for organ and orchestra Op. 31, 1934. As is expected of a master of this type of composition like Dupré, this three-movement work gives us striking themes in a very clear and comprehensible form which can be easily identified, without the musicianly impulse which characterizes this lovely work being inhibited in the slightest.

I Allegro con moto with the main idea

These motifs alternate between organ, strings, woodwind and brass.

Contrapuntal rhythmic groups ♫♫♩ ♪ are next heard on the organ, after which the roles are reversed and the orchestra takes the rhythmical part instead. The second theme in long note values only appears briefly but nevertheless creates a mood which contrasts with the precise, almost rigid section with the first set of themes.

II Large (largo) with a melodic theme which is developed in just a few bars, and a second trio section with its own motif added on. In the third section Dupré combines the ideas in the first two so skillfully that the lively contrast between the two themes is hardly perceptible.

III Vivace is the finale, with swift runs in organ and orchestra and only short motifs:

It is like a rondo, enlivened by the inclusion of the Allegretto motif from the second movement, and shortly before the end, after a ponderous cadence, the theme of the first movement makes a fleeting appearance as well. This is a virtuoso competition between organ and orchestra.

Further works: Three preludes and fugues Op. 36; Second symphony Op. 26, 1926; Psalm 18 Op. 47, 1950; Suite Op. 39, 1944; Tryptich Op. 51, 1957; 79 chorales Op. 28, 1931.

Publishers: Bornemann; Leduc.

HERMANN GRABNER

b. Graz, May 12, 1886;
d. Bozen, July 3, 1969

In 1909 Grabner earned a doctorate in law at Graz and then studied with Max Reger in Leipzig. He taught theory in Strasbourg, Heidelberg and Mannheim, after 1924 in Leipzig and from 1938–46 in Berlin. He succeeded in freeing himself from Reger's strong influence and developed a modern musical language in which to express himself. Apart from organ music he mainly composed for voice, and he also wrote books on musical theory.

Media vita in morte sumus (In the midst of life we are in death) Op. 24, 1957. This is composed on the antiphon of the same name, and is divided into prelude, passacaglia and fugue. The Gregorian chorale is first heard in unison, then in parts, and leads into the passage work of the prelude, which is imitatively worked, each time within the scope of a few bars. In the pedals the cantus firmus is heard in the following rhythm:

The Passacaglia, marked Adagio, is based on an eight-bar theme derived from the antiphon itself. The counterparts to the ostinato are traditional in form, starting slowly and growing gradually. The theme is also heard on other tonic notes, and a harmonized line from the chorale comes at the end. The fugue has the following theme:

The development of this very lucid work contains inversions and stretti, and soon the part writing gives way to a toccata finish which takes up and merges the themes of fugue and passacaglia. The somewhat modal basic harmonies of this very pleasant sounding piece are ideally suited to the character of an antiphon.

Psalm 66, 1957. This is thematically built on the chorale melody "Jauchzt, alle Lande, Gott zu Ehren" (Rejoice, all ye lands, to the glory of God). The opening Grave e sostenuto with its heavy, dotted chords and runs in sixths soon opens into the Chorale, which alternates between soprano and alto. Both the short Andante tranquillo and the Fugue marked più mosso build their themes on the chorale, sections of which with contrasting counterpoint also dominate the second half of the Andante moderato after the repeat signs. The final Allegro vivace recalls the chorale in 3/8 time, with movement in the other parts and a close in toccata style with pedal solo and chords as at the beginning of the work.

Toccata Op. 53. An effective work with colorful changes between vigorous, fugal and short homophonic sections, culminating in a merry, playful fugue.

Further works: Prelude and fugue Op. 49; Hymn "Christ ist erstanden" (Christ is risen) Op. 32; Fantasia on the Lord's Prayer Op. 27; Concerto for organ and string orchestra.

Publisher: Kistner.

HEINRICH KAMINSKI

b. Tiengen, Upper Rhine, July 4, 1886;
d. Ried, Upper Bavaria, June 21, 1946

Kaminski came to music relatively late in life, but apart from two years teaching in Berlin he lived entirely from his compositions. His main fields were orchestral and choral—e.g. Psalm 69—and also chamber music. All his works are based on polyphonic structure.

Toccata and fugue. The toccata is full of contrasts in the greatest sense of the word: from a swift opening with 32nd-notes in the manuals and stretching pedal triplets in rhythmically confusing parts, through the peaceful 3/4 Andante to the Adagio with the metronome marking ♩ = c.42. It does sometimes gain in tension through frequent changes of time signature and precisely given tempos, but still runs the risk of seeming a bit amorphous.

The listener gets the same impression in the fugue, which is difficult to follow because of the lack of a rhythmic figure as guideline for the often complicated passage work. The triplet theme in 2/2 time is changed into quarter-notes, and the nucleus of the theme is worked on with various motifs towards the end.

Chorale sonata, 1926. Various chorale tunes are handled freely and follow each other without a pause. On the whole the impression is of three sections distinguished by their tempos, which might be "Andante tranquillo, Adagio, Allegro". The first takes the chorale "Ach Gott, vom Himmel sieh darein" (Ah God, in mercy look from heaven) and the second, marked Adagio molto, "Ich ruf zu dir, Herr Jesu Christ" (I call on thee, Lord Jesus Christ), an extremely complex movement in four distinct parts, with the cantus firmus in the soprano.

All the parts revel in melodic phrases and then calm down and die away in the last line of the chorale. "In dich hab ich gehoffet, Herr" (In Thee have I hoped, Lord) brings the middle section to a close and leads into the last, marked Allegro, on the words "Glori, Lob, Ehr und Herrlichkeit" (Glory, praise, honour and majesty), with easily recognized quotations from the chorale in the pedals and the upper part on the manuals.

Toccata on the chorale "Wie schön leucht uns der Morgenstern" (How brightly shines the morning star), 1923. The composer has indicated that the swell mechanism of pulleys and shutters should not be used because it goes against the spirit of the work. This is Kaminski's most concise work. Its brisk pace gives it a taut form and more immediate and convincing parlance than the others. It begins with a great pedal solo, continues in chords and soon slows down to a Sehr ruhig (Molto tranquillo), quasi recitativo. After brief references to the beginning comes the three-part Adagio, which at first varies the chorale motifs fugally. Finally comes the Chorale, always open and full of movement, building to a climax at the end on the words "praise o praise such love o'erflowing."

Publisher: Bärenreiter; Universal.

HERMANN UNGER

b. Kamenz, October 26, 1886;
d. Cologne, December 31, 1958

Unger earned a doctorate in ancient philology before studying music with Reger. He later became a university professor in Cologne, composed operas, orchestral works and chamber music, and wrote about music as well.

Concerto for organ and orchestra Op. 45. I Invocation, in three sections—Maestoso, Appassionato with cadenza, Maestoso; II Funeral march; III Consolation; IV Chorale and figue. The fugue is preceded by some introductory tutti bars for the organ, which also present the theme. A broad chorale passage ends the piece.

Publisher: Tischer.

FRANK MARTIN

b. Eaux Vives (Geneva), September 15, 1890;
d. Naarden, The Netherlands, November 21, 1974

His studies were lengthy and he taught in Geneva until 1938, when he gave this up almost entirely to concentrate more on composition, though he returned to teaching at the music academy in Cologne from 1950 to 1957. His oratorios Le vin herbé (The herbal wine), Golgotha *and the* Mystère de la nativité (Mystery of the nativity) *and his orchestral and chamber works are well known. After his early association with French impressionism his music showed influences of the Schönberg school of twelve-tone writing.*

Passacaglia, 1944, duration 12 minutes. It begins *pianissimo,* and the first line in the manuals moves as peacefully as the theme in the pedals.

The melodies in bass and soprano remain ostinato over long stretches of the work, but the theme soon changes by dropping in semitones from the last A and ending on D. After a pedal point on D-sharp the ostinato also changes to:

and:

A surge of chromatics based on the repeated theme then rises by a semitone in each of the following variations from B major to A minor, and culminates in B-flat major, with a recurrence of the soprano ostinato from the opening. A pedal point on D-sharp with the theme in the manuals brings the work to a *piano* close.

The **Church sonata,** 1938, duration 13 minutes, is in one movement, and two versions exist, one for viola d'amore and organ, and one for flute and organ.

Publisher: Universal.

ARTHUR HONEGGER

b. Le Havre, March 10, 1892;
d. Paris, November 27, 1955

Honegger studied in Paris with d'Indy and Widor among others, and continued to live there as an independent composer. He drew his inspiration from earlier composers such as Debussy and Florent Schmitt and was equally receptive to all new musical ideas. Best known among his extensive works are the stage oratorios Le roi David (King David) *and* Jeanne d'Arc au Bûcher (Joan of Arc at the stake) *and the symphony in one movement* Pacific 231, *while his organ works are of only marginal significance.*

The **Fugue in C-sharp minor,** 1917, has a regular exposition in four parts. Only the pedals carry no theme throughout the work, but begin shortly before the fourth entry with trivial supporting figures, as though they were the lowest manual part. Entries follow at once on D-sharp and A, and after a rising chromatic passage the head of the theme appears on E-sharp. Once again A is the dynamic climax. The recapitulation runs over a pedal point on C-sharp. The sublime musical language and colorful chromatics of this fugue offer us a wonderful late work in the spirit of Brahm's A-flat minor fugue.

Choral, in D minor throughout. The title obviously refers to César Franck's conception of the genre as a freely invented tune unconnected to any traditional chorale. It begins in 12/8 time:

but does not adhere to it, and the melody quoted next appears twice with the changed time signature, in the tenor and soprano registers. At the end comes a thematic reference to the opening bars.

This Choral is one of the few organ works which can be called impressionistic. Naturally the timbre is orchestral and therefore difficult to reproduce with the relatively "brittle" resources of the organ. The performer needs to steep himself long and intensively in both work and instrument.

Publisher: Chester.

DARIUS MILHAUD

b. Aix-en-Provence, September 4, 1892;
d. Geneva, June 22, 1974

Milhaud studied in Paris, where he was particularly influenced by the music of Debussy, Mussorgsky and Stravinsky. He went to Rio de Janeiro in 1916 as secretary at the legation, and on his return became a controversial innovator in French music. During World War II he went to the United States and from 1947 to 1962 taught both at Mills College in Oakland, California and the Paris Conservatoire. He wrote important works for orchestra, stage and ballet, but the organ is represented by only a few pieces.

Sonata, 1931. The first movement is marked "Étude" (Study) and is the best kind of flowing, graceful music to play, born of superb musicianship. Apart from short flourishes which are not developed further it contains only one theme mostly encountered in the upper part

while the other three or four parts accompany it. The final passage is broadly emphasized by the appearance of the theme in the pedals.

The "Rêverie" (Dream) following also has only one theme, the first two bars of which often recur, always as the top part of a homophonic, cantabile movement.

The Finale marked Animé is a rondo with varying treatments of the theme (one treatment in 6/8 is particularly striking) and an exact recapitulation in virtuoso manner which is technically very difficult to master.

Nine preludes, total duration 19 minutes. This is a series of essentially unconnected little pieces, which last between 40 seconds and two minutes each. Their themes are idiosyncratic and they give completely different impressions. A few examples of the themes follow:

Further works: Pastorale, Little suite.

Publishers: Eschig; Gray; Heugel; Schott.

PAUL HINDEMITH

b. Hanau, November 16, 1895;
d. Frankfurt-am-Main, December 28, 1963

This "Classical modern" composer not only studied musical theory and taught at the universities of Berlin, Yale and Zürich, but was himself a performing musician. He was the concertmaster of the Frankfurt opera orchestra and the violist of the Amar Quartet. He mostly wrote symphonic music and operas. His theoretical work Unterweisung im Tonsatz (The Craft of Musical Composition) *is widely studied.*

Works for organ solo

First sonata, 1937, duration 15 minutes.

I Mässig schnell (Allegro moderato). The first theme is developed in short

motifs, only to be completely replaced by a second theme marked "lebhaft" (vivace) in 3/8 time. Widely contrasting fugal passages occur, and at the end the two themes are given almost equal importance.

II Sehr langsam (Molto lento). Ornamented, far-reaching lines are followed "without a break" by the Fantasia, marked "frei" (libero).

This contains two separate sections, the first in toccata style, sometimes recitativelike and sometimes lively, vigorous but strict in tempo, and the second marked "Ruhig bewegt" (Andante tranquillo), a markedly melodic finale with the following theme:

The whole sonata has great impetus and sparkles with life, largely on account of its imaginative construction.

Second sonata, duration 10 minutes. Of the three similar works this one is the most like chamber music.

I Lebhaft (Vivace) consists of swift and often surprising changes between homophonic bars, vibrant passages written in three parts, and mechanical-sounding runs. The recapitulation repeats the first section in its entirety.

II Ruhig bewegt (Andante tranquillo). Changes between the two manuals (Great and Swell).

III Fugue: Mässig bewegt, heiter (Andante moderato, sereno). The fugue is very translucent, like a pastel painting. The interludes occur in a consistent series, clearly differentiated from the thematic sections.

The extremely playful basic pattern continues to the end, with the parts fading away until only one part is left to state the theme for the last time. This is a rare example of a fugue which sounds relaxed and imaginative while being soundly constructed.

Third sonata, on old folk songs, 1940, duration 11 minutes.

I "Ach Gott, wem soll ich's klagen" (Ah God, to whom should I complain), marked mässig bewegt (andante moderato), is in the rocking 12/8 time which in earlier times was used to give pastorals and laments their special character. The tune is only heard at the end of the movement:

II "Wach auf, mein Hort" (Awake, my delight) is a lovely, melodic, cantabile four-part movement with the tune in the tenor. At the beginning the upper part anticipates the melody very tenderly:

III "So wünsch ich ihr" (So do I wish for her). Ruhig bewegt (Andante tranquillo), is consistently constructed with the tune in the pedals and several upper parts elaborating on it freely, with references to the motifs.

These major-minor folk song tunes are convincingly combined with the contrapuntal parts by means of the tonal style which still prevailed in Hindemith's writing.

Works for organ and orchestra

Concerto for organ and chamber orchestra Op. 46, No. 2, 1927, duration 14 minutes. Orchestra: two flutes, oboe, two clarinets, three bassoons, horn, trumpet, trombone, cellos, double basses.

I Nicht zu schnell (Non troppo allegro). The continuation of the main theme, given in the motif in bars 3–5 of the example, characterizes this movement.

A second motif is only used in brief episodes:

II Sehr langsam and ganz ruhig (Lentissimo e tranquillo). A song form, in three parts, with the theme stated first by the organ, and the upper parts in canon.

Later the theme also appears among the solo instruments of the orchestra, is taken up again in canon by the organ and there remains until the end.

III A movement marked only " ♪ up to 184." A furious finale, characterized particularly by the nucleus of the theme from the fugal opening:

A calmer, legato second theme contrasts with the staccato motion of the wind instruments.

Concerto for organ and orchestra 1962, written for the opening of the Lincoln Center in New York: duration 25 minutes. Orchestra: two flutes, two oboes, two clarinets, two bassoons, contrabassoon, two horns, two trumpets, three trombones, tuba, timpani, percussion, glockenspiel, celeste, string quintet.

This was Hindemith's last work and has quite different features from those of his first organ concerto. Composition and structure are noticeably more symphonic, the orchestral treatment is less conventional and the instrumentation is very inventive.

I Crescendo. The marking says it all. The cellos open in unison with the theme over a long, sustained C on the organ:

This extended theme then appears *piano* on the organ, an octave higher, and the woodwinds come in with the strings, which apart from the cellos and double basses have so far been silent, while the organ maintains a single line. A new motif is stated in the organ part but little developed, and the brass finally enters *forte* with the theme in the first trumpet and the organ part in stretto with it. After a strongly rhythmic transition the theme appears in an orchestral tutti, with the organ half a bar ahead. Towards the final climax the final motif is heard alternating between organ and orchestra.

II Allegro assai. An ostinato string passage supported rhythmically by timpani and trombones opens the movement, and the organ states a theme which is either emphasized or interrupted by the ostinato.

There follows a melodic section marked Dolce e semplice with a theme that moves through woodwinds, organ, brass, organ again, and strings. After the cadenza with its references to the slow theme, the ostinato figure from the beginning briefly reappears.

III Canzonetta, with two ritornellos. The canzonetta theme is stated in the organ, mostly with basic chordal harmonies, and then a ritornello enters in the strings, clearly differentiated by its dotted eighth-note rhythm, marked "grazioso".

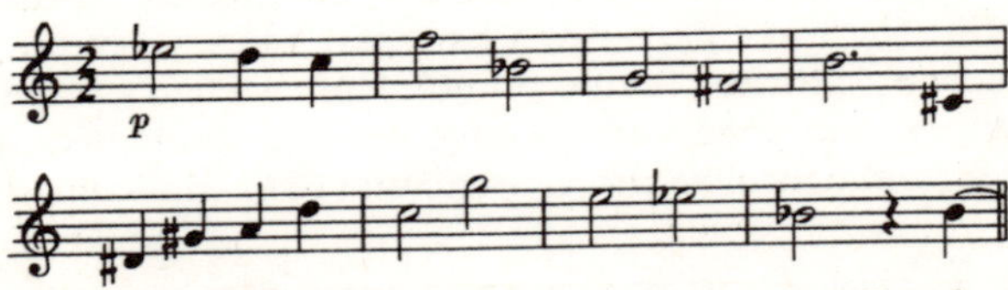

Glissandi, and trills for flute and horn in the second ritornello, characterize these passages. The organ brings the movement to a close with the theme in large note values and a brief cadenza.

IV Fantasia super "Veni, creator spiritus". The organ opens and is soon answered by agitated figures in the orchestra.

The Allegro energico employs the cantus firmus in the following form:

The organ takes up the theme in a 9/8 gigue rhythm and the instruments follow it. The great cadenza with the composer's registration markings flows into an Arioso with new thematic material, which after a few bars gives way to the Largamente. Now the cantus firmus sounds once again, antiphonally between the brass of horn and trumpet, and the organ. The movement ends in a grandiose climax.

Publisher: Schott.

JOHANN NEPOMUK DAVID

b. Eferding, Upper Austria, November 30, 1895;
d. Stuttgart, December 22, 1977

David first worked as organist and choirmaster in Wels and in 1934 was called to Leipzig to teach composition at the provincial conservatory. After the war he went via Salzburg to the Stuttgart music academy as professor of composition. He grew up in the shadow of Bruckner but later succeeded in combining a sensitive romantic feeling for musical sound with his original talent for counterpoint. His organ works occupy an important position between his rich output of symphonic music and his sacred choral works. In his last years his part writing became increasingly strict in form.

Works for solo organ

Free works

Ricercare in C minor, 1925. This is like a trio sonata, in three movements and superbly contrapuntal, as well as being rendered so musically beautiful by its melodic lines and related harmonies that it is a jewel among its peers, and can even bear comparison with J. S. Bach's trio sonatas—the greatest yardstick of all.

I Ganz still: The three parts run a bar apart, in canon at the upper fifth.

II Im gleichen Zeitmass (Tempo primo): Here we find a convincing blend of fugues and canons combined with passage work in double counterpoint. It all sounds very light and dancelike and gives no hint of the difficulties it poses for the organist.

III Ein wenig belebter (Un poco più mosso): The same treatment as in the second movement, but here starting at once in two parts. At the end, marked "etwas breiter" (un po più largo), there is a quotation from the theme and counterpoint from the second movement.

Chaconne in A minor, 1927, duration 15 minutes. It begins *fortissimo* as an improvisation, marked "frei". After a few bars the theme enters,

but is not allowed to retain its original shape as in Classical variation form; here at the second entry the ostinato appears in the manuals, the pitch is changed and the individual parts are woven closely together in canon. In the middle the opening bars are recalled.

This is an incomparably imaginative work, bubbling over with original ideas and superbly written for organ, yet it is entirely coherent and highly successful.

Passamezzo and fugue in G minor, 1928. A very lucid work in two sections. The short passamezzo, based on a 16th-century Italian dance, is followed by a fugue which forms the head of its theme out of the inversion of the passamezzo theme. In the course of the fugue the parts are often alarmingly closely woven but still audible, in a manner reminiscent of old Dutch polyphonic masterpieces.

Fantasia super "L'homme armé" (The armed man), 1929. The old familiar tune can already be clearly heard, especially in the pedals, in the first bars marked "Langsam, aber äusserst rhythmisch" with their sustained, inverted dotted rhythm.

It then emerges in the soprano, is further elaborated in the pedals (marked Andante maestoso),

next appears in changed form in a three-part canon with a free fourth part, and finally appears in the pedals in the fugal finale, while the upper parts make simple statements.

Toccata and fugue; Chaconne and fugue, both of 1962. Both works show the strong consistency which characterized David's later compositions: concision of form with content of unparallelled contrapuntal wealth. Connoisseurs can feast their eyes on a score which will inspire many people to get involved with both works. The combination of sounds made by the strongly blended individual parts does not seem to have concerned the composer, and as a result the work's harmonies make a weaker effect than does its form.

Into the Allegro energico toccata, where the overwhelming trio character is maintained in a constant swift motion, a short three-part movement marked "Quasi Adagio" is inserted. Here the two lower parts proceed normally with "expansion", while the upper parts "contract" the inversion of a canon. This slow section works with further compositional devices like retrograde, and later ends the toccata and moves into the fugue, the theme of which was already heard on the pedals in the toccata and prominently in the upper part of the Quasi Adagio canon.

The technical sophistication here is outstanding.

The ostinato of the chaconne is as peaceful as usual:

The variations which unfold vary in motion and force. The fugue is as contrapuntally dense as the toccata fugue but nonetheless full of impetus.

Partita on B-A-C-H, 1964. The compass of the eight clearly divided sections is too broad for brief description, and only a study of the score will serve to guide and help the listener. The four notes of Bach's name first appear in the pedals like this:

while the manuals create contrasts:

In the later sections themes such as are given below form the basis for further fugal elaboration:

In the third section:

In the fourth section:

In the eighth section:

The chromaticism of the four-note theme gives the work its highly individual character.

Twelve fugues for organ in all keys Op. 66, 1968. This important volume can be described as a compendium of the art of fugue writing from the old master of counterpoint. The individual pieces are often incomprehensibly densely intertwined. They offer every key, ascending in whole tones from C to B-flat and descending from B to D-flat. The strictness is relaxed by combining the fugues with other forms which sometimes precede them and are sometimes woven in with them—a fantasia with the fugues in D and G-sharp, a chorale with the fugue in E, a chaconne with the fugue in B-flat and a musette with the fugue in G.

Works related to chorales

David's chorale compositions, written between 1932 and 1974, comprise the most extensive work on song cantus firmi since Bach. At first he favored small forms such as Chorale Prelude, Little Fantasia, Little Partita, Toccata, etc., but later grand cycles like the study "Christus, der ist mein Leben" (Christ, who is my life), the partitas "Unüberwindlich starker Held, Sankt Michael" (St. Michael, the strong, victorious hero), "Es ist ein Schnitter, heisst der Tod" (There is a reaper, called Death) and "Lobt Gott, ihr frommen Christen" (Praise God, good Christians), or the sacred concerto "Es sungen drei Engel ein süssen Gesang" (Three angels sang a sweet song). In volume 13 various chorales are combined, as for instance "Aus tiefer Not- Ach Gott, vom Himmel" (Out of the deep—Ah God look down) or "Ach Gott, vom Himmel—Vater unser—Aus tiefer Not" (Ah God look down—Our Father—Out of the deep). Volume 14 of 1962 contains "Fantasias for organ". Several works allow for performance on the Positive organ. Because the structure of the smaller works can be easily appreciated they need little explanation—e.g. the "Vater unser" (Our Father) and "O Welt, ich muss dich lassen" (Oh world, I must leave you) from volume 2 and the partita "Vom Himmel hoch" (From highest heaven) from volume 7—only some of the larger-scale works are discussed here.

Christus, der ist mein Leben (Christ who is my life) from volume 6, is headed "Ein Lehrstück für Orgel" (A study for organ), which indicates that it demonstrates the whole far-reaching and soundly based contrapuntal art of the composer, and indeed it does so most convincingly. Obviously it will not have great audience appeal as a result, but David's other works can also be recognized by just such a dense structure, which even leads to musical rigidity.

The individual movements are headed as follows: I Aria: "Einfach, nicht schleppend"; II Double counterpoint at the sixth: "Im gleichen Zeitmass"; III Double counterpoint inverted at the twelfth: "Immer stürmisch voran"; IV Canon at the seventh: "Mit sanftem Schwung, ohne Hast"; V Canon in diminution at the tenth: "Äusserst flüchtig"; VI Canon at the octave, direct, inverted, retrograde, and retrograde inversion: "Sehr feierlich, nicht schleppend"; VII Canon inverted at the second: "Gehend"; VIII Canon in unison: "Langsam schwebend, sehr zart"; IX Double counterpoint at the ninth: "Gehend"; X Canon at the fourth: "Im Schuss, leicht lärmend"; XI Double counterpoint at the seventh: "Langsam vorwärts tastend"; XII Chaconne-fugue: "Grossschreitend"; XIII Canon at the fifth: "Ganz still voran"; XIV Canon at the sixth with double counterpoint at the tenth: "Leicht und gehoben".

Es sungen drei Engel ein' süssen Gesang (Three angels sang a sweet song) from volume 8, marked "Geistliches Konzert für Orgel" (Sacred concerto for organ), 1941.

I The old familiar air is first heard in the pedals, once some introductory bars hinting at the motifs have been played.

A fugue runs through the three upper parts at the same time. When the tune of the chorale "O Haupt voll Blut and Wunden" (O sacred head sore wounded) comes in *pianissimo* there are three parts with a repeated theme in the upper part—as in the fugue—and cantus firmus in the pedals. The parts fill out towards the close.

II "Sehr langsam" is in free lines formed of great, sweeping melodies and delicate rhythms. The middle section is swift and fugal.

III This is the longest movement and is based on a free theme (in canon, in fugue and inverted) in contrast to the cantus firmus of the song, which is heard to great effect in the pedals and in the upper manual part.

The cantus firmus appears in stretto in the pedals and the orchestral octaves in the manuals prepare for a stretto which brings the section to a final climax.

Through the flow of their music the two outer movements of this piece communicate even with listeners unable to grasp their precise construction—a quality one might wish for many other works, however well-fashioned contrapuntally.

Partita "Unüberwindlich starker Held, Sankt Michael" (St. Michael, the strong, victorious hero) from volume 9. This is the most forceful work in the whole series.

I Begins in unison *fortissimo,* then presents the nucleus of the theme in varied treatment. Further sections of the theme and later also lines from the chorale serve as bases for the following sections. The counterpoint is made of descending runs. Before the end of this movement, which is in even, quarter-note motion, the cantus firmus appears in the soprano and tenor.

II "Sehr ruhiger Dreischlag". This consistently beautiful movement has a stately rhythmic measure 𝅗𝅥 𝅗𝅥. ♩, and sounds agreeably "homophonic". It is based

on quotations from the cantus firmus in the pedals, which give it an even more tranquil and balanced feeling. The continuously sustained e^2 in the last bars may surprise and even alienate the listener before the last line of the chorale emerges from that note. A short "Recitative" with directions for changing manuals between Great and Positive leads into the

III Fugue. As usual with David, the long exposition is lacking, so that

after three entries on the manuals the theme already appears in augmentation in the pedals, and the inversion which then immediately follows comes as no surprise.

The phrasing of the theme lends a transparency to the movement, in spite of all its density, so that the listener can follow the essential divisions in the concentrated workings.

Finally the cantus firmus of the song appears in the pedals with the fugue theme (as in Reger's fantasia fugues), while motifs from the cantus firmus are still alluded to in the upper parts. The final lines of the chorale are heard in canon in the pedals below the towering manual parts.

Partita "Es ist ein Schnitter, heisst der Tod" (There is a reaper called Death) from volume 10. This is David's monumental view of death and destruction. Its folk original is spiritually enriched and uplifted by association with the Gregorian chant "Dies irae, dies illa," which is textually appropriate and also musically fruitful.

I Adagio. The theme of the song is written for the pedals, where it appears in a different rhythm and forms the basis for passagework figures.

II Molto moderato with free upper parts developed from the theme.

III Andante, a trio movement.

IV Allegro, with the theme first in the pedals and then in the upper manual parts.

V "Dies irae" as a bicinium. During the repeat of the *Dies Irae,* after "Tremens factus sum ego," the accompaniment plays double notes reminiscent of progressions in medieval *organum.*

VI Andante con moto. This variation is the most immediately gripping and the easiest to remember, because a figure in the pedals portrays the rhythmic scything action of the reaper:

Above it the theme from the *Dies Irae* is heard, and later the tune from the folk song too. Part writing and figuration build to a climax.

VII Andante, a calm finale which ends this impressive work by combining the two themes, though the "Dies irae" is only alluded to through the notes E, D, E, D.

Works for organ and orchestra

Introit, chorale and fugue, 1939, duration 20 minutes, written for organ and nine wind instruments on a theme by Anton Bruckner.

Orchestra: four horns, two trumpets, three trombones.

Here is Bruckner's theme, which he wrote for an organ recital:

The Introit which starts "Feierlich und breit" introduces it in retrograde inversion, and soon after in its original form, in manuals and pedals. A *pianissimo* middle sec-

tion, mostly of ascending and descending chromatic lines, is clearly defined and contrasts with the third and last section, which is definitely and audibly dominated by Bruckner's theme. Up to this point the organ has been playing alone, but now in the "Chorale" the wind instruments join in. At first the exposition of the fugue is again only given to the solo instrument; to Bruckner's theme are added motifs and phrases from the middle section of the introit and later from the chorale as well. Another theme is stated by trumpets and trombones, while the horns continue with

their theme from the chorale. This multiplicity of themes is combined with Bruckner's idea, first in G major and then, intensified, in C major. However splendid and convincing this movement looks on paper, it is almost too complicated to execute well, as we see from the horn theme. It is all too easy for the listener to be only aware of a grandiose torrent of sound.

This work mounts to a hymnlike climax and is in its entirety a magnificently successful glorification and honoring of Bruckner's spirit.

The **Concerto for organ and orchestra** Op. 61, 1965, duration 20 minutes, is in three movements and scored for two flutes, three trombones, timpani, percussion, harp and strings.

Further works: Ricercare in A minor; Toccata and fugue in F minor, 1928; Preamble and fugue in D minor, 1930; Sonata for violin and organ Op. 75; Hymns, Fantasias and Fugues.

Publisher: Breitkopf.

HANS FLEISCHER

b. Wiesbaden, November 10, 1896;
d. Bayreuth, February 20, 1981

Fleischer studied composition with Johanna Senfter and then worked independently in Wiesbaden. In 1941 he became deputy director of the regional music college in Luxembourg and after the war lived in Bayreuth as a freelance composer. The extensive catalogue of his works contains many songs, nine symphonies and other orchestral works, chamber music and sacred music. His special qualities are best expressed in his orchestral works.

Concerto for organ and orchestra Op. 155, duration 23 minutes.

I "Sehr lebendig", begins in the pedals to triplets from the oboes, and then the following theme appears in the manuals:

The transposed string entry with dotted triplets offers some fresh material to elaborate. The organ states the second theme marked "Ein wenig ruhiger" (Poco più tranquillo).

The subsequent contrasting exchange between the two ideas produces a heightened tension which seems to slacken and tighten again spontaneously, thereby making this music extremely lively. Each occurrence of the first theme can be recognized by its triplet rhythm.

II "Sehr langsam" (Lentissimo) begins and ends with an organ solo. The expressive melody only appears in the organ part, apart from a few imitations of its opening, while the orchestra, particularly the first violin, is given a sort of second theme not heard on the organ.

III "Zügig, aber nicht zu schnell" (Allegro, ma non troppo) starts with raging chords in strings and trumpets, leading into a theme which substantially fills the whole movement, apart from the opening chords. At the marking "Ruhiger" (Più tranquillo) a cantilena appears and returns twice. Shortly before the end the organ plays a fugato as a sort of cadenza, which leads into a reprise of the opening chords.

The broad ending is in C major. This is a very colorful and musicianly work which offers the organist great musical opportunities.

Music for organ and brass Op. 167, in manuscript. This work is in three movements, marked "Lebendig, Langsam, Zügig" (Vivace, Lento, Allegro) and scored for two trumpets, two horns and three trombones. Sometimes the wind instruments are independent within the polyphonic writing, and in the second movement describe peaceful, soaring lines and even solo flourishes, while the organ plays in the background. Fleischer has succeeded in composing a piece in original style which underlines the organ's brass characteristics while simultaneously contrasting its linear potential with the brass complement.

Further works (all in manuscript): Concerto for organ and string orchestra Op. 156; Theme with twelve counterpoints Op. 33/1; Three organ pieces Op. 45.

Publisher: Schultheiss.

JOHANNES WEYRAUCH

b. Leipzig, February 20, 1897;
d. ibid., May 1, 1977

Weyrauch studied with Karg-Elert and in addition to his work as a private music teacher he was from 1936 to 1941 cantor and finally from 1946 on lecturer at the Leipzig music academy. He wrote a St. John Passion, motets, cantatas and chamber music.

Prelude, aria and fugue. The prelude is planned on a theme which continues its first rhythmic figures and contains frequent descending "flights of steps".

Aria: Solo on a reed stop—the composer's instruction. Fugue: A regular exposition with clearly defined interludes. A second theme appears and in the last bars is combined with the first.

Partita "O Heiland, reiss die Himmel auf" (O Saviour, open the heavens). I Descending figures in fourths characterize this movement. The cantus firmus is treated line by line in the alto. II Solo in the soprano with ornamented chorale melody. Two parts which imitate each other serve as background. III Trio with cantus firmus in the middle part and ostinato below. IV Cantus firmus in the bass against triplets in the manuals. V Chorale, with cantus firmus in the soprano and hints at a canon in the pedals.

This work is suitable for concerts as well as church services.

Further partitas: "Singet frisch und wohlgemut" (Sing with fresh and merry heart); "Jesu, deine Passion" (Jesus, Thy passion); "Heut triumphieret Gottes Sohn"

(Today God's Son doth triumph); "Nun bitten wir den Heiligen Geist" (Now pray we to the Holy Ghost); "Unüberwindlich starker Held" (Strong victorious hero); "Ich weiss ein lieblich Engelspiel" (I know a lovely sport of angels).

Publisher: Breitkopf.

PAUL MÜLLER

b. Zurich, June 19, 1898

He studied in Zurich and Paris, and since 1927 has been teaching at the conservatory in his home town. His music belongs in spirit to the Baroque era and employs many Classical forms, while its language has remained tonal with hints of the church modes. He also composed works for orchestra, chamber orchestra, stage and voice.

Prelude and fugue in E minor Op. 22. The close relationship between the two sections is emphasized by the motif appearing in both.

The prelude works almost exclusively with this motif, which is imitated in the upper parts and interrupted by short, slow episodes, while in the fugue it appears as the head of a second theme inverted to create the actual fugue theme. In the exposition, marked "ruhig fliessend, stufenweise steigernd", the first theme of the fugue is treated conventionally to begin with;

later comes a stretto treatment of the combined themes, the first theme in fifths and finally in four-part chords. The end "wie am Anfang" (come primo) contains the motif and references to the themes.

Toccata in A minor Op. 50. The pedal solo which opens this work programmatically is very forceful in character and contains the motifs for further development.

After the short introduction comes a three-part middle movement marked "tranquillo, quasi improvisando" with simple but extremely melodic lines, and a final fugal section which demonstrates the composer's technical skill and effectively leads the way into a slow closing phrase.

Their openness and simplicity make Müller's works suitable for audiences who are to be gradually initiated into contrapuntal music; they are all relatively easy to understand and absorb.

Of note are his **Chorale fantasias with wind instruments.** Those on the chorales "Wie schön leuchtet der Morgenstern" (How brightly shines the morning star) and

"Ein feste Burg" (A Mighty Fortress) are each scored for two trumpets and two trombones. Further works: Toccata in C major Op. 12; Concerto for organ and string orchestra.

Publishers: Bärenreiter; Schott.

FRANCIS POULENC

b. Paris, January 7, 1899;
d. ibid., January 30, 1963

The main influences on Poulenc were Satie and Auric, and he became a member of the Groupe des Six. *His vocal chamber music, choral compositions, chamber music and concert and stage works distinguish him among 20th-century French composers, who all wrote music reflecting their own feelings and intuition.*

Concerto in G minor for organ, string orchestra and timpani, 1938, duration 21 minutes.

This unusual work is a continuous composition with clear subdivisions. The subtle string writing produces a splendidly colorful sound in contrast to the organ's effective role as a wind instrument. Sometimes both components merge into one homogeneous sound and the solo organ makes a strong virtuoso impact.

It opens Andante with a programmatic statement from the organ:

After only two bars the chords dissolve into peacefully flowing lines, and this introduction and the transition into the Allegro giocoso builds to a climax with the theme:

The organ plays only runs and scales while the orchestra states the theme with verve and passion, but soon the strong, sweeping melodic lines of the

Andante moderato unfold. The dotted rhythms at first make this movement sound like a stately dance, but later when the orchestra plays contrapuntally against the organ it is like a pastoral dialogue. There is a dynamically broad transition to the Allegro, molto agitato, where references to the first Allegro are heard, but it makes a much more impetuous impression than the opening movement. Once again, though only for a few bars, its course slows to a "Très calme, lent" in the Solo register of the organ. The end is a mirror image of the beginning: an Allegro like an Allegro giocoso mentioned above, only without the theme quoted there, and a Largo like the first bars of the work. Maurice Duruflé cooperated with the composer on providing the registration instructions.

Publisher: Salabert.

WILLY BURKHARD

b. Leubringen nr. Biel, April 17, 1900;
d. Zurich, June 18, 1955

He taught temporarily at the conservatories of Berne and Zurich, and was one of the most important Swiss composers of this century, whose deeply intense works are based on polyphony. Apart from sacred choral music, represented by two oratorios, cantatas, etc., Burkhard shone in his numerous works for orchestra and in his chamber music.

Prelude and fugue, 1932. "In der Art einer Improvisation" consists of descending scales, and smaller descending figures in the pedals. The brief fugue is in four to five parts and its theme also appears inverted and in stretto.

Chorale Triptychon Op. 91, 1953.

I "Ich steh an deiner Krippen hier" (I stand here at Thy cradle). A very complex movement marked Andante, Allegretto, Allegro. The cantus firmus appears in various parts, mostly accompanied by joyful Christmas tunes which play around it.

II "O Mensch, bewein dein Sünde gross" (O man, bewail thy grievous sin). After the chorale in four parts the movement divides into smaller sections, each with a part of the text. "Von einer Jungfrau rein und zart" (From a virgin pure and fair) is a duet with delicate sixteenth-notes in the right hand painting a tone picture. "Den Toten er das Leben gab" (He brought the dead to life) is a dense, heavy movement which repeats the previous theme in the pedals, and "Dass er für uns geopfert würd" (That He were sacrificed for us) is a trio lament with clear imitation of the chorale.

III "Christ lag in Todesbanden" (Christ lay in the bonds of death) is like a toccata. The improvisatory theme given here also serves as the leading theme of the fugue which follows, and the first notes of the chorale are appended to it. Towards the end the chorale is heard in unison and then builds to six parts.

Fantasia and chorale "Ein feste Burg ist unser Gott" (A Mighty Fortress is our God) Op. 58, 1939. This is a grandly laid out fantasy with very free and even fragmentary use of Luther's chorale. Only verse four of the hymn which starts "And were the world all devils o'er" is clearly and appropriately developed. The chorale itself is in five parts with short interludes.

Concerto for organ and orchestra Op. 74, 1945, duration 20 minutes. Scored for two trumpets, two horns, trombone and strings.

I Tempo moderato. A broad introduction in quarter-notes for organ and strings. The brass sound the most-quoted motif. There follows an Allegro as a fugato in three parts on the organ with an orchestral accompaniment, and then a reprise of the introductory bars and the fugato Allegro again, this time in the brass. The main motif returns with much use of the rhythm ♫♫♩ from the end of the fugato theme.

II Adagio. Primarily a solo piece for the organist's right hand, marked "cantabile". After being interrupted by a passionate section in which the organ plays in loving lines and the strings quote the chorale from the third movement, the first theme returns in the violins.

III Allegro. The rising fifth in various rhythms dominates the opening while the organ plays repeated figures. Soon the motif from the first movement appears as the beginning of a kind of chorale theme then heard in the organ.

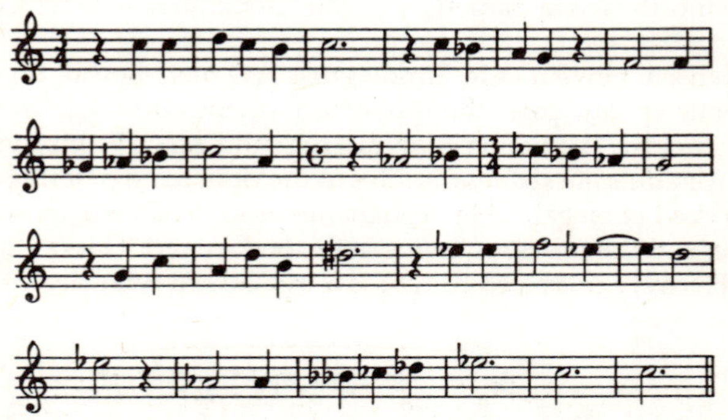

The orchestra accompanies in broken chords without thirds. The powerful recapitulation contains an inversion of the theme with the fifth from the beginning, followed by the chorale in the brass and its inversion in the organ pedals. This impressive work closes on a great dynamic climax.

Further works: Sonatina; Fantasia Op. 32, 1931; Variations on two chorale movements by H. L. Hassler Op. 28, 1930; Partitas on "Grosser Gott, wir loben dich" (Great God, we praise Thee) and "Wer nur den lieben Gott lässt walten" (He who relies on God's compassion); Hymn for organ and orchestra Op. 75, 1945.

Publisher: Bärenreiter.

ERNST KRENEK

b. Vienna, August 23, 1900

Krenek studied composition in Vienna with F. Schreker, lived in Zurich, Kassel and Wiesbaden and in 1938 went to the United States. After his atonal period he was widely acclaimed for his jazz opera "Jonny spielt auf" (Jonny strikes up), and later he took to twelve-tone and serial composition. The organ is marginal to his oeuvre, which does however include a little Concerto for organ, piano and chamber orchestra Op. 88, 1940.

Sonata Op. 92, 1941, duration 8 minutes. This is a continuous composition, but can be divided into three clear sections—Allegro, Andante, Allegro scherzando.

The first movement has two themes but hardly any development. In the Andante there is a little three-part A B A form which returns in the last movement. The theme of the swift finale is derived from the final phrases of the slow movement. By reverting to the first theme of the opening movement the composer gives the impression of a recapitulation.

The four winds, 1975, duration 11 minutes, has movements called Euros, Notos, Zephyros and Boreas.

Publishers: Gray, Bärenreiter.

LEO SOWERBY (b. Grand Rapids, MI, May 1, 1895; d. Port Clinton, OH, July 7, 1968) was an American composer who did not deny his musical origins in late French Romanticism. Many of his works bear witness to this: **Interlude, Arioso, Requiescat in pace,** the 1937 **Concerto** and the 1944 **Classic Concerto** for organ and strings. Beside his splendid, fluid **Toccata** there are character pieces—the lyrical **Carillon** and the dramatic **Fanfare. Pageant,** dedicated to the Italian organist Fernando Germani, is an extremely difficult demonstration piece for pedal technique. Publisher: Gray.

AARON COPLAND (b. Brooklyn, NY, November 14, 1900) has a more aggressive, but tonal modern, style. Among his many chamber and orchestral works there is only one **Symphony for organ and orchestra,** 1924, duration 25 minutes. It is in three movements and requires a full symphony orchestra. Publisher: Boosey & Hawkes.

SAMUEL BARBER (b. West Chester, PA, March 9, 1910; d. New York, NY, Jan. 23, 1981) wrote a splendid **Toccata festiva** Op. 36, 1960, duration 14 minutes, for organ and orchestra. The climax is reached by means of a solo cadenza in the pedals. Publisher: Schirmer.

CONRAD BECK

b. Lohn, Schaffhausen, June 16, 1901

Beck studied in Zurich and Paris and in 1933 settled in Basle. He is a prolific composer of almost all kinds of vocal and instrumental music, and his organ works can be classified as chamber music. His writing is basically linear; in spite of its clarity, it demonstrates certain deeply-rooted brooding features.

Sonatina, 1927. The first movement, a Passacaglia, knits its series of variations loosely together. Before the ostinato figure first appears, a manual passage formed from the same notes is heard:

The ostinato also occurs in the middle and upper parts. The Andantino is a duet which moves at a calm pace, while the Allegro sparkles in runs and playful staccato. Particularly from this final movement the whole sonata derives its merry, varied charm.

Two preludes, 1932. These are basically very tranquil works but their harmonies shimmer with varied tone colors, like a veil through which the dreamy music shines. The general calm does not deny these preludes their flowing character; though there is slowness it is not the prevailing mood. The great, moving contrast to any mechanical motion makes a strong impression. In the **first,** marked Maestoso, the beginning of the opening section quoted here returns like a recapitulation after the Cantabile, a melodic piece with a canon, sometimes over pedal points.

The **second,** marked Andante sostenuto, is constructed similarly. Its opening is based on tense intervals of a second; linear passages follow in two or more parts, only to lead back into a "tempo primo" with the original thematic material.

Chorale sonata, 1948. As in all works with this title, the individual sections are based on a chorale melody, and sometimes also on the words. In I the model is "Von Gott will ich nicht lassen" (I will not part from God), marked Andante sostenuto, with clear quotations from the chorale in soprano and bass, though in unrelated keys. II "O Lamm Gottes, unschuldig" (O spotless Lamb of God), marked Lento e semplice, develops the cantus firmus in the tenor. III "Komm heiliger Geist, Herre Gott" (Come Holy Ghost, Lord God), marked Allegro con fuoco, runs as loosely as a toccata and has two middle sections with quite different figures. The sweeping cantus firmus of the song is heard twice in its entirety—at the beginning in the soprano and at the end in the pedals.

Publisher: Schott.

ERNST PEPPING

b. Duisburg, September 12, 1901;
d. Berlin, February 1, 1981

Pepping studied in Berlin, lived as a freelance musician in Mühlheim and Essen, in 1934 became a teacher at the school of church music in Spandau and in 1953 a professor at the Berlin academy of music. He was one of the most important figures in contemporary Protestant church music, and his organ works and choral compositions take precedence over his orchestral and chamber music. He wrote in contrapuntal, neo-Baroque style without ignoring the opportunities for creating tone colors.

Concerto I, 1941. Intrada. Unison opening with octave leaps

which help to shape the movement's thematic material. This happy, rewarding piece suffers a little from its articulation which is occasionally unsuitable for the instrument. Some interpreters can make it sound dry and wooden, although it is nothing of the kind. Aria alla passacaglia. The ostinato figure is a descending scale of C minor, which is later inverted and changed. Above it play the variations, the last being like a recapitulation of the opening with the parts sometimes exchanged.

Fugue. A double fugue with separate developments, later combining the two themes.

Concerto II, 1941. Prelude in a very attractive three-part form. The opening section is dominated by a motif with emphatic fifths:

A quiet section suggests a new motif:

but only the fifths heard earlier are elaborated and lead into the recapitulation. This is a very close-knit movement with an easily understood structure and a certain agreeable feeling of exhilaration. Canzona like a dance with long steps (*Schreittanz*). Chaconne with the following ostinato theme:

At first the counterpoint is calm and is a single line, but other parts are gradually added. In the course of the inventive variations which increase in speed the cantus firmus also appears in the tenor and the soprano. A cadenza leads into the massive final bars.

Three fugues on B-A-C-H, 1943. The theme of the **First fugue,** Allegro sostenuto, starts in true Classical style with the four specified notes in half-notes. This multiple fugue in its many parts is most successfully carried out, and among other devices the theme appears inverted. The **Second fugue** is equally effective and begins in two parts with a counterpoint to the theme.

The composer's feeling for sweeping musical lines combined with contrapuntal artistry is most clearly shown in the **Third fugue,** Maestoso passionato, which is planned as a double fugue. The first theme is thoroughly stated and developed, and

after a break—clearly identified by ritardando and unison—the fast second theme enters. Its runs do not suit it well for the pedals, and so the exposition is written in four parts for the manuals. After some interludes the two themes appear together three times and the work ends with chords.

The second idea gives this fugue an almost concertante feeling, complementing the long B-A-C-H of the first section.

Toccata and fugue on the chorale "Mitten wir im Leben sind" (While we are in the midst of life), 1941. Quotations from the chorale, one line at a time, occur in all parts in the first section as well as ostinato figures in the pedals. This piece has the character of a toccata because of its ample, fluctuating motion, not restricted to sixteenth-notes but enhanced by lively runs with glissandi and indeterminate rhythms. The fugue's theme which soon appears in expanded form, i.e. starting in quarter-notes, is combined with the cantus firmus, first in its inversion and then in its original form. This is a concentrated and highly articulate work.

Partita "Mit Fried und Freud ich fahr dahin" (In peace and joy I go from hence), 1953. Here the cantus firmus lies mostly in the pedals and can thus be easily heard.

I Sostenuto, uses as counterpoint a theme with fifths like the chorale itself. Each line of the chorale in the pedals is answered by the same line in the soprano.

II Moderato, has the cantus firmus in the pedals below agitated upper parts with many chordal phrases.

III Andante, with ornamented cantus firmus in the alto, to be played on the pedals. The upper parts play in descending legato lines, interrupted to great effect by staccato motifs.

IV Allegro. This is a dramatic toccata movement with cantus firmus in the pedals leading into a closing chorale section in four parts.

The **Partita "Wer weiss, wie nahe mir mein Ende"** (Who knows how near my end may be) is of interest, because it uses a variety of contrapuntal devices with the cantus firmus, such as the simple canon, free canons and double canon.

Pepping wrote a quantity of **Chorale preludes,** the most important being the series to be found in his *Grosses Orgelbuch (Large organ book)* of 1939, which contains preludes and organ chorales on tunes arranged for the cycle of the church year. Among them are free toccata movements as well as settings of the cantus firmus written in parts and simple chorales for organ. The composer used this last form deliberately in the sense of the chorale, i.e. each piece is the same length as a cantus firmus verse, like the pieces in Bach's *Little Organ Book,* and varying numbers of imitative parts exist alongside the unornamented melody. Further works: Sonata, 1958; Partitas; Fugues; Chorale settings; Preludes and postludes for 18 chorales, 1969.

Publishers: Bärenreiter; Schott.

MAURICE DURUFLÉ

b. Louviers, January 11, 1902;
d. Paris, June 26, 1986

He was a pupil of Vierne, Tournemire and Dukas. In 1930 he became organist at St. Etienne-du-Mont, and in 1943 professor at the Paris Conservatoire. His strict style has a hint of impressionistic tone painting which makes his compositions very attractive. He was not a prolific composer, but each of his works is a masterpiece. The most important is the Requiem *Op. 9. His organ works reveal their author as a virtuoso and passionate organist.*

Prelude, adagio and chorale variations on the theme "Veni creator" Op. 4, duration 20 minutes. In the prelude there is a continuous motion in triplets which characterizes almost all Duruflé's fast pieces. They are joined by motifs and a theme showing a distant relationship to the Gregorian "Veni creator" by using its strongly expressive intervals of seconds and fourths.

Lento, quasi recitativo leads into the Adagio which opens with the head of the cantus firmus but does not use it again. Not until the Choral varié does the theme appear, in the following form:

The first variation has the cantus firmus in the bass with the third line of the chorale in the right hand. The second has the cantus firmus in the soprano and sets triplets and duplets against each other. The third is a canon between the top parts in manuals and pedals and the last one, marked "Final", is like a toccata. The cantus firmus is heard both in the top notes of the runs and in the pedals.

This is a satisfyingly unified work to listen to.

Suite Op. 5. Prélude, Sicilienne, Toccata. The prelude is a very concentrated piece with a theme which is clearly heard at the beginning and dominates its whole course, thus giving it cohesion in spite of frequent tempo changes.

The Sicilienne also has a prominent theme which keeps appearing in a new light because the accompaniment is always different. The Toccata, unfortunately the only part of the work to be played frequently, has great impetus, achieved by means of sixteenth-note runs, sometimes in unison and sometimes in chords. (The title of the piece refers to this technique. In recent French organ music "toccata" means a work in which the musical motion remains constant, and has nothing to do with Buxtehude's works of that name. Though this new use of the term is not derived from J. S. Bach's toccatas in D minor and F major BWV 538 and 540, it was certainly influenced by works such as Schumann's piano toccata, which was well known in France.)

After the introductory bars the theme is first heard in the pedals which then pass it on to the right hand on the manuals.

A second theme appears and oscillates between quadruple and triple time. In the recapitulation the figuration on the theme in the pedals is enhanced by virtuoso 32nd-note and staccato chords in chromatic sequence. The work closes in grandiose style.

Prelude and fugue on the name Alain Op. 7, in memory of Jehan Alain, duration 14 minutes. Out of a name not in the least suitable for setting to music Duruflé creates a motif by arbitrarily using later letters of the alphabet for the notes in the upper octave, so arriving at the following theme:

Out of this motif he shapes the passage work of the prelude,

contrasting it effectively with tied chords, which need

for their performance a mellifluous and not strident Voix Céleste such as is usually found only on French organs. A third motif finally anticipates the triplet rhythm for the theme of Jehan Alain's *Litanies* (see below, p. 213) which is quoted at the end of the prelude.

The first part of the prelude is in D minor and the second, quite separate, part in G minor. Once the *Litanies* theme appears the speed which had been slackening does so even more and the volume of sound decreases as well so that a moment of total repose is reached from which the fugue springs to life. Its first theme, taken from the ALAIN motif, is stated and forms a transition to the second theme, which after three entries is combined with the first theme. Stretti of the first theme and a

constantly increasing tempo produce a dynamic, symphonic progress to a splendidly vigorous close. This fugue is one of the most accomplished contemporary examples of that demanding contrapuntal genre.

Further work: Scherzo.
Publisher: Durand.

HANS FRIEDRICH MICHEELSEN

b. Hennstedt, June 9, 1902;
d. Glüsing, November 23, 1973

Micheelsen studied with Hindemith in Berlin, where he was organist at St. Matthew's church. From 1938 he was a teacher and professor in Hamburg. He devoted most of his composition to church music, such as motets, passions, cantatas for solo voices and works for organ.

Organ concerto on the tune "Es sungen drei Engel ein süssen Gesang" (Three angels sang a sweet song), 1943.

I Toccata. Among the passage work individual lines of the theme are heard in massive chords. Duet and trio sections follow with quotations from the cantus firmus and a return to the manner of the opening.

II Canzona. A melodic trio movement. The top part describes a decorated, sweeping line around the nucleus of the cantus firmus, which itself only appears briefly in the pedals at the end.

III Fugue. In the development only the head of the theme is discussed, but it is then effectively used in stretti.

Third organ concerto, 1947, duration 12 minutes.

I Introduction. Restless, unison runs in varying tempos open this concerto and lead into a polyphonic movement,

immediately followed by the freely-moving

II Toccata, in which the pedal part is particularly prominent. After some brilliant passage work, the last part of the toccata refers to the introduction quoted above.

III Fugue, with the theme marked "heiter bewegt, nicht schnell". The combination of the "gioioso", or merry, element with impish boldness is supremely successful.

Appropriately the development of the fugue is not pedantically strict but unusually relaxed and free. This is a joy for both organists and audiences, who so often must plough their way through a mass of complicated counterpoint. It finishes in toccata style with renewed references to the introduction.

Fifth organ concerto on "Christe, der du bist Tag und Licht" (Christ, who art day and light), 1954. It has the usual three divisions of Toccata, Chorale and Fugue. In the first and third Micheelsen uses no time signature, so that the lines enclosing the chorale can move with complete freedom. The result is some enchantingly lively music, especially in the toccata.

Sixth organ concerto on "O dass ich tausend Zungen hätte" (O that I had a thousand tongues), 1961, duration 15 minutes. Again we have an opening toccata, which elaborates on the first five notes of the chorale. There is a dual tonality here, which produces some very widely varying sounds:

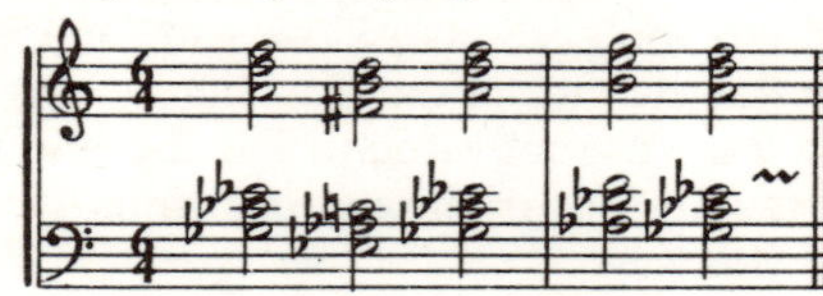

In the second part the cantus firmus is developed in the tenor; the third is a Fugue.

The **Seventh organ concerto** on "Der Morgenstern" (The morning star), 1963, has several movements:

I Sostenuto, very free, like an improvisation.

II Andante cantabile, continuously alternating between unison lines and blocks of chords.

III Adagio, with a freely treated song cantus firmus in solo style.

IV Andante, chordal, with a prominent solo part.

V Maestoso-Vivo, with showers of falling chords, and passage work with fragments of the cantus firmus.

The **"Grenchener Orgelbuch Teil I und II"** (Grenchen organ book, parts I and II), 1964–65. Part I contains organ music on chorales and chorale motifs intended for study purposes, according to the composer's own words. Apart from simple organ chorales there are canons, partitas and ostinato forms. Part II, *Meditationen für Orgel (Meditations for organ)*, is a collection of five completely free pieces which were meant to stimulate organists to create "new organistic sound effects".

Further works: Organ concerto in A minor; *Das Holsteinische Orgelbüchlein (Holstein little organ book)* with pieces for a small instrument; Organists' exercises: chorale settings.

Publisher: Bärenreiter.

GÜNTER RAPHAEL

b. Berlin, April 30, 1903;
d. Herford, October 19, 1960

After studying both privately and at the Berlin academy Raphael went to Leipzig in 1926 to teach at the conservatory. He was forbidden to work professionally during the Hitler regime, but thereafter was a lecturer in Duisburg and Mainz and finally professor at the Cologne music academy. Like Pepping he saw his main duty as writing music for the Protestant church, which he did in great quantity, with settings of the Lord's Prayer and the Creed and a Requiem for choir and orchestra, motets, choral works and works for organ. He also wrote symphonies, a concertino for saxophone, and orchestra and chamber music. Counterpoint formed the basis of his musical language.

Fantasia in C minor Op. 22/2. A single theme appears impressively in all possible combinations and thus in varying guises. The Sostenuto introduces the work with free figures, after which the theme is presented as a bicinium. Some bars

marked Largo lead to a short Adagio which takes the first bar of the theme as its motif. There is a reference to the opening, an Allegro in fugato form, another Adagio similar to the previous one, and a closing Allegro.

Variations on "Durch Adams Fall ist ganz verderbt" (Through Adam's fall all is lost) Op. 27/2. The variations are not built on the chorale melody, but rather on the strongly expressive bass line from Bach's arrangement in the *Little Organ Book* which graphically illustrates Adam's fall.

In the first bars that whole bass part is stated in unison: then follows a two-part treatment which presents the theme twice in two different upper parts. Next come two trio sections with mounting tempo, the first in triplets and the second in sixteenth-notes. The Allegro with its runs and dotted passages in canon over the cantus firmus bass calms down first into the Allegretto—another bicinium with cantus firmus in the top part—and subsequently into the Adagio, in which the bass accompanies an arioso movement.

A three-part variation marked Allegro vivace has a toccata motion, with the cantus firmus in the outside parts and effective octaves in the manuals. The Allegro molto overflows with abundant expressiveness and leads into the chorale melody, the individual lines of which are interrupted by the Bach bass line in unison. The grandiose conception and development of this work makes it one of Raphael's most important creations.

Toccata in C minor Op. 27/3. This work has two themes, the first of which is heard again at the end,

thus thematically embracing the Adagio fugue which elaborates this expressive theme:

Raphael wrote three works on Finnish chorales—"Fantasia and fugue", "Passacaglia" and "Partita". Without wishing to denigrate the first two, I will discuss only the third, as it is a very original and rewarding composition to play.

Partita on a Finnish chorale Op. 41/2, duration 11 minutes. The *Chorale* section presents a simple chorale melody in four parts. The *Trio* is a canon for the cantus

firmus between tenor and soprano while the bass provides a free third part. *Bicinium* presents the cantus firmus against a stormy counterpart. *Minore* brings the chorale in minor. *Cantus firmus im Pedal* is an enchanting trio movement with the two upper parts imitating and contrasting effectively with each other in strict legato and staccato phrases. *Pachelbel form* has anticipatory pedal entries and the cantus firmus divided into lines. *Choral* is marked fortissimo and has an ostinato bass.

Fantasia on the chorale "Christus, der ist mein Leben" (Christ who is my life), 1945, has an introduction in which the major third from the beginning of the chorale is persistently turned into a minor third. The chorale is developed seven times with different tone colors.

Sonata Op. 68, 1949, duration 13 minutes. This work marks a change in Raphael's musical language. Instead of being loyal to and even dependent on his great forerunners, he had become consistently and often harshly severe and unconventional. Untroubled by actual sound, he was pursuing his vision of form, and through it created a work of great density, especially in the first and third movements. The sonata is difficult to listen to; only the last movement appeals to its audience by quoting from the cantus firmus.

I Preamble "Et incarnatus est de spiritu sancto" (And was incarnate by the Holy Ghost). The theme is particularly insistent in the pedals, while in the manuals the continual fluid motion in eighth-notes predominates. There is an Andante sec-

tion within the movement with a theme in the lower manual part and in the pedals. At the end the entries follow quickly after each other, emphasizing and intensifying the theme.

II Canzona "Crucifixus etiam pro nobis" (He was crucified for us). The two upper parts develop an extensive and rich melisma while the bass rises slowly in stages through an octave from the D below middle C.

III Soprano ostinato "Et resurrexit tertia die" (And rose on the third day). To the ostinato melody

is added the following theme, mostly in fourths and fifths and therefore sounding rather monotonous:

Later contrapuntal treatment breaks up the ostinato also used in the lower manual part, and in broader note values in the pedals.

Little partita on the chorale "Herr Jesu Christ, dich zu uns wend" (Lord Jesus Christ, turn to us), 1958. Although composed as one piece, there are the following divisions: 1. Cantus firmus in the soprano with two lower parts. 2. Trio in 9/8 time, with cantus firmus in the bass. 3. Trio in 3/4 time, with cantus firmus in the bass. 4. Cantus firmus in the bass, with chords in the manual parts. 5. Chorale.

Concerto for organ and orchestra in D minor Op. 57. Scored for three trumpets, timpani and strings.

I Improvisation. The title primarily refers to the organ part, which is written like an improvisation, often in two parts with the melodic material in the manuals and sustained bass notes in the pedals. There are also recitative pedal solos in the style of a toccata. The whole piece is linked by the orchestra, especially the strings, which play the following motif at significant points in the score:

II Ostinato adagio, achieves extremely attractive sounds through simple chord progressions in the orchestra. After extensive rests for the solo instrument, which at first had been playing by itself, the tempo and dynamics mount to a free cadenza-style transition into the

III Chorale on "Ein feste Burg ist unser Gott" (A Mighty Fortress is our God), the first line of which gives thematic substance to the powerful orchestral prelude, where the chorus of trumpets is always contrasted with the string section. At once the organ enters, playing motifs from the second half of the chorale against a counterpoint of strangely antagonistic triplet and duplet phrases. A fugato introduces the finale,

in which the whole chorale is presented in dramatic grandeur as excerpts from it alternate between organ and orchestra.

The effectiveness of this work lies in the very simplicity of its construction.

The **Sonata for violin and organ** Op. 36—Andante sostenuto, Molto vivace—is full of strongly imitative work, fugatos and little canons, unlike the similarly scored church sonatas by Joseph Haas. There is a tempestuous violin solo at the beginning of the second movement. Raphael made a version for violin and organ from the Largo of his **Violin sonata** Op. 12 no. 1.

Further works: Introduction and chaconne in C-sharp minor Op. 27/1; Prelude and fugue in G major Op. 22/3; Organ chorales; Toccata, chorale and variations on "Wachet auf, ruft uns die Stimme" (Sleepers, awake, the voice is calling) Op. 53.

Publishers: Bärenreiter; Breitkopf; Müller (Organ concerto).

FLOR PEETERS

b. Tielen, Antwerp, July 4, 1903;
d. July 4, 1986

Peeters studied in Mecheln and Paris with Dupré and Tournemire. Since 1923 he has been organist at Mecheln cathedral and organ teacher in Ghent and Antwerp. On the one hand his compositions are symphonic in concept; on the other they respond to the stimulus of Gregorian chant and vocal polyphony. Apart from organ and church music he wrote songs, instrumental concertos and chamber music.

Passacaglia and fugue Op. 42. Traditional passacaglia form, dominated by an eight-bar pedal ostinato. There are only a few parts as the calm variations begin, but the music soon grows in intensity. The ostinato occurs in the soprano and the tenor as well. The fugue is unfortunately not very striking, and also rather too long to serve as a cogent finale to the passacaglia. After time changes and increases in tempo with an organ point on B, the work does in fact come to a majestic finish with the theme heard in augmentation.

Three preludes and fugues Op. 72. These are short pairs of strongly contrasted works in church modes. The Prelude and fugue in the lydian mode employs a descending scale as a source of themes for the prelude, and the regularly developed fugue returns to this thematic material.

After the peaceful Prelude and fugue in the dorian mode—marked Sostenuto espressivo, Molto andante, all in large note values—comes the Prelude and fugue in mixolydian mode in the lively style of a toccata. It starts with a pedal solo, and a relaxed structure fluctuating between part writing and chords makes it sound like a fantasia, leading easily into the fugue with its merrily dancing theme.

Thirty chorale preludes on Gregorian hymns. Peeters composed these small-scale compositions with mastery, and their style shows his neo-impressionistic sensitivity as well. The forms are quite varied and include melisma on Classical models, elaborate canons, strict part writing and, in contrast, strongly vigorous pieces with the characteristics of toccatas. This collection of individual pieces penetrates deeply into the essence of the Gregorian chorale.

One particularly impressive work for soprano and organ is his impressionistically colorful **Speculum vitae,** which portrays in four movements—Night, Morning, Noon and Evening—the course of the day and thus of life itself.

Further works: Toccata "Ave maris stella"; "Heures intimes" (Intimate hours); Concert piece; Concerto for organ and orchestra; Concertino for organ and harpsichord; Partita "Puer nobis nascitur" (A child was born for us); Sonata quasi una fantasia.

Publisher: Lemoine; Peters; Schott.

HERMANN SCHROEDER

b. Bernkastel, March 26, 1904; d. Bad Orb, October 7, 1984

He studied in Cologne where he became a teacher at the music academy, being appointed professor in 1946. He also taught in Trier where he was cathedral organist from 1938 on. He wrote choral and chamber music, one symphony and one opera.

Sonata in B minor, 1957.

I allegro risoluto. The main idea, and particularly the two intervals of a fourth with which it begins, form the leading thematic substance of this movement, for

these intervals are even heard in the top parts which play in canon at the beginning of the two *piano* trio interludes, in E minor and B minor respectively. The accompaniment consists of ostinato bass figures with intervals of a sixth.

II Larghetto cantabile. This movement in three sections has a prominent soprano solo accompanied by two or three other parts in the first and last sections. The middle trio section develops all its parts equally.

III Allegro con spirito. Quick passage work, with *forte* sections once again alternating with softer episodes, characterized by the same intervals.

The whole sonata is "entertainment" in the best sense of the word, for the performer as well as the audience.

Partita "Veni, creator spiritus", 1959.

I Toccata. Free, virtuoso figure work with emphasis on fourths, directly related to the Gregorian cantus firmus:

II Ostinato in the pedals, with the cantus firmus in the upper part in long note values.

III Bicinium, with imitative texture.

IV Arioso, again with an ostinato bass, in octaves. The solo part circumscribes the cantus firmus with ornamentation and broad melodic arches.

V Fantasia ricercare. After the introductory fantasia bars the ricercare can be recognized as consisting of fughetta sections composed on each respective line of the chorale. The rhythmic cantus firmus is heard at the end of each.

The **Marian antiphons** are shorter pieces on Gregorian cantus firmi, in the case of "Regina coeli" as a prelude, "Ave regina" as variations, "Alma redemptoris mater" as a chorale and "Salve regina" as a toccata.

Little intradas. These short movements—toccata, ritornello, aria with variations, pastorale and passacaglia—are cheerful entertainment pieces and provide an effective contrast to chorale arrangements because they are not connected to a cantus firmus. Among themselves they offer some rich diversity.

The whole idea of the **Beethoven variations,** which are meditations on the "Hymn of thanksgiving . . . in the lydian mode" from Beethoven's string quartet Op. 132, and the **Trilogies on chorales** is a felicitous one. They comprise lyrical, virtuoso intonations, meditations and finales on each chorale and can be played together as a concert piece or used individually in the liturgy.

The **Duo da chiesa** (Church duet) is concertante music for violin and organ in six movements, of which the Scherzo is downright comical.

In the **Canticum triplex**—three songs for soprano and organ—the solo voice rises in broad, free arcs of melody above the accompanying chords. Only in the third song—Jubilus-alleluja—do the parts blend in concertante style.

Further works: Prelude and fugue "Christ lag in Todesbanden" (Christ lay in bonds of death); Second sonata; Sonatina; 5 sketches; Cycle of inventions; Motif variations; Concerto piccolo; Concerto for organ and orchestra.

Publishers: Breitkopf—*Marienstatter Orgelbüchlein (Marienstatt little organ book)*; Brockhoff; Gerig; Müller; Peters; Schott; Schwann.

JOSEPH AHRENS

b. Sommersell, Westphalia, April 17, 1904

Ahrens studied mainly in Berlin where in 1925 he became organist and in 1928 teacher at the academy. His sacred vocal works are overshadowed by his countless organ compositions, which clearly show that their author was himself an active organist.

Toccata eroica, 1934. This is a passionate piece, marked "Mit Schwung" (with impetus), beginning with extensive unison runs in the manuals. The opening section shows the characteristics of a typical contemporary toccata—multiple rhythms, free metric structure, runs and massed chords to be played ad lib—and makes no coherent impression. The fugue which follows develops regularly with a transition into the final toccata section.

Organ mass, 1945. The style of composition varies between the individual sections: there are homophonic movements with a short motif, often in consecutive fifths and fourths, dialogues and fugal pieces. They are arranged as follows: Introit, Kyrie, Gloria, Gradual, Creed, Offertory, Sanctus, Benedictus, Agnus Dei, Communion, Dismissal.

Triptychon on B-A-C-H, 1949.

I Toccata. An improvisation with broad passage work. Here and in the third section it becomes apparent that in the 19th century Schumann, Liszt and Reger blazed the way, and set precedents, for settings of B-A-C-H, or perhaps have virtually exhausted all the melodic and harmonic possibilities of this magical theme.

II Ostinato in the bass, derived from the B-A-C-H sequence, with free upper parts, but a brief quotation from the theme as well.

III Ricercare, in four parts, sometimes with sustained counterpoint. The three themes of the movement are first individually developed and then appear simultaneously at the end.

The Christian year. Chorale for organ, 1952. This is a large collection of short pieces, intended primarily for liturgical use. Thematically they start with Advent, the beginning of the church year, and take us through Christmas, Easter and Pentecost to the Eucharist, praise to the Virgin and praise to God. Once again the composer uses the most diversified forms, sometimes strongly contrapuntally connected, sometimes freely imaginative, to achieve good contrasts. Particularly successful are the pieces with graphic titles, such as the toccata "O Heiland, reiss die Himmel auf" (O Savior, Open the heavens), the Christmas pastoral "Wachet auf, ruft uns die Stimme" (Sleepers, awake, the voice is calling), or the toccata "Christus ist erstanden" (Christ is risen).

The **Canzona "Du Wunderbrot"** (Thou wondrous bread) with the following first theme is most beautifully developed:

The partitas "Es ist ein Ros entsprungen" (A rose has flowered) and "Vom Himmel hoch, da komm ich her" (From highest heaven I come) have very different musical characteristics.

Cantiones gregorianae, 1957, is a general title embracing a collection of 24 shorter compositions which are each based on the eponymous chorale. It is prefaced with St. Augustine's words: "Quia fecisti nos ad te et inquietum est cor nostrum, donec requiescat in te" (Thou hast made us for Thyself, and our hearts find no rest until they rest in Thee).

A representative selection of Gregorian cantus firmi have been used here: some are from the Ordinary of the Mass: Kyrie, Gloria, Creed, Sanctus, Agnus; some are hymns: "Puer natus", "Vexilla regis", "Victimae paschali laudes", "Christ ist erstanden" (Christ is risen), "Veni, creator spiritus"; and some are settings of the Lord's Prayer, the "Salve regina" and the "Te deum". The Gregorian tune is printed before each piece and should also be played, to help the listener follow the spiritual content of the music.

Following the soaring lines of the Gregorian chorale, Ahrens makes no formal division into bars but merely indicates basic pulses, usually 1/2 or 1/4, intended to inspire the interpreter to "perform with improvising verve," but he does give instructions for registration.

Thematically the pieces adhere very closely to the cantus firmus. Single motifs, often of only two or three notes, are isolated and worked on in many different ways. The basic character of each piece is established from the very first notes, and in some cases—for instance the Creed—they are joined by a kind of counterpoint in most of which the cantus firmus origins can be heard. Harmonically the style avoids all mannered modern devices and sounds tonal, in the sense that each cantus firmus has its own key coloring in spite of not being actually written in any precise key.

Herewith a few examples of the use of the Gregorian tunes, each taken from the beginning of the piece:

Credo in unum Deum

This entire work is a profound glorification of the primeval and enduring strength of Gregorian music and its role in Catholic worship.

Further works: Hymns "Veni, creator spiritus" and "Pange lingua"; Chorale partitas "Christ ist erstanden" (Christ is risen), "Lobe den Herren" (Praise the Lord) and "Verleih uns Frieden" (Grant us Thy peace); Metamorphoses I-III; Civitas Dei (City of God)—Seven visions from the Apocalypse—1960; Five *Leisen* (Sacred medieval songs), 1969; Fantasia and ricercare on a theme by Joannis Cabanilles, 1967; Trilogia contrapunctica.

Publishers: Bärenreiter; Müller; Schott.

JEAN LANGLAIS

b. La Fontenelle, February 15, 1907

Langlais trained in composition with a pupil of César Franck's, and having also studied organ was appointed in 1945 to Franck's organ at St. Clotilde's in Paris. This blind virtuoso player and improviser also taught at the Paris Schola Cantorum and excelled in expressing himself in his organ compositions. In addition to his sacred works he has also written orchestral and chamber music.

Te deum. The Gregorian cantus firmus rings out in unison at the start and is followed by cascading chords which are often repeated in the course of the work:

In the second section the lines of the cantus firmus (from "In te domine speravi") are counterbalanced by triplet runs and mount to a freely-constructed finale which quotes from the beginning of the cantus firmus. Runs marked "con fantasia" and a Maestoso section provide a grandiose ending.

Nine pieces. This collection contains three chorale preludes and two free works—a prelude and a rhapsody—in addition to the songs with programmatic titles such as "chant de peine", "chant de paix", "chant de joie" and "chant héroique" (songs of grief, of peace and of joy, and a heroic song).

His organ chorales are interesting:

In dulci jubilo has dense texture and a prominent melody. The upper part continues in the same motion throughout and somewhat resembles the tone painting of Bach's eponymous chorale from the *Little Organ Book.* A series of diversified musical sounds is achieved through the free treatment of tonality.

Aus tiefer Not (De profundis; Out of the deep) develops the cantus firmus in the soprano. At the beginning, middle and close of this piece there are dark, restless figures and sighing chords.

Mon âme cherche une fin paisible (Herzlich tut mich verlangen; I desire with all my heart) is a simple polyphonic chorale movement with unconventional and rather thin harmonies.

Gregorian rhapsody starts stormily but after a few bars the first theme marked "sacris solemnus" enters and is densely elaborated in each of the following bars.

Verbum supernum is heard in the pedals while the manuals play sustained chords. The cantus firmus then appears in the soprano and the alto.

Lauda Sion joins in, and in the last section all three themes are combined with great artistry.

This work shows off Langlais's improvisational skills particularly well, as also his skill in subordinating older technical principles to his new, but not excessively modern, musical language.

Homage to Frescobaldi. Eight pieces for organ.

In his reverence for the old Italian master Langlais here employs a predominantly polyphonic technique.

The Prelude to the Kyrie has attractive harmonies in the upper parts, later joined by the tune of the "Kyrie cunctipotens".

The Offertory is similarly conceived: Motifs consisting mainly of combinations of the figure ♩ ♫ are joined after about 20 bars by another Gregorian quotation, from "Lucis creator". The simplicity of this material produces a solemn tranquillity in both pieces.

In the Elevation, which contains chromatic runs, and in the Communion more well known Gregorian themes can be heard. In the latter there is a development which was to influence later compositions: Langlais no longer writes in specific meters but in free rhythms, and is placing his bar lines according to the dictates of the tune or the motifs mostly as a guide to the player. The resulting fluctuation of meter makes these two movements very lively

This is particularly evident in the Fantasia:

"Antienne" and "Theme and variations" follow, the variations being full of charm and easily demonstrating their relationship to the theme. The final Epilogue on a theme by Frescobaldi is written for solo pedals, with the exception of the last bars. This is a considerable compositional achievement; it demands equal talent from the performer if it is to sound exciting. It will in any case be incomprehensible to many people that an organist can play three parts with two feet, but as a performer himself Langlais naturally knew exactly where to draw the line between what can and cannot be done. A fugato on Frescobaldi's theme follows the fantasia opening which is still technically easier.

Then come references to the beginning, more quotations from the themes and final runs helped out by the manuals. This short virtuoso piece is not exhausted by its technical problems, but rather shows some lovely musical aspects.

Mosaic, pieces for organ, is a fantasia for four hands consisting of an Allego with tightly woven textures of sound and a tempestuous final fugato.

Further works: Short suite; French suite; Essay, 1962; 2 concertos for organ and orchestra.

Publishers: Combre; Bornemann; Philippo.

KARL HÖLLER

b. Bamberg, July 25, 1907; d. Hausham, April 14, 1987

Höller grew up in a musical family, as his father was cathedral organist in Bamberg. After his studies he first taught at the musical academy in Munich, and after a period at the Frankfurt college of music he returned to Munich in 1949 as professor of composition, subsequently becoming president of the academy. His early acquaintance with the organ characterizes many of his other compositions, for instance those for orchestra.

Chorale variations "O wie selig seid ihr doch, ihr Frommen" (O how blessed are ye, the faithful) Op. 1. Variation 1—bicinium; variation 2—trio, with cantus firmus in the tenor and bridge passage to variation 3—cantus firmus in the bass; variation 4—cantus firmus in the alto, with quick triplets in the upper part and a quasi pizzicato pedal; variation 5—cantus firmus in the soprano, followed by a quiet close.

Chorale variations "Jesu meine Freude" (Jesus my joy) Op. 22/2, duration 17 minutes. Before the true variations begin the chorale is heard in its own bold and interesting harmonization.

Variation 1—duet, with cantus firmus alternating between upper and lower parts.

Variation 2—a free theme treated in canon, interspersed with lines from the chorale.

Variation 3—trio, with imitation in the lower parts and free melodic lines in the upper part around the chorale.

Variation 4—free, virtuoso variation with leaps and runs which are difficult to play, marked "sehr lebhaft und leicht" (molto vivace e leggero).

Variation 5—harmonic elaboration of the lines from the chorale, repeating motifs to intensify the effect.

Variation 6—free bars, consisting of chromatic descending lines in the pedals and dotted figures in one manual, leading into parts related to the cantus firmus on the other manual. The parts are exchanged several times, and all the lines of the chorale are heard clearly and in context.

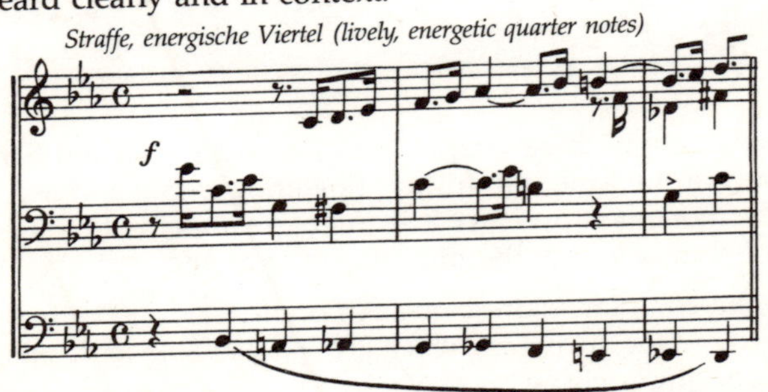

The intense finale contains concentrated motifs and leads through a transition into the Chorale, which has the same harmonies as the beginning, extended upwards and downwards with octaves to produce greater musical sonorities.

Chaconne Op. 54, duration 16 minutes. It begins traditionally with the theme,

continues in the manuals *pianissimo* with chords and then broad, sweeping melodic lines. Soon a fugato is heard, the theme of which even appears over the ostinato bass and then in the bass itself. The repeated bass line changes position, even moves to the soprano; then, after a further fugato, it rings out *fortissimo* in the original key of B minor as the climax of the work. The *pianissimo* close is in a romantic, evening mood and sometimes returns to the peaceful music of the opening. This is a work of symphonic character, as is "Jesu meine Freude", which can sound superb on the organ.

Höller wrote two more works on chorales—the **Variations "Helft mir Gottes Güte preisen"** (Help me praise God's goodness) Op. 22/1 and the **Chorale passacaglia "Die Sonn hat sich mit ihrem Glanz gewendet"** (The sun has changed in its glory) Op. 61. A kind of introduction sets the mood of the chorale most beautifully. It rises in a soft register and fades away again, *pianissimo*. Only then appears the basic motif of the passacaglia, consisting of a falling fourth from tonic to dominant, which is heard, clearly recognizable, after a few bars:

It is then repeatedly altered, both in rhythm and key, but the falling fourth is always present as a harmonic foundation. After a surging wave the motion ebbs away and the chorale is heard again in a tempo marked "sehr breit und ausdrucksvoll" (molto largo e expressivo) as it develops the sixth and the last verses. The closing chords die away.

Concerto for organ and chamber orchestra Op. 15, 1930, revised 1966, duration 27 minutes. Orchestra: two trumpets, two horns, two trombones, tuba, percussion, cellos, double basses.

I Un poco maestoso, Agitato. This begins like a toccata with the head of the theme in the trumpets and horns and runs in the organ which then takes up the

theme. The last figure in this example, and the way the second bar of the theme builds the notes of the tune into further flowering music and accentuates them, characterize the movement and give it an intensive impetus. Other groups of notes arise like motifs but have not the importance of themes.

II Larghetto con gran espressione. An orchestral tune with an ostinato bass forms a background for the organ, which is to play its solo parts imaginatively and freely, "as though improvising".

III Allegro con brio. This feels and is formed like a dance in 3/8 time to begin with, but moves into a section in 4/8 time dominated by the organ and marked "Risoluto", with a fugue on the following theme:

The theme is expanded in the brass before the music returns to the opening and ends on a climax.

The **Improvisations on "Schönster Herr Jesu"** (Beautiful Savior) for cello and organ belong musically to the late Romantic era and sound like a successful cello concerto.

Further works: Fantasia Op. 49 for violin and organ; Triptychon on the Easter chant "Victimae paschali laudes" Op. 64.

Publishers: Leuckart; Schott; Peters.

WOLFGANG FORTNER

b. Leipzig, October 12, 1907

Fortner studied with Hermann Grabner in Leipzig. He taught theory in Heidelberg from 1931 to 1954, then in Detmold until 1957 and in Freiburg until 1973, and was a co-founder of the Kranichstein musical institute. Among his varied oeuvre the main compositions are symphonic and chamber music, but he did write some classic examples of the oratorio. In his later works he has adopted twelve-tone technique.

Toccata and fugue, 1930. Both are in D minor. The toccata is full of contrast and its themes are clearly differentiated. The opening, marked "ziemlich bewegt", is written for both hands in unison throughout and flows into a "Più maestoso" section in which a motif reminiscent of Buxtehude is developed. This same section returns after the three-part Andante molto tranquillo; the closing passages echo the beginning.

The four-part fugue, Andante con moto, at first provides variety through a counterpart in dotted sixteenth-notes and later with a theme in insistent chords. A short reference to the toccata and a peaceful Molto andante ending with the fugue theme round off the work.

Preamble and fugue, 1935. The preamble in "mässigen Vierteln" (moderato quarter-notes) has a pedal point in C major with scales, tied chords and another pedal point in G major, and leads to a very dense five-part fugue, Grave, in three sections which in turn elaborate the basic theme, its inversion and its retrograde version. The drawback of writing in five parts is obvious here, because the texture is almost too dense for the parts to be separately distinguishable.

The **Intermezzos,** 1962, comprise three pieces—Fantasia, Contrapunctus and Conclusio.

Further works: Concerto for organ and string orchestra, 1932: Prelude, passacaglia, fugue.

Publisher: Schott.

HUGO DISTLER

b. Nuremberg, June 24, 1908; d. Berlin, November 1, 1942

After studying with Hermann Grabner and Günther Ramin in Leipzig, he went to Lübeck in 1931 as organist at St. James's church, and then taught at music academies in Stuttgart and in Berlin, where he moved in 1940. His organ and choral works gave decisive stimulus to the Protestant church during a period of upheaval, by enriching traditional forms with a new and personal content. He wrote an important book—Funktionelle Harmonielehre (Study of functional harmony).

Partita "Nun komm, der Heiden Heiland" (Come, redeemer of our race) Op. 8/1, 1933, duration 23 minutes.

I Toccata. First comes the cantus firmus in the pedals, then passage work and further references to the cantus firmus.

II Chorale with variations. After a theme by Balthasar Resinarius with cantus firmus in the pedals come the following variations: 1. Bicinium with the cantus firmus alternating between the two hands and equivalent alternation of the free part. 2. Cantus firmus in the pedals with a two-part imitative piece above. 3. A four-part section in abbreviated Pachelbel form. 4. Passage work with the cantus firmus as notes for the pedals.

5. In four parts with runs throughout in the upper part and an ostinato for the pedals. 6. Cantus firmus in canon at the fifth in the bass and alto. 7. In three parts with quotations from the cantus firmus and a free upper part.

III Chaconne on the first line of the chorale.

IV Toccata as I.

Partita "Wachet auf, ruft uns die Stimme" (Sleepers, awake, the voice is calling) Op. 8/II, duration 12 minutes.

I Toccata. In this movement the characteristic fifths from the beginning of the theme—C,E,G—are primarily used. A graphic idea of Distler's treatment of his model can be gained from a passage for manuals and pedals which occurs after 12 bars.

II Bicinium. The cantus firmus appears in both parts.

III Fugue. The theme is first stated alone in four parts and later combined with the cantus firmus. The escalating finale resembles a toccata; it has runs, the cantus firmus in the pedals and then in the manuals in octaves, and is in several parts.

Sonata Op. 18/II, 1939. A strict three-part trio, less expressive and impressive than the partitas.

I Swift, energetic half-notes with the main theme quoted here and the upper parts sometimes in canon, while the pedals also echo the head of the theme. The recapitulation and the coda are easy to identify with the pedal point on B.

II Introduction: very agitated eighth-notes in free tempo. Runs lead into what is actually the slow movement and can be omitted if registration is technically difficult. "Gehende Viertel. Gelassen" (Andante quarter-notes. Relaxed) is the heading of the peaceful section, which consists of a dialogue between the two upper parts. This whole movement is decidedly melodic in character, and the pedals only serve as support.

III Very quick eighth-notes. The main theme is thoroughly developed;

then the second theme immediately appears, and after a middle section in E minor turns into the ostinato of a short final chaconne.

Distler recommends that the registration should be "certainly like chamber music, but not too thin and tinkly; rather somewhat bolder, especially in the finale."

Further works: Little arrangements of chorales for organ Op. 8/III; 30 pieces for playing on the small organ Op. 18/I, 1938–39.

Publisher: Bärenreiter.

OLIVIER MESSIAEN

b. Avignon, December 10, 1908

Messiaen studied at the Paris Conservatoire, where his teachers included Dukas and Dupré. Early in his career he began to concern himself with Greek and Indian rhythms and with the symbolism of the stars, which were to dominate his later work, and with folklore and birdsong. An avantgardist par excellence in his compositions, he is also a deeply devout Catholic and mystic and dedicates all his work to the praise of God. Since 1931 he has been organist at the church of the Holy Trinity in Paris, and since 1942 has taught several subjects at the Conservatoire. Apart from countless works for organ he has composed for orchestra, choir and piano and has written one opera.

La Nativité du Seigneur (The nativity of the Lord) Nine meditations on various aspects of the nativity in Bethlehem. In his foreword the composer gives detailed theological, instrumental and musical information about the work. A listener more interested in the musical picture will enjoy a direct experience of what is outlined here:

I The Virgin and Child. A quiet, intimate conversation. II The shepherds. After introductory chords comes a pipe tune:

III Eternal purposes. A solo part is set in a mystical accompaniment. IV The Word. A meditation with contrasting dynamics. V God's children. A single crescendo and decrescendo with a cry of "Father, father" at the summit. VI The angels. A visibly and audibly exciting vision of the heavenly hosts:

VII Jesus accepts the suffering. A premonition of his terrible passion and death.
VIII The Wise Men. The procession of the magi beneath the guiding star.
IX God among us—"The Word was made flesh and dwelt among us." A hymn of praise to God divided into sections with the following opening:

If it is impossible to explain the exact structure of these movements in a short space, it is equally impossible to describe their spiritual and sacred content in a few words. The explanations given above are only pointers and should simply inspire the listener to meditate on the theme set out in the title.

Le banquet céleste (The celestial feast). A meditation on the Last Supper with three entries of a theme in four parts; on the third occasion the pedals play a staccato solo. The end comes on a dominant seventh chord on F-sharp!

Apparition de l'église éternelle (Vision of the everlasting church). This is a vision of the church which will be built in eternity. A whole tone interval, extremely richly harmonized in Messiaen's usual style, develops from *pianissimo* through a gigantic crescendo to the maximum volume of which the instrument is capable and back again.

This is a thrilling work which clearly illustrates the composer's visionary powers.

Mass for Pentecost. The five single sections are marked as follows: I Introit—tongues of fire. II Offertory—things visible and invisible. III Consecration—the gift of wisdom. IV Communion—the birds and the springs. V Dismissal—the wind of the Spirit.

Throughout this work Messiaen uses Greek and Hindu rhythms, expanded or contracted, which have a life of their own as separate "personalities". Understandably these puzzling constructions are hidden from the audience, just as the indications in the score, such as "staccato goutte d'eau" (staccato drop of water), "oiseau" (bird), "rossignol" (nightingale), "chant de merle" (blackbird's song), "le vent" (the wind) or "chant des alouettes" (song of the larks) are only there to encourage the player in his style of performance. The listener just hears a flat, two-dimensional sort of music, perhaps associated with Pentecost because of the headings, but completely improvisatory, a characteristic to which the absence of any time signature also contributes.

The same can be said of the **Organ book,** 1951, duration 45 minutes, which contains seven pieces. I Reprises by permutation, using three Hindu rhythms—

pratapacekhara, gajajhampa and sarasa. The first two are slightly modified on each repetition but the third remains unaltered. The three sections are built respectively on the music in its normal form, its retrograde and a combination of the two.

II Trio. Written for the feast of the Trinity, using new and old Hindu rhythms.

III The hands of the deep. For days of penitence, the rhythms varied as in I.

IV Songs of birds. For Eastertide. As in the other sections, Messiaen marks precisely the time and place when the work was conceived, in this case the landscape where he heard the birds singing: "1951—pré Perrin de Fuligny; forêt de St-Germain-en-Laye; branderaie de Gardépée; Charente." In the course of the music we hear the "afternoon of the birds: blackbird, robin, song thrush—and the nightingale when evening comes."

The next three pieces—

V Trio. For the feast of the Trinity,

VI Eyes in the wheels (Ezekiel 1:18 and 20). For Pentecost, and

VII 64 durations, the equivalent of I, sometimes use more foreign rhythms or sometimes are formed from reversal, expansion and contraction of note values. The audience will only recognize the voices of birds in general, while the player will find it an effort to execute all the rhythms precisely. An odd effect is hard to avoid.

The Ascension. Four symphonic meditations on this theme.

I The majesty of Christ as He begs His Father for His reward. This is a short piece, its idea derived mainly from the first two bars, which return frequently with heavy harmonic support. There are very effective dynamic transitions from *pp* to *mf* or *ff* and back again.

II Blissful alleluias from a soul yearning for heaven.

The theme first appears alone and is then joined by a second one. They are then combined contrapuntally but not developed. At the end the first theme is heard again, and towards the close it is greatly expanded against a continuous trill.

III Transports of joy of a soul gazing on Christ's glory which it shares. The introductory *fff* chords, pedal figures, runs and quick passage work, marked "presto, più presto, ancor più presto", make this sound like a toccata.

IV Prayer of Christ as He rises to His Father. This is an emphatic solo melody above accompanying chords:

All four meditations sound heavy and have a trace of late Romantic sentimentality.

That Messiaen's works are unique in all contemporary music—composed without forerunners or father figures—can be partially explained by the fact that he works strictly without any traditional form. "I have remained free and belong to no school," he says of himself. "The freedom I am talking about has nothing to do with fantasy, disorder, rebellion or indifference. It is a constructive freedom, won through self-control, respect for others, standing in awe of creation, meditation on mysteries and search for truth."

Méditations sur le mystère de la Sainte Trinité (Meditations on the mystery of the Holy Trinity), 1969, duration 80 minutes. This is Messiaen's greatest organ work, one which breaks all barriers. In length it might be compared to Bach's *Organ Mass* (see p. 85ff) and shares the same profound theological background. In Bach's case one assumes that he chose to compose it in three sections—the Catechism chorales, flanked by a prelude and fugue in E-flat major—as a symbol of the Trinity, but Messiaen spells out his intention and by multiplication reaches nine sections, similar to the ninefold Kyrie, Christe, Kyrie of earlier masses. Musically this work, which alone can provide an evening's listening, can be described as the apogee of his expressive technique. This is the whole Messiaen, and the whole wealth of his musical imagination, in a single work, albeit a very long one.

The composer writes in the preface:

> The various languages we know are above all instruments for communication. Generally they are vocal in character, but is this the only way of conveying meaning? One can well imagine a language which relies on movements, images, colors and scents, and everyone knows that braille uses the sense of touch. In any case one must start from existing conventions, whereby people agree that x is expressed by y. Music on the other hand does not express anything directly; it can suggest or evoke a feeling or a frame of mind, touch the subconscious and widen one's capacity for dreaming, and these are enormous powers, but it cannot ever 'speak', or give exact information.

Messiaen goes on to mention Wagner's method of using leitmotifs before postulating his own language for communication. Starting with the use of letters to identify notes, he develops a musical alphabet by assigning to each letter a note, an octave and a duration. To demonstrate the name of "the King of Kings, the divine name" he has invented a theme which appears both in its basic form and in inversion, "like two extremes gazing at each other, which could be pushed apart indefinitely."

The eight basic letters:

The composer has supplied a musical and theological commentary for each of the nine movements, and as it would be excessive to give them here in their entirety, herewith some brief summaries of his notes:

I The father of the stars, with the movement of the stars in their courses.

II The holiness of God "in two panels [and a conclusion]". "God is holy" is expressed by means of the Gregorian Alleluia for the dedication of a church.

III Meditation on a saying by St. Thomas Aquinas: "In God a really existing relation has the existence of the divine nature and is completely identical with it."

IV "He Is."

V Meditation on the divine attributes: God is immeasurable, omnipresent, eternal, changeless.

VI Dedicated to the Son or the Word, the second person of the Trinity, "in two panels".

VII The Father and the Son love [each other and us] through the Holy Ghost. This is flanked by chords and the song of an unknown bird.

VIII God is one Being, expressed through the Gregorian Alleluia for the feast of All Saints, "The three in one" (*Tres sunt*).

IX "I am that I am."

Further works: *Les corps glorieux (Glorious bodies)*—seven short visions of the lives of the resurrected.

Publishers: Leduc, Lemoine.

HARALD GENZMER

b. Blumenthal, Bremen, February 9, 1909

Genzmer studied with Hindemith, worked as a voice coach and since 1946 has been a teacher of composition, first at the music academy in Freiburg and since 1957 in Munich. He has written orchestral, chamber and piano music.

First sonata, 1952. The first movement is called Toccata, and its passage work is strongly dominated by sextuplets which run up and down the scale, end in chords and result in little figures in the bass. Its middle section, however, is melodious, with a main idea

which returns repeatedly, and the end is marked *come primo.* The second movement is an Adagio trio with flowing, expressive lines and little motifs in canon, followed by a Chaconne with a seven-bar theme. The usual progress of a chaconne is effectively interrupted and enlivened with "glittering" variations which only hint covertly at the theme. The very convincing build up to the close of this short work is achieved through dynamics and stretti of the ostinato.

Second sonata, 1956.

I Moderato, starts with introductory chord progressions:

and arpeggios, before a Largo in several parts is interpolated and leads back to the homophonic bars of the opening.

II Chorale "Du grosser Schmerzensmann" (Thou great man of sorrows) has a simple, three-part development with the tune in the tenor and an upper part which sounds decidedly like a solo:

III Toccata, has a lively opening:

which, however, ebbs away when the solos for the pedals and manuals enter. At the close the opening theme returns to great effect.

Tripartita in F major, 1945. Prelude—moderato, in two sections, to be performed with Organo Pleno Mixture and Solo registration; Intermezzo—Adagio; Fugue with the following theme:

There are stretti in the course of the development.

Third sonata, 1963, duration 15 minutes. The first movement is a Fantasia, a lively piece which opens stormily and closes more peacefully with the ascending tonic scale inserted near the end. In the Chaconne there is an ostinato containing all 12 chromatic notes. After a few strangely harmonized passages comes a calm farewell song which leads into the Meditation—a very slow trio with the bass supporting the upper parts in canon. The Fugue is very relaxed, because it is not technically strictly composed, and the interludes which provide contrast are not in linear form. A second theme, tranquil compared with the first, joins in and is combined with it.

The times of day, 1968, duration 17 minutes, is a series of chorale variations divided into "Evening", "Night I and II" and "Morning". Typical chorale melodies like "Die Sonn' hat sich mit ihrem Glanz gewendet" (The sun has changed in its splendor) or "Er weckt mich alle Morgen" (He wakes me each morning) are used in simple presentation, variation and in the lively toccata finale.

Seven impressions is a collection of pieces which can be played separately: Meditation—a canon: Pastorale—a simple duet; Largo festivo, Andante—musically very attractive; and Toccata with chorale.

More demanding is the **Easter concerto,** 1980, duration 15 minutes. The movements are chorales for the liturgical calendar: I Passion, "Aus tiefer Not" (Out of the deep); II Meditation and chorale, "O Lamm Gottes" (O spotless lamb of God); and III Finale "Christ ist erstanden" (Christ is risen).

The **Concerto for organ and percussion,** duration 13 minutes, requires a large quantity of percussion instruments such as blocks, cymbals, tam-tam, kettle-drums, vibraphone, xylophone and tubular bells. The outlay is worthwhile, for a brilliant tone painting is created by the contrasting color values of the sustained tone of the organ and the fading sounds of the percussion.

The **Sonata for cello and organ** is another example of beautiful, intimate chamber music, in spite of some blaring chords in the last movement.

Publishers: Peters; Schott.

GASTON LITAIZE

b. Menil-sur-Belvitte, August 11, 1909

Litaize was a pupil of Dupré's at the Paris Conservatoire and then organist at several churches, including St. Francis Xavier in Paris. He works as a teacher and concert organist, and most of his compositions are for organ.

Low mass for all seasons, consisting of five pieces for liturgical use.

"Prelude". Starts quietly with intervals of a fifth, then grows in broad lines to a *fortissimo* climax and returns to a peaceful, soft close.

"Offertory". Introductory bars which return later prepare for the "Theme of the Bread":

This continues for a few bars until the "Theme of the Wine" takes its place.

Both themes are heard again repeatedly.

"Elevation". A musical interpretation of this point in the Eucharist. Again two themes represent the Body and the Blood.

"Communion". This is a "sacred dance", expressing the joy of the faithful as they receive their God. Themes from the Offertory and the Elevation are incorporated.

"Finale". A prayer of thanksgiving, in the course of which all the themes of the work are developed, sometimes in canon and sometimes fugally. It ends with mounting chords. These settings show both Litaize's deep faith and his total mastery as a composer over a musical style only slightly inspired by the Gregorian chorale and representing a fusion of the mystical and the ornamental—both typical features of French art.

Litaize strikes quite a different note in his **Prelude and dance fugue.** After the bizarre prelude comes a dancelike fugue with syncopated thrust and phrasing against the bar-line. The theme:

Further works: Liturgical preludes; Twelve pieces for organ, including Variations on a Christmas carol and a Prelude and fugue in B-flat minor.
Publishers: Bärenreiter; Leduc.

JEHAN ALAIN

b. St-Germain-en-Laye nr. Paris, February 3, 1911;
killed in action near Saumur, June 20, 1940

Alain's premature death deprived us of an outstandingly gifted composer who sometimes based his music on counterpoint, without being reliant on the Classical forms of organ music, and sometimes used novel chords and keys he had invented. His significance in France is comparable to that of Distler in Germany.

Variations on a theme by Clément Jannequin. The theme below,

which does not exceed the span of a fifth, is first presented in the soprano in this very lucid three-part composition. After a repetition in D minor with a slightly different accompaniment, the melody is broken into ornamentation and highlights one single motif. It ends as it started in part writing.

Litanies. Both the melodies and the rhythms are dominated by the litany-like theme. This work is an expression of Alain's motto: "When in its despair the Christian soul can find no new words with which to plead to God in His mercy, it calls out ceaselessly in the same words in lasting faith. Reason has its limits, and only faith can continue its flight towards heaven." The continuous repetition and its intensification through chord progressions on different manuals, and finally through the appearance of the theme in a pedal *accelerando* evoke a state of ecstasy. At this point the organist must overcome the obstacle of a theme in three-note chords which the composer himself admitted was extremely difficult.

Two dances "à Agni Yavishta" (Agni Yavishta is an ancient Indian deity). These are two highly idiosyncratic and unusual works. The first, Allegro, uses only the theme quoted here to a mostly repeated accompaniment, while the second derives its flickering character from a continuous interplay between two ideas—Plus vite (più allegro) and Plus animé (più animato).

Among his other pieces, most of them short, mention should be made of **Le jardin suspendu** (The hanging garden) with its magical sounds, the **Berceuse** (Lullaby), the **Aria** and the two **Fantasias.** The recommendations for registration are by the composer.

The **Three dances,** duration 23 minutes, became Alain's main composition, which he was working on in the last months of his life. Their subtitles "Joies" (Joys), "Deuils" (Bereavements) and "Luttes" (Conflicts) are intended to represent human life, consisting of joy and sorrow and the constant struggle between these two opposites. "Joies" is built from two themes: the first is a fanfare, opening the dance in a progression of chords which are later repeated in altered rhythmic structure. The second theme is the dance itself.

The absence of pedal notes produces a syncopated stress which gives the dance its impetus. The two themes, both in keys Alain has worked out for himself, are combined in the second half in a cumulation of sound which builds up to the tutti and leads into "Deuils", which begins with this theme.

As it progresses further the tune is filled out with overtones like a Mixture stop, which produce impressionistic parallel layers of sound. In the middle section, Molto scherzando, new thematic ideas evolve from motifs taken from the theme and almost suppress the mourning of the opening tune.

"Luttes", which is compressed into a shorter space, offers the themes from the first two pieces, at first next to each other, then simultaneously, to illustrate the synthesis of the two ideas. The closing passage is a great musical apotheosis, further strengthened with multi-note chords.

The works of this composer are little known and rarely played, which is unfortunate because they especially bear witness to the enormous explosive outburst of French organ music after Guilmant and Widor.

Further works: Preludes; Intermezzo, Monody, Suite, Variations on "Lucis Creator".

Publisher: Leduc.

Organ Music in the 20th Century

A change in attitude towards the organ occurred among the generation of composers born around or after 1900. All that remained of Romanticism was discarded in favor of linear structures suitable for the organ as a wind instrument. This development was encouraged by Albert Schweitzer's movement for organ reform and by the renaissance of hymns and liturgical music in the Protestant church, together with a new evaluation of the Protestant chorale. Admittedly the chorale had dominated Reger's and Karg-Elert's music, but now it regained its prominence as an integral part of composition technique, as in Baroque music, and its texts again inspired composers. An interesting example of text-oriented music is provided by EBERHARD WENZEL (b. Pollnow, Pomerania, April 22, 1896; d. Künzelsau, January 27, 1982) in his **Psalm 90 for speaker and organ.** This is not a music drama with the music illustrating the words, but a cooperation on equal terms between the two media. The speaker's scansion is matched to the music and is therefore mostly written out exactly. In his **Sonata** Wenzel composed a fugue, a toccata, a recitative and aria, and another fugue all on the same theme. Publisher: Bärenreiter.

The chorale is the nucleus of the partitas by FRITZ WERNER (b. Berlin, December 15, 1898; d. Heilbronn, December 23, 1977)—**"Christe, du bist der helle Tag"** (Christ, Thou art bright day), and GOTTFRIED MÜLLER (b. Dresden, June 8, 1914)—**"Nun komm, der Heiden Heiland"** (Come, redeemer of our race). Both works produce unified effects by repeated interpretation of the notes of the cantus firmus. Werner's **Toccata and fugue in D major** is a persuasive, musicianly work, tonally conceived. Publisher: Merseburger.

LOTTE BACKES (b. Cologne, May 2, 1901) wrote two meditations for organ, . . . **et spiritus dei ferebatur super aquas** (and the Spirit of God rested upon the waters) and . . . **et repleti sunt omnes spiritu sancto** (and they were all filled with the Holy Spirit). She also created an entrancing musical picture of Christmas in her **In sacratissima nocte** (On the most holy night) with its images of "angeli—pastores—infans in praesepio" (angels, shepherds, babe in the manger). Publishers: Deutscher Verlag für Musik; Heinrichshofen.

HANS CHEMIN-PETIT (b. Potsdam, July 24, 1902; d. Berlin, April 12, 1981) added a string orchestra and timpani to the organ in his **Concerto,** which consists of a fantasia and a fugue. The fantasia is formed from short and dramatic motifs with tranquillo passages, while the sixteenth-note theme of the fugue is strictly developed, artfully varied and fused with a second subject, before ending in a powerful climax which takes up the theme of the fantasia.

The **Organ concerto** by REINHARD SCHWARZ-SCHILLING (b. Hanover, May 9, 1904; d. Berlin, December 9, 1985), written for solo organ, is a virtuoso piece and in the third movement—"Fuga alla passacaglia"—dense and vigorous. Publisher: Merseburger.

The **Hymn to the universe** by ANDRÉ JOLIVET (b. Paris, August 8, 1905; d. ibid., December 19, 1974) is another purely concert piece which makes high virtuoso demands and is only to be played on large and well-equipped instruments. Its rich chords and colors make it a typically French work, but the intimate chamber music character of its passage work with novel melodies gives it a wider significance. Jolivet's **Mass for the day of peace** should be mentioned because of its odd scoring, for voice, organ and tambourine. Publishers: Boosey & Hawkes; Heugel.

WALTER KRAFT (b. Cologne, June 9, 1905; d. Amsterdam, May 9, 1977) was for many years organist at St. Mary's in Lübeck. He painted a powerful, rousing musical picture in his **Triptychon St. Michael,** with New Testament quotations set above the individual movements. It was published by Schott, together with his **Toccata "Ite missa est"** and the **Fantasia "Dies irae".**

HELMUT BORNEFELD (b. Stuttgart, December 14, 1906) is not only a prolific composer but equally well known as a dedicated writer, committed to the interests of the organ, organ building and church music in general. His remark that "Once an organ starts to sound, all speech comes to an end" establishes his priorities. Through his organ works one can detect his steady stylistic and technical development, for instance within the **Begleitsätze** (Accompanying movements) for liturgical use and the **Chorale partitas,** written 1944–1950 and 1937–1956 respectively. Best of all is the **Te deum.** He produces interesting new ideas like the **Organ pieces** as "Intonations for old and new choral works for which there are no appropriate preludes." Two large-scale works by him are the rather difficult **Sonata** and the **Chorea sacra** on the Last Supper. His 12 studies entitled **Homage to Chopin** and the **Sonatina** are pure concert music free of any liturgical application but always serving a high spiritual purpose. The composer wrote: "I wanted to write music with a substantially simplified score which could nevertheless permit a concertante performance to unfold." As an organist Bornefeld supplies his compositions with detailed instructions for registration which greatly aid performance. In addition he has a predilection for arranging music, for instance Busoni's **Fantasia contrappuntistica** on a fragment by Bach, Bach's own **Sonata** BWV 1005 and **Partita** BWV 1004. Works for organ and singer, e.g. **Psalm of night,** and for organ and percussion round off the picture of a versatile composer. Publishers: Bärenreiter; Breitkopf; Hänssler; Universal.

The **Seven meditations** by GÜNTER BIALAS (b. Bielschowitz, Upper Silesia, July 19, 1907) were planned as interludes for the choral work *Im Anfang (At the beginning)* but can also be played on their own. They are short, exciting pieces and musically and rhythmically sophisticated. Publisher: Bärenreiter.

KERSTIN THIEME (b. Niederschlema, Erzgebirge, June 23, 1909) shows her close affinity with the polyphonic chorale technique of the old masters in two works, the **Toccata "Vom Himmel hoch"** (From highest heaven) and the **Chorale fantasia "Verleih uns Frieden gnädiglich** (In Thy mercy grant us peace), while breaking through the barriers of traditional harmonic and melodic systems. While in contrast to the toccata one notices in the chorale fantasia a freer, broader and musically tougher structure, the **Invocazioni per organo** (Invocations for organ) in three movements, duration 12 minutes, are even more open to the most recent composition techniques. Thieme forms a most effective link with the distinguishing musical characteristics of contemporary French organ music. Her **Triptychon of psalms** consists of three sacred concertos scored for organ with soprano and alto voices, which together form a sort of cantata. Publisher: Müller

RUDOLF VON OERTZEN (b. Neuhaus, February 16, 1910) published a collection of **Chorale meditations** and **Chorale sonatas** without meter markings, which therefore have a free impetus and offer an opportunity for ad lib execution and use. Publisher: Bärenreiter. In contrast, CESAR BRESGEN (b. Florence, October 16, 1913) and FRIEDRICH ZIPP (b. Frankfurt am Main, June 20, 1914) contributed free organ works: Bresgen a **Toccata and fugue** on a ricercare theme by Hans Leo Hassler, published by Peters, and Zipp his **Free organ pieces,** which according to the composer close a gap in contemporary organ music independent of the chorale. They are planned so that at various points they can end, or they can be assembled into cycles. Publisher: Merseburger.

Two composers must be mentioned, although their connection with organ music does not immediately spring to mind—JEAN FRANÇAIX (b. Le Mans, May 23, 1912) and BENJAMIN BRITTEN (b. Lowestoft, Suffolk, November 22, 1913; d. Aldeburgh, December 4, 1976). Françaix depicts the nuns most enchantingly in his **Suite Carmelite:** the simple, devout Soeur Blanche, the bright Soeur Constance and the resolute Soeur Mathilde, not forgetting the maestoso entrance of Mère Marie de Saint-Agustin. Publisher: Transatlantiques. Britten elaborated on a theme from Vittoria in his **Prelude and fugue**—a short piece, especially interesting for its harmonies. Publisher: Boosey & Hawkes.

SIEGFRIED REDA (b. Bochum, July 27, 1916; d. Mülheim, Ruhr, December 13, 1968) was organist in Gelsenkirchen and Berlin and director of the church music department at the Folkwang school in Essen. In 1947 he wrote his first **Organ concerto.** The first movement, Allegro, has the theme as its A-section, followed by B and

C sections with new motifs, in the style of a concerto grosso. The ♫ ♩ ♫ ♩ rhythmic group from the third bar of the theme is particularly important in the development of the movement. The second movement, "Siciliano", is a pastoral piece which often varies its triple time from 6/8 through to 12/8, and thus sounds almost free in rhythm, being only tied to groups of three eighth-notes:

The "Ciacona" of the third movement consists of 20 variations on a repeated bass in typical 6/4 time.

Reda's third **Chorale concerto,** 1948, "Christ unser Herr zum Jordan kam" (When Christ of old to Jordan came), takes the motto of its first movement from the first verse of Luther's hymn and develops a free composition, by taking up and continuing motifs from the chorale. Sometimes the figures become ostinato, especially in the pedals. In the second movement, "Kanon", the fifth verse provides the motto. The canon at a fifth in the two upper voices is joined by the chorale with its tonic, G, in the pedals, enriched by octaves on the manual with fifths and sixths like a Mixture stop.

"Intonation and ciacona" follows with the seventh verse as its motto. The intonation only lasts a few bars, in two parts with cantus firmus, and leads at once into the chaconne. In the course of the free variations over the ostinato the cantus firmus is quoted line by line in the manual parts, transposed by octaves. As it approaches the end the motion becomes faster until the last ostinato is heard again in the broad tempo of the opening.

His **Images of the Virgin**—Annunciation, Magnificat, Choir of angels: Salve regina, Vespers: Burial, Pietà—has no cantus firmus (unlike the chorale concertos) and only quotes briefly from the ninth psalm mode in the "Magnificat". Here Reda renounces any formally clearly defined development which the listener could follow through motifs and themes; instead he paints pictures which move past in bright colors, and for which he gives the required registration. References to Stravinsky's *Symphony of Psalms* are explicitly mentioned in the "Magnificat" and are also heard elsewhere in the work. When listening one should be prepared to surrender entirely to sheer musical impact; then this work will fulfill its purpose.

The **Sonata,** 1960, duration 30 minutes, makes maximum demands on both player and audience. It is too complex to follow without the score, in which the composer mercifully gives exact instructions for registration and notes on its technical structure. The movements are: Exposition, Development in the form of a fugue, Recapitulation as a slow movement, Finale like a passacaglia. Publisher: Bärenreiter.

The organ sonatas of JOHANNES DRIESSLER (b. Friedrichsthal, January 26, 1921) stand on the margin of his extensive oeuvre dominated by vocal music such as motets and oratorios. According to the composer's own words the individual movements of the **Chorale sonatas for the church year** Op. 30—usually three or four—can be performed as chorale preludes, and this extends their application into the liturgy.

Each piece has a title such as toccata, fugue, hymn, partita, prelude, ricercare, canzona, fantasia, bicinium, passacaglia or aria, and each has a chorale tune as its theme, used as the basis for its melodic development and joined by motifs and figures which are either free, or only slightly related to it. The compendium of forms from the Classical age of organ compositions assembled here should not deceive one into thinking that Driessler adopts any one form as it is; in fact he expresses himself entirely freely in these works.

1st sonata, Advent: "Toccata"—"Nun komm, der Heiden Heiland" (Come, redeemer of our race) is introduced by the first notes of the chorale in the pedals

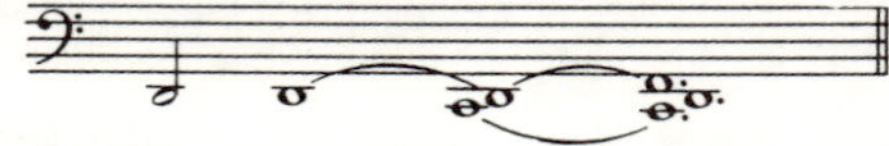

and then continues like a toccata in runs and this motif:

The cantus firmus joins in in almost all parts and is usually immediately varied or continued in its original form.

"Aria"—"Es kommt ein Schiff geladen" (There comes a ship laden). Cantus firmus in the alto register of the pedals with two free melodic parts in canon above it.

"Fugue"—"O Heiland, reiss die Himmel auf" (O Savior, open the heavens). The theme of the fugue is heard in the pedals only after some introductory passage work with references to the chorale. Thereafter the cantus firmus lines are distributed throughout the development of the fugue.

Frequent use of the chorale melody does produce a certain monotony, but also a convincing thematic unity.

9th sonata, *Passion,* is a trio sonata: Andante—"Ein Lämmlein geht und trägt die Schuld" (A little lamb goes and bears the guilt). The chorale appears in various positions in the pedals: The first line is heard twice, beginning on A and D, and the other lines also alternate between the keys of C, G and D (the trio is strictly developed with two upper parts which sometimes imitate each other), and as a result the movement has an unusual shimmering atmosphere.

Largo—"O Traurigkeit, O Herzeleid" (O sorrow, O heartfelt grief). From the descending thirds of the cantus firmus a melody emerges which almost earns the status of a theme.

The tune of the chorale is heard twice in its original form, first in the left hand and then in the pedals.

Allegro moderato—"Wir danken dir, Herr Jesu Christ" (We thank Thee, Lord Jesus Christ). A free movement with ostinato figures in the pedals and only distant echoes of the chorale.

Toccata and hymn on "Wach auf, wach auf, du deutsches Land" (Awake, awake, o German land) Op. 46/1, duration 15 minutes, is a concentrated work with the following structure: "Toccata"—toccata: runs, and lines of the chorale to the first half of the cantus firmus; trio: three-part canon of the complete chorale with a free part; mirror image toccata: chorale lines of the second half of the melody.

"Hymn"—hymn: in Organo Pleno, with dotted rhythms and echoes of the chorale; double canon: a free part and the cantus firmus developed in its entirety; hymn: in Organo Pleno. Publishers: Bärenreiter; Breitkopf.

The development of organ composition and its notation since about 1960 can be recognized by the various factors which apply in general to New Music of this period. The quest for new paths led to the discarding of the predominant traditional style of composing in major and minor keys, together with its extension into serial or tone row techniques developed from Arnold Schönberg's method of composition. This resulted in exhaustive analysis of rhythms and a rejection of the bar line. In order to eliminate any sustained meter, use was made both of a distinctive, precisely established notation and of a vague, suggestive manner of composition which gave the performer room for free interpretation. Aleatory music with its haphazard association of sounds and drawing of lines was similarly aimed at a new type of composition in which the performer participated. Composing with electronic devices, that is, with electrically produced sounds, led mainly—and in fact only—to scoring for organ and electronic tape when creating new works for organ. Experiments with coloring and other effects led further, and the results were collectively named "post-serial". Finally, mention should be made of instrumental dramatics, which require the organist to perform body movements such as nodding the head, clapping or running, or to recite words.

Apart from these technical changes in methods of composition, a change has taken place in the spiritual basis of these works. In many recent compositions one can see an attempt to move away from performance and concertante elements towards an introverted art with a literary motto to establish programmatically the composer's purpose—a movement which might collectively be termed "meditation music".

Since these two poles of the new organ music—meditation versus mechanization—are not only diametrically opposed to each other but reach such extremes in both directions that they come together again under different names, we have in this apparently enigmatic picture an image of the entire musical development of today.

The earliest post-serial organ work to appear in print is the **Volumina,** 1961/62, revised 1966, by GYÖRGY LIGETI (b. Dicsöszentmárton, Transylvania, May 28, 1923). The composer wrote in his performance notes: "The piece consists exclusively of stationary clusters and clusters which move in various ways."

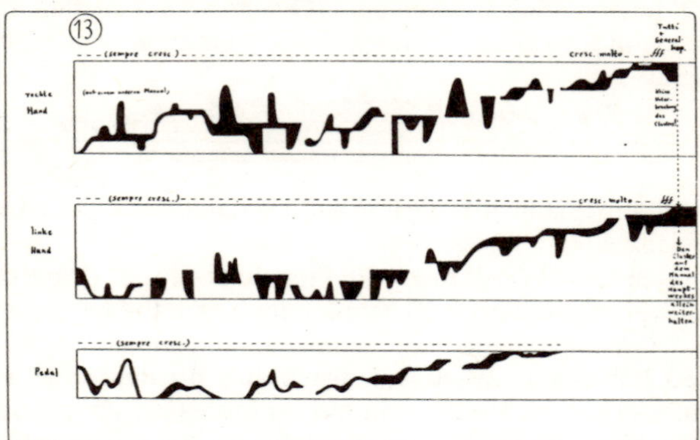

From Peters Edition 5983, by kind permission of C. F. Peters, Frankfurt am Main

We can amplify this: it consists solely of sounds which change in color, dynamics and pitch, and these sounds are the actual innovations in this kind of organ music. One can hear the enchanting, swirling clouds of sound of a 4′ Rohrflöte, the dark, growling timbre of a 16′ stop, shreds of sound from reed stops or the shuddering, challenging roar of the tutti.

This sounds unfamiliar, because clusters of notes have rarely been heard in organ music before. They were in fact used by Abbé G. J. Vogler (1749–1814), who was not regarded in many circles as a serious writer of organ music. In Vogler's tone painting (cf. p. 111f.) there is something obvious: many clusters of notes together, especially the louder ones, give the impression of menace and depict something sinister by making the noise of a machine. The organist and Stuttgart court music director Justin Heinrich Knecht (1752–1817), composer of a symphony called *Tongemälde der Natur (Tone paintings of nature)* described it in similar terms.

Sounds alone do not by any means signify a new development in the course of a work. Ligeti demands that the "large scale of the piece," which lasts some 16 minutes, is to be "shaped like a single great arc," which seems difficult to achieve with such static sounds. The immobility of this music and above all the lack of meter and rhythm pose the danger of fatigue and lapse of attention. Colors alone have no plastic power, and effects such as the starting and stopping of an engine soon wear off. Ligeti's two studies, **Harmonies,** 1967, and **Coulée,** 1969, use conventional notation. The first study consists of soft chords constantly varying by semitones, their duration longer or shorter at the player's whim. The second, however, is "to be played extremely fast, so that the single notes can hardly be heard and the motion almost fuses into a continuous sound." Publishers: Peters; Schott.

ISANG YUN (b. Tong Young, Korea, September 17, 1917) uses a more sophisticated scoring technique in his **Tuyaux sonores** (Resonant pipes), 1967. He distinguishes between chords with few harsh dissonances, fairly harsh chords with diminished seconds and augmented sevenths, and very harsh chords with many neighboring tones. However, on the whole even such nuances will produce the same basic sound of friction between seconds, the effect of which wears off in the long run. Publisher: Bote.

KLAUS HASHAGEN (b. Semarang, Java, August 31, 1924) explicitly includes in the basic idea of his **Timbres,** 1967, both musical gestures and tone colors, and progressively changes these two components to considerable effect in the course of the nine-minute piece. Another of Hashagen's works, **Jan Pietersz Sweelinck 1562–1621,** 1971, is a sort of organ concerto with vocal and instrumental groups. By adding other sources of sound Hashagen reaches beyond post-serial organ music, and because of this the organ's role seems more important and effective. Post-serial musical language takes a more appropriate position in light of traditional sounds, and as a contrasting element achieves better effects. Publisher: Peters.

Understandably only a few contemporary composers let themselves be tied to just one of the new techniques and restricted as a result. Most of them have gone through a period of development which included polyphonic writing as well as an approach to twelve-tone technique, and are now examining even more progressive rhythmical and metrical problems.

To the realm of this music belong the **Variations** of JOHN CAGE (b. Los Angeles, CA, September 5, 1912), **Fabliau** by MILKO KELEMEN (b. Podravska Slatina, Croatia, March 30, 1924) and the **Transformations** and **Sons brisés** (Broken sounds) by JUAN ALLENDE-BLIN (b. Santiago de Chile, February 24, 1928), though each work lies on the margin of its composer's oeuvre.

The three pieces by the Swede BENGT HAMBRAEUS (b. Stockholm, January 29, 1928), **Konstellationer, Interferenser** and **Nebulosa,** rank as an alphabet of modern musical language. Hambraeus also wrote an extremely concertante **Concerto for organ and harpsichord,** 1951, duration 20 minutes—a vigorous, thrusting work in several movements. Publisher: Hansen.

MAURICIO KAGEL (b. Buenos Aires, December 24, 1931), whose **Improvisation ajoutée,** 1962, had already been written sometime before, brought some humor into this serious subject with his **Rrrrrrr . . . Eight organ pieces,** duration 19 minutes. His **Rauschpfeifen, Repercussa** and above all **Rosalie** are notated normally and have none of the "horror" this sort of music provokes in many listeners. Publisher: Peters.

The **Toccata senza fuga** by HANS WERNER HENZE (b. Gütersloh, July 1, 1926) is scored like a chaconne, but its title is its most original feature, while DIETHER DE LA MOTTE (b. Bonn, March 30, 1928) wrote freely rhythmic pieces, often relieved by figure work and well suited to the organ—**Prelude** and **Organ piece with windows,** 1970, the latter an elaboration on a three-note motif from Stravinsky's **Symphony of Psalms.** Publishers: Schott; Bärenreiter.

TILO MEDEK (b. Jena, January 22, 1940) went to live in West Germany in 1977. He adopted old models for his **Retrograde passacaglia** but looked at them afresh, i.e. the development goes in the opposite direction from the listener's expectations. His **Buried peasant flute** appeared in 1969. Publisher: Hansen.

WOLFGANG STOCKMEIER (b. Essen, December 13, 1931) is one of the most prolific composers of his generation, who wrote extensively for organ. His early works were influenced by Hindemith, and the later ones by twelve-tone music, which he tried out in his **1st organ sonata,** 1961. Several sections—sometimes corresponding to one another—make up this piece, and they are both linked and divided by one connecting bar which appears at the beginning like a motto. Rhythmically this sonata is fairly conservative. The **2nd sonata,** 1966, consists of four metrically free meditations on the main ideas in the Old Testament Book of

Jonah, and the **3rd sonata,** 1970, is a mass for organ comprising Kyrie, Gloria and Credo using various chorale tunes. Stockmeier tries by means of appropriate indications to induce the performer to play freely and to improvise—notes with ad lib durations and rests of indeterminate length will always produce different music from players with different temperaments.

In 1969 he wrote the *Symphonia sacra* as a large-scale meditation on chapter 5, verse 19 of Corinthians II: "God was in Christ, reconciling the world unto himself." Here also the notation is left metrically free for the organist to shape the music, so a listener will hear a new version with each performance. According to the composer the **Symphonia** is "a kind of reckoning with a certain branch of modern theology which is making an effort to misunderstand Christianity as solely a matter of social behavior. In contrast, this passage points to the act of salvation itself with the chorale quotation 'Now rejoice, dear Christians together.' The series of different sections can be regarded as different stages of the meditation and partly as an emotional reaction to the theological standpoint just mentioned." The **2nd Toccata,** 1970, approaches a quintessence of the methods of composition previously considered. "It begins hesitantly, with notes alone or in groups, chords which follow each other increasingly closely and thicken with a crescendo into a massive block. Chords like clusters roaming about with contrapuntal motifs alternate with bizarre polyphonic passages, until the whole resolves into a kind of passacaglia with an ostinato bass held rhythmically in suspension. A passage similar to the opening leads into the final recitative, its rhythmic form based on the words of verses 9–13, chapter 4 of John I."

The most radical are his **Two organ pieces,** 1966, which break with all tradition. They carry further some of Frescobaldi's specific ideas on form which aimed at a certain flexibility. In the first piece, "Capriccio", the performer is offered a number of fully composed little passages which he can assemble into a whole in many different ways. The second, "Te Deum", also contains a number of small sections that can be put together, but only the beginning of each passage has been fully composed and the rest is to be improvised on the basis of the beginning. Variable formation and aleatory style are in evidence as components of a piece of music; they determine the sounds that will be heard.

From: **The Organ,** Series 1, No. 14. By kind permission of Fr. Kistner and C. F. W. Siegel & Co., Cologne.

The **4th sonata,** 1973, is an examination of the Classic-Romantic sonata form. Several movements are boxed inside one another, and in place of themes we have differently constructed sections, sometimes in precise notation, sometimes aleatoric. Entitled "Mysteries", it is a great virtuoso organ work.

Other works by Stockmeier include the two **Cycles of variations** on a theme by Johan Kuhnau, 1961, and on the Bach chorale "Herrscher Über Tod und Leben" (Lord of death and life), 1962; the **Organ pieces,** 1967; **Meditation,** 1961; **2nd toccata,** 1963; the **Variations on a theme by Arnold Schönberg,** 1977; and chorale preludes and inventions. He wrote two **Concertos for organ and instruments.** The first, 1962, with string orchestra, has the following movements: Fantasia allegro, Toccata allegro, Canzone moderato, Variations allegro. The second concerto, 1973, has Fantasia, Capriccio, and Variations and is scored for two flutes, oboe, clarinet, two bassoons, horn, trumpet, trombone, two cellos, and double bass. Publishers: Gerig; Kistner; Möseler; Schwann; Breitkopf—*Marienstatter Orgelbüchlein.*

HELMUT EDER (b. Linz, December 26, 1916) can also look back on an impressive number of organ works. He bases his work audibly and visibly on polyphonic ideas and is a supreme master of his technique. Apart from his brief, capricious **Five pieces** Op. 40 and the **Partita on a theme from Johann Nepomuk David's Ezzolied** Op. 42, 1965, he was very concerned with chorales, which is by no means automatically the case with contemporary organ composers. In **Op. 47,** 1968/70, he combines five organ partitas, duration between 8 and 12 minutes, and Op.48 consists of a chorale suite—**Seven little chorale preludes on "Der Weg des Herrn"** (The way of the Lord). All these are written conventionally, but the Op. 53 meditation, **Vox media,** 1969, is partly written in symbols because of its clusters. There are movements full of atmosphere in the **Partita on old folk songs** Op. 67.

Eder's most important contribution to contemporary organ music is probably contained in his two concertos. **L'homme armé** Op. 50, 1969, a "concerto in three movements", duration 20 minutes, has the style of a virtuoso concerto of grand dimensions with a symphony orchestra as accompanist. The program notes for the world première ran as follows:

> The theme, at one time one of the most common in vocal polyphony, had always fascinated the composer with its musical simplicity and commitment to expressing the words, but especially by its extremely topical contemporary relevance. He now takes this cantus firmus as the foundation for an organ concerto and carries the logical dependence of his melodic-harmonic progressions on the old tune into the most minute figures. Beside relatively traditional principles of elaboration is arrayed a whole series of modern elements, such as the expressive sound clusters brought in stiffly by the organ while the orchestra provides mobile clusters contrapuntally.

A clear hallmark of Eder's technique here, as in his later concerto *Memento,* is the "carpet of sound," a dense but never compacted foundation, which he achieves through various simultaneous subdivisions of one beat, e.g. eighth-notes, eighth-note triplets, sixteenth-notes, quintuplets, sextuplets and dotted notes, all played together on the same quarter-note. This may happen in wind groups such as horns and trumpets, but mostly in the strings, with the violins divided into as many as eight parts.

The second concerto, **Memento** Op. 57, 1971, duration 15 minutes, for positive organ and two string groups, has a similar kind of sound on a smaller scale: a string quartet and a string orchestra play against the positive organ's sharp, rather compressed sound to produce every possible kind of contrast between winds and strings, whether plucked or bowed. Publishers: Breitkopf; Doblinger.

ERNST PFIFFNER (b. Mosnang, Switzerland, December 6, 1922) contributed some "meditation music" with his **Meditations on the chorale "O Lamm Gottes unschuldig"** (O spotless lamb of God), a very calm piece, with dissonances to make it sound deliberately sorrowful. Publishers: Bärenreiter; Peters. The same applies to ROBERT M. HELMSCHROTT (b. Munich, 1938) who wrote a **Meditation on Psalm 137,** our psalm 138, "Feiern will ich Dich, Herr, aus ganzem Herzen" (I will give thanks unto Thee, O Lord, with my whole heart). This is a spirited hymn of praise which exhausts all the organ's potential. Publisher: Kistner. Another work which belongs here is the **Vater unser im Himmelreich, Nine verses for organ** (Our Father, who art in heaven), 1963, by MANFRED KLUGE (b. Unna, July 16, 1928; d. nr. Mölln, betw. February 27 & April 11, 1971), but this is not a partita in the traditional sense which develops the chorale, but variously structured pieces which decipher its essence. Publisher: Breitkopf.

BERTHOLD HUMMEL (b. Hüfingen, Baden, November 27, 1925) treated the Gregorian chorale with very modern techniques. In his **Halleluja,** 1972, there are tone clusters as background chords for little phrases from the chorale, short passages with ostinato rhythms and quick, wide-ranging runs over the entire keyboard. Between, above and below sounds the cantus firmus, often in chords. This is a piece for cathedral organs. Among Hummel's free works there is a very beautiful **Adagio,** duration 10 minutes, dominated by the opening thirds which are later extended into chords and interrupted by short linear phrases. The contrasting sections are given to different manuals, but the player is advised "to avoid too much change in registration". The introduction to the **Fantasia** gives a prominent position to the thirds heard in the **Adagio,** as though it were a sequel to it. The second movement, "Passacaglia", develops in six variations an ostinato which is stated in the introduction. An arioso ends the work. His **Tripartita** achieves very distinctive effects in its third movement, "Toccata", by expanding and contracting its motifs. Mention should also be made of the **Three Marian frescoes,** 1970, and particularly a kind of organ concerto called **Metamorphoses on B-A-C-H** for organ and 11 wind instruments, 1971.

The **Invocations** for organ and trumpet are very difficult for both performers to play. The three movements are entitled "De profundis", "In te Domine speravi" and "Non confundar in aeternum". Publishers: Simrock; Schott.

ARIBERT REIMANN (b. Berlin, March 4, 1936) has as yet unfortunately contributed only one work for organ, **Dialogue I.** It is a continuous composition, alternating between chords and figures, with very precisely marked agogics. It culminates in a boisterous fugato in which the exuberant theme is inserted above and behind itself. Publisher: Schott.

JOSEF FRIEDRICH DOPPELBAUER (b. Wels, August 5, 1918), like Hindemith, declares his support for tonality as a system to which the human ear is accustomed. This is borne out by his works, which are very well-suited to the organ and offer some interesting technical solutions. This applies both to the **Seven chorale preludes** and to the **Aphorisms and versets** for liturgical chants, the latter being especially suitable for use in worship.

The **Four new pieces,** and above all the **Sonatina** of 1956, demonstrate that Doppelbauer is a genuine composer for the organ with a sure touch in presenting three-dimensional themes. The especially attractive last movement, "Rondo", is in a form not found elsewhere in organ works. The partita called **Ornaments** of 1969, the **Concerto for organ and string orchestra** and the **Ten studies** for solo pedals deserve a closer look. The latter are more than mere exercises for foot agility. Publishers: Coppenrath; Doblinger. The works of KURT-JOACHIM FRIEDEL (b. Stettin (now Szcecin), April 5, 1921) also give the impression of a composer committed to church music who is a performer as well. The arrangements for manuals only entitled **Chorale preludes and organ chorales** and the partitas **Wie schön leuchtet der Morgenstern** (How brightly shines the morning star) bear witness to this, for they comprise good musical invention simply realized. The partita on **Jesus Christus unser Heiland** (Jesus Christ our Savior) is more demanding; it begins with a variation for solo pedals and ends with a concertino section in tonal style made unfamiliar by sparse chromatic modulation. He also wrote a **Concerto** for trumpet in B-flat and organ. Publisher: Merseburger.

HANS LUDWIG SCHILLING (b. Mayen, March 9, 1927) comes from the school of Hindemith and Genzmer and has already written extensively for organ. After experimenting with serial and electronic techniques he is now working "with the emphasis on melody carried by harmonies which have not been exhausted, and dancelike rhythms." Apart from his three **Partitas,** these principles are especially demonstrated in the **Eight interludes,** which are imaginative and colorful miniatures for pedalless organ. There is no hesitation to use clusters. The chorale element, founded on colorful chords, appears in the **Four chorale preludes** for organ with trumpet—or oboe or cor anglais. This is music which sounds as good in a concert as in a church service. **Carillon**—a piece for percussion and organ—is completely free from traditional ties, and betrays no trace either of the organ's association with liturgy or of the loftier forms of counterpoint. Playful sounds dominate; this comes out particularly well in the concertino passages for one line of organ music and vibraphone. Other compositions for organ with other instruments (trombone, viola, cello, horn, alto saxophone) exist in manuscript form. Publishers: Breitkopf; Hänssler; Schwann.

MAX BAUMANN (b. Kronach, November 20, 1917) scored his **Concerto for organ** (1963) for string orchestra and timpani. A Grave introduction precedes the first quick movement, the organ plays solo in the third movement, marked Largo, and the Allegro vivace finale is riotously fast. His **Sonatina** unfolds more traditionally, but his **Three pieces** of 1963 are of unusual and inventive caliber. Publisher: Merseburger.

JEANNE DEMESSIEUX (b. Montpellier, February 14, 1921; d. Paris, November 11, 1968) was well known as a concert organist. She wrote the famous, or infamous, **Six studies,** in which she concentrated on multiple notes in the pedals, and a **Te deum** Op. 11, 1958, which is a great work for organ, partly toccatalike and full of rich harmonies. Publishers: Bornemann; Durand.

ANTON HEILLER (b. Vienna, September 15, 1923; d. ibid., March 25, 1979) mostly wrote choral music. His organ works include **Chorale preludes, Partitas, Four pieces for the Feast of Corpus Christi,** and his **2nd sonata,** displaying a cool, strict, uncompromising style. The other aspect of his artistic leanings is demonstrated by the exuberant **Dance toccata** and the three-movement **Organ concerto,** duration 22 minutes, which has an almost Baroque vigor. It is scored for woodwinds, timpani and strings. Publisher: Doblinger.

The Czech composer PETER EBEN (b. Zamberk, January 22, 1929) won early fame through his **Sunday music,** 1958, duration 31 minutes. The title indicates that it is a festive, ceremonial work for the splendid-sounding instrument the organ is—a rare positive attitude from a modern composer. **Fantasia I** is a variation on a theme elaborated on again in **Fantasia II,** together with some new ideas. "Moto ostinato" and "Finale", the two best known movements, were inspired by the toccatalike French organ works of the late 19th century, and the main theme of the finale is a fanfare which augments this effect. The **Lauds,** duration 23 minutes, composed somewhat later, is a strongly declamatory four-movement suite. Only the second movement, Lento, is distinguished by its more spiritual and religious atmosphere. Publisher: Bärenreiter.

AUGUSTINUS FRANZ KROPFREITER (b. Hargelsberg nr St. Florian, September 9, 1936) wrote partitas, versets, canons and variations which are entirely rooted in the chorale. Larger-scale works are the **Triplum super "Veni, Creator Spiritus"** and the two **Sonatas.** Publisher: Doblinger.

CURTIS CURTIS-SMITH (b. Walla Walla, WA, 1941) has composed a number of works for various forces, but his **Masquerades,** composed in 1978, is a witty, enjoyable, often ironic collection of organ pieces. Published by author, Western Michigan University, Kalamazoo.

WILLIAM ALBRIGHT (b. Gary, IN, October 20, 1944) wrote the words and music of **The King of Instruments** for the dedication of an organ. It is a musical pageant in verse for organ and speaker, lasting 19 minutes. In a charming way the author describes the king of instruments and how to play on it, beginning with an introduction and describing manuals, pedals, flutes, and finally the organist. He uses every technique of organ composition, old and new, in virtuoso style, albeit with a certain detachment and irony. He also composed **Halo** for organ and percussion. The "Triumphal march" at the end of *The King of Instruments* is dedicated to the organist and bears these words:

Over the keys his fingers dance.
Across the pedals his tootsies prance.
He huffs and puffs; he frets and sweats.
Up and down the bench he slides
As over the beastie he presides.
He rips his seams; his girdle pops
At last, he's pulled out all the stops.

Further work: **Sweet Sixteenths, A Concert Rag for Organ.**
Publishers: Peters; Piedmont.

Two postscripts

An unprecedented independent school of organ music has recently emerged in the Soviet Union. Russian orthodox churches had no organs, and until now only a meager amount of music had been composed for organ while concerts on the few existing secular instruments were rare. The decades since World War II have provoked a wave of new organ building in the larger towns and a marked increase in the quantity of concerts, which has encouraged a number of composers to write for the organ. Some interesting works are listed here:

V. G. KITKA (b. 1941), organ suite **Five scenes from Orpheus;** G. MUSCHEL (b. 1909), **Suite,** containing an Aria and a Toccata; A. MURAVLEV, **Idyll;** I. ASSEYEV (b. 1921), **12 Symphonic fugues;** V. SUSLIN (b. 1942), **Poco a poco II;** J. JUZELIUNAS (b. 1916), **Organ concerto;** A. KHATCHATURIAN (b. 1903), **Introduction and fugue;** O. JANCHENKO (b. 1939), **Concerto for organ and orchestra.** Publishers: Peters—*Orgelwerke sowjetischer Komponisten (Organ works by Soviet composers),* ed. Leonid Roisman; Sikorski—*Sowjetische Orgelmusik (Soviet organ music);* Moscow Music, the original publisher of these and other works.

Arrangements for organ have always existed. Previously the aim has been to publicize works or to adapt for organ those the arranger thought suitable for the instrument, but nowadays works by composers who have not written for the organ at all are being rewritten for it. Towards the end of the last century Wagner transcriptions were already lying on the music stand of every organ, and Reger's and Karg-Elert's organ arrangements of Bach's piano works were also widely known. Today the publishing house of Forberg is particularly active in bringing out organ arrangements, for instance Richard Strauss's **Prelude in B-flat major** and Rossini's **Religious prelude,** both edited by J. Dorfmüller; Prokofiev's **Toccata** Op. 11 and **March** from Op. 33, edited by J. Guillou; and Liszt's **Legend No.1, the Sermon to the birds,** edited by G. Berger.

Addenda:
Contemporary British and American Composers

by
Lee Garrett
Region 8 Councillor, American Guild of Organists

INTRODUCTION

The history of organ music is one of immense stylistic diversity, associated to a large degree with the different characteristics of organs from one region to another. In the Baroque period, for example, the styles of both organ music and organ building were vastly different in France, Germany, Italy and Spain; by contrast, the violin's evolution has been characterized at any given time by a high degree of uniformity in sound and appearance from builder to builder and region to region.

Comtemporary British and American organ music appropriately reflects diverse influences from evolved musical styles and, perhaps even more significantly, from an extraordinary range of thinking about what constitutes a good organ. While the first few decades of the 20th century continued to favor the orchestrally-conceived organ, any number of developments (even beginning with Albert Schweitzer's views on the proper organ for playing Bach) have resulted in a prominence of organs built since World War II favoring a return to classical, e.g., 17th and 18th century principles of design and construction. To a degree this is more the case in the United States than in the United Kingdom, where the organ for the most part has had a continued association with cathedral music and British anthem accompaniment, though British organ builders are increasingly incorporating mechanical action and other aspects of classical organs (including, in some instances, flexible winding and adaptions of unequal temperament) into their current output.

If America is sometimes seen as "the melting pot," absorbing and amalgamating various ethnic and cultural influences in its immigrant history, the 20th century American organ can appropriately be seen as an instrument with mixed ancestry. Though there have been attempts to emulate Anglican traditions, typical American churches largely lack the acoustic characteristics very much a part of the British esthetics. A King's College stoplist will not produce a King's College sound in any American building. North European traditions have surfaced most strongly in the last half of the 20th century, influenced initially by the work of European builders such as Rudolph von Beckerath and Dirk Flentrop, whose instruments gained prominence in post-war restorations, and through the attention of such figures as E. Power Biggs—an American who immigrated from England.

While organists might rejoice in the diversity of organ building styles available to them (including, in some cases, virtual reconstructions of historic instruments complete with meantone tuning), mainstream American composers by and large have been more skeptical of an instrument whose sounds can be so unpredictable. Stravinsky (whom we can consider American) complained that the organ never breathed. Norman Dello Joio was once asked why he had written so little for the organ, and his reply was that he couldn't be sufficiently certain how the music would sound unless it were written for and played on a specific instrument. To be sure, other composers have recognized and been encouraged by the organ's diversity today, but that diversity along with, in the minds of some, the instrument's association with liturgical functions seems to have discouraged many gifted composers from writing on a scale similar to their output for other instruments. We can be grateful, then, to organizations such as the American Guild of Organists and to individual performers who have commissioned new works from both established composers and from those whose styles have yet to meet the test of time.

The following survey highlights representative compositional styles and calls attention to recent works for organ by well-known composers who may be venturing into the genre for the first time. I focus primarily on works composed since 1960, and exclude those which are more likely to have been conceived for church rather than concert use, an obvious assumption being that something conceived for concert use is perfectly suitable for some church contexts. Admittedly, the converse is also true, and the sensitive composer, organist and listener will delight in discovering those pieces which can and should have a place in both concert and church repertoire.

Contemporary organ music ranges from the decidedly conservative to the avant garde. Although some compositional styles parallel mainstreams of works for other genres (e.g., in aleatoric works), organ music has seldom become a part of the mainstream—perhaps for reasons cited above. At the same time, one can cite works as rich in craft and imagination as those written for any other medium, and one simply hopes for broader recognition of these compositions.

A survey of the contemporary is, *a priori,* incomplete and immediately out of date. Readers may rightfully question inclusion of some title or composers at the expense of others, and will have their own interesting lists of works. Indeed, I have searched for some consensus on this thorny topic among many highly prominent and respected organists and organ teachers. While the names of certain composers predictably surface, few titles were included on everyone's list. I simply hope my own list is sufficiently representative to capture something of the flavor of the fascinating array of styles found in the works of contemporary British and American composers.

As should be expected in a survey of contemporary times and tastes, information is not always at hand regarding a composer's activities, place of birth, etc. Suffice it to say, most composers' names should at least be recognized—often as much because of their own performing career as for their work as composers. Though their pedalling may be known more widely than their pen, I hope this survey can bring us to a further understanding of their creative energies.

L.G.

HERBERT HOWELLS

(b. Lydney, Gloucestershire, England, Oct. 17, 1892; d. Feb. 27, 1983)

Howells studied at the Royal School of Church Music, London, and was a pupil of Charles Stanford and Charles Hubert Parry. He held posts at Salisbury Cathedral, Royal College of Music, St. Paul's Girls' School and St. John's College, Cambridge. His lush harmonic style is typical of English cathedral music traditions, and symphonically conceived organs in resonant rooms provide the greatest possibility to realize his music most effectively. His concert works include four Rhapsodies composed over a 40-year time period, three sonatas, and two sets of Three Psalm Preludes. His rhapsodic, improvisatory style is tonally centered but without traditional, functional harmonies. A typical scale basis reads (from C): C, D, Eb, E, F-sharp (rarely F), G, B-flat, C, though he avoids the augmented second from E-flat to F-sharp.

Most of Howells's compositions are published by Novello.

VINCENT PERSICHETTI

(b. Philadelphia, June 6, 1915; d. August 14, 1987)

A winner of many awards, including two Guggenheim fellowships, Persichetti applied his very eclectic style to nearly every musical medium. He was associated with church music and with higher education, having held appointments at the Philadelphia Conservatory and the Juilliard School of Music. His concert organ works include *Auden Variations* Op. 136, commissioned by Leonard Raver and based on Persichetti's setting of the W. H. Auden hymn, "Our Father, Whose Creative Will." Other concert works include choral preludes on *Drop, Drop Slow Tears* Op. 104, and *Give Peace, O God* Op. 162; *Do Not Go Gentle* Op. 132; *Dryden Liturgical Suite* Op. 144, *Parable VI* Op. 117, *Shimah B'Koli,* Op. 89, *Sonata for Organ* Op. 86, *Sonatine for Organ, Pedals Alone* Op. 11, and *Song of David* Op. 148. *Shimah B'Koli,* commissioned for the inaugural concert of the organ in Lincoln Center's Philharmonic Hall, uses a 12-tone row in which the second half is an exact inversion and retrograde of the first half. The work's five sections correspond to verses of Psalm 130.

The *Sonatine,* for pedals alone, is a relatively short three-movement work of virtuosic proportions, demanding numerous registration and dynamic changes.

Also for pedal solo is *Do Not Go Gentle,* based on the poem of the same name by Dylan Thomas.

Elkan-Vogel publishes Persichetti's organ music.

Measures 23–38, Movement I, of *Sonatine,* Op. 11, by Vincent Persichetti.

JOHN COOK

(b. Maldon, England, October 11, 1918; d. Boston, Mass, Aug. 12, 1984)

John Cook was an organ student of Boris Ord and David Willcocks, received his undergraduate degree at Cambridge University, and is a Fellow of the Royal College of Organists. He has held numerous church and academic positions. His popular *Fanfare*, inspired by Psalm 81 (verses 1–3), is typical of much contemporary British writing for the organ, presenting prominent melodic lines against somewhat dissonant accompaniments.

Measures 1–12 of *Fanfare*, by John Cook. Reproduced by permission of Novello and Company Limited.

DANIEL PINKHAM

(b. Lynn, MA, June 5, 1923)

Pinkham attended Harvard University, and studied with Walter Piston, Aaron Copland, Arthur Honegger, Samuel Barber, and others. In addition to being a prolific composer he has held numerous academic posts, and has received a Fulbright scholarship and Ford Foundation Fellowship. He is a Fellow of the American Academy of Arts and Letters.

Pinkham's over 40 organ compositions include works for solo organ, organ with instruments, and organ with pre-recorded tape. Many pieces have a basis in scripture, and are works of concert proportions in length and technical demands, featuring complex harmonies and textures. Most allow considerable freedom to the organist, designating general timbres and pitches, leaving the performer free to choose specific registers most suitable on a given instrument. The harmonic language may be triadically based or favor clusters, while tonal centers may be achieved by simply sustaining one or more pitches either manually or by means of weights or wedges on the keyboard.

Among the works for organ and tape, two are significant and representative of contemporary practices in that genre. His *Shepherd's Symphony* calls for the organist and one or more other performers on melody instruments to somewhat randomly select from among several brief melodies, to the background of a variety of sounds on the tape. The organ is thus one of many solo instruments (utilizing its many timbre possibilities) in this mildly aleatoric work which can also include optional (light) percussion instruments. *When the Morning Stars Sang Together* calls for a large organ and is a work of virtuosic style, requiring careful coordination between the organist and tape sounds occurring at carefully timed intervals.

Epiphanies, for solo organ, composed in 1978 for the Fisk organ at House of Hope Presbyterian Church in Minneapolis, takes advantage of the organ's unequal temperament in favoring tonal centers of G, C, and D. The five movements of this large-scale work are based on scripture passages, with the third movement ("By the Waters of the Jordan") utilizing the organ's flexible winding system to suggest a gentle river turbulence (see the following page). This is accomplished through the active bass line moving against a more sustained upper part; the wind requirements for the lower line produce a mild and interestingly uneven tremulant effect on the sustained lines.

The fourth movement calls for lead weights to be placed on eight keys for which stops are then drawn and removed to present a quick succession of timbres over static pitches.

Most of Pinkham's compositions are published by Ione Press (E. C. Schirmer).

First three lines of "By the waters of the Jordan" (*Epiphanies,* Movt. 3), by Daniel Pinkham. Copyright 1980 by Ione Press, Inc., Boston. Reprinted with permission.

NED ROREM

(b. Richmond, Ind., Oct. 23, 1923)

Well known for his compositions in a variety of genres, Ned Rorem brings a particularly lyric quality to his compositions for organ—perhaps influenced by his many compositions for solo voice. Rorem attended Northwestern University and the Curtis Institute, and received an MA degree from Juilliard, his teachers having included Aaron Copland and Virgil Thompson. He has won a Pulitzer Prize, two Guggenheim Fellowships and three Ford Foundation grants, among other awards. He is also a noted author.

In writing for the organ he has no specific sounds or instruments in mind. Apart from dynamic and tempo markings (and occasionally specifying two manuals) he leaves the organist free to choose the registers that seem most appropriate for the instrument at hand. His published organ compositions include *A Quaker Reader,* commissioned by Alice Tully for Leonard Raver, and *Views from the Oldest House,* commissioned by the Washington, D.C., Chapter of the American Guild of Organists for its 1982 national convention.

A Quaker Reader is in 11 movements, each headed by a quotation from a Quaker personage and having a programmatic title such as "First-Day Thoughts," "The

World of Silence," "Bewitching Attire of the Most Charming Simplicity," "No Darkness at All," and "Ocean of Light." The writing is very idiomatic to the organ, and encompasses the entire range of textures: occasional unaccompanied melodies, toccatas in the grand French style and well-developed counterpoint. While freely chromatic, the music always has a sense of tonal orientation.

Views from the Oldest House was inspired by Rorem's contemplation of the so-called Oldest House, a landmark structure built in 1686 near Rorem's home in Nantucket. Rorem is inspired by the vista from the hill where the house is situated, and the titles of this six-movement suite reflect those views. "Sunrise on Sunset Hill," which opens the work, is cast in an arresting toccata style; "Elms" is a short, lyrical piece for manuals alone, while "The Nest of Old North Church" employs a highly improvisatory style in passages preceding a section in hymn style.

Rorem's two suites constitute a major contribution to contemporary organ composition. Far from revolutionary in their style, they are well-crafted works in a largely traditional idiom. Their programmatic basis is not critical to the success of the music, and indeed the movements of the suites can be played singly or in groups of the performer's choosing.

Mr. Rorem is represented by Boosey & Hawkes Publishers.

KENNETH LEIGHTON

(b. Wakefield, Yorkshire, England, October 2, 1929, d. August 24, 1988)

Leighton studied at the Royal College of Music and at Oxford University, and has held academic posts in Great Britain. Well known for his choral music, his organ music is equally well crafted, usually highly rhythmic and often sharply dissonant. His most extended work, calling for a large instrument, is his *Prelude, Scherzo and Passacaglia.*

Martyrs, for two organists (either at two consoles or both sharing the same bench—the parts are carefully written to avoid awkward overlapping), was written in 1976 for Stephen and Nicholas Cleobury, and is an extended variation treatment of the hymn tune of the same name from the Scottish Psalter, 1615. Much of the work is based on the opening rhythm and contour of the hymn tune (see the following page).

PETER HURFORD

(b. Minehead, Somerset, England, November 22, 1930)

Hurford holds degrees in music and law from Cambridge University, and maintains a very active performance schedule as a concert organist. He has composed numerous shorter works for organ, many based on hymn tunes. His compositional style is mildly dissonant, not unlike his contemporaries Kenneth Leighton, William Mathias and Simon Preston. His music is in the catalogues of Novello Publishers and Oxford University Press.

Measures 28–34 from *Martyrs,* by Kenneth Leighton. Reproduced by permission of Novello and Company Limited.

WILLIAM MATHIAS

(b. Whitland, Carmarthenshire, South Wales, Nov. 1, 1934)

Mathias studied at the University College of Wales, and has held various posts in Great Britain. In 1965 he became a Fellow of the Royal Academy of Music. His compositions, even his shorter works, reflect the cathedral traditions, being best suited for large, eclectic instruments. Most of his works incorporate a sharp, rhythmic style with a strong tonal center in spite of a fairly dissonant idiom. His *Processional* is probably his best known organ work, contained in the anthology *Modern Organ Music,* published by Oxford University Press.

WILLIAM BOLCOM

(b. Seattle, May 26, 1938)

Bolcom received his undergraduate degree at the University of Washington, and his Master of Fine Arts degree at Mills College. He holds the Doctor of Musical Arts degree in compostion from Stanford University. Further studies were at the Paris Conservatory, where he won the Prix de Composition. He has held academic appointments at the University of Michigan as well as at Yale, Washington and Stanford universities, and was composer in residence at New York School of the Arts. His awards include three Rockefeller Foundation grants and two Guggenheim fellowships.

Black Host was written for organ, percussion (chimes, bass drum and suspended cymbals) and pre-recorded electronic sounds. It is a collage of styles, incorporating a Genevan Psalm tune as well as elements of rock and theater organ music. It requires an organ of very large resources and a virtuoso performer with an assistant. Performance instructions include "slow, inflexible rock tempo, 'flat' sound, everything deliberate and brutal." Graphic notation, in a style often associated with Ligeti, closes the work. The boldest graphs, at the bottom of each system, represent sounds on the tape.

Three Gospel Preludes represents the application of very contemporary concepts of sound density and articulation to very traditional melodies: the gospel hymns "What a Friend We Have in Jesus," "Rock of Ages," and "Just As I Am."

In "Rock of Ages," the long beams over half notes illustrate the free treatment of rhythm and meter. The *Maestoso* which follows brings the melody in the left hand.

Mysteries is a four-movement work commissioned in 1976 by the organ builder Walter Holtkamp, Jr. Significantly, Bolcom in this work states that registration is left to the organist, with the object being that the pieces can be played on an organ of any design, including electronic instruments. "The Endless Corridor" calls for "cool" sounding but contrasting eight-foot stops, and is cast in a trio texture for two manuals and pedal. Frequently changing meters occur through this first movement. The second movement, "Eternal Light," is unmetered, calling for soft, pointillistic treatment of chord clusters or isolated pitches, executed by the organist playing on various manuals at the opening and closing of the work; the middle section contains bold, sustained chords building toward, then moving away from full organ sound. "La lugubre gondola" suggests a gently rocking gondola through soft dynamics and an emphasis on lower registers and gently moving chord changes. "Dying Star" incorporates many fast, fleeting figurations on an eight-foot stop in the manual. Fragments from Bach's chorale "An Wasserflüssen Babylon" appear near the close of the work, interspersed with the figuration and periods of silence ranging from 9–13 seconds.

Bolcom's music is published by Hal Leonard Publishing Corporation.

Page 20 of *Black Host,* by William Bolcom. By permission of Editions Jobert, Paris.

Measures 53–62 of "What a Friend We Have in Jesus!" (from *Three Gospel Preludes*), by William Bolcom.

Page 15 of "Rock of Ages" (La Cathédrale Engloutie), by William Bolcom. Copyright © 1980 by Edward B. Marks Music Company. Used by permission. All rights reserved.

SIMON PRESTON

(b. Bornemouth, England, August 4, 1938)

Simon Preston was a pupil at the Choir School at King's College, Cambridge, where he later was an organ scholar under David Willcocks and received his MusB and MA degrees. An international concert organist, Preston made his debut in Festival Hall in 1962; he subsequently held appointments at Westminster Abbey and Christ Church, Oxford.

His widely performed *Alleluyas* is strongly influenced by Olivier Messiaen, with figured outbursts and polytonal chord clusters in a relentless rhythm. Principal motives of a descending fourth and ascending seventh are best heard on a solo trumpet stop.

The work is inspired by the text associated with the Liturgy of St. James:

At his feet the six-winged Seraph;
Cherubim with sleepless eye,
Veil their faces to the Presence,
As with sleepless voice they cry,
Alleluya, Alleluya, Alleluya, Lord most high.

Preston's music is published by Oxford University Press.

First three lines (3 measures) of *Alleluyas,* by Simon Preston. Copyright Oxford University Press.

WILLIAM ALBRIGHT

(b. October 20, 1944, Gary, Indiana)

(See also p. 226f) A graduate of the University of Michigan, Albright studied both organ and composition at that institution. The recipient of numerous fellowships and awards, he explores various timbres of the organ in a fashion usually requiring a very large instrument and, ideally, a resonant room. His style ranges from highly transparent to enormously dissonant, and in the latter idiom he sometimes calls upon the organist to produce tone clusters with the arm or fist. His *King of Instruments* is an affectionate parody of the instrument, introducing the organ to the listener through music and verse, with a narrator describing the instrument's sound and aspects of its mechanical features. Three volumes of *Organbook* represent Albright's adaptation of the classic French "Livre d'Orgue," collections of discrete movements exploring timbre or texture. While the 18th-century practice was for each movement to be used in alternation with sung portions of the liturgy (e.g. in settings of the Mass), Albright's collection has no liturgical purpose. *Organbook II* calls for prerecorded tape and is best heard on a large instrument (as is the first volume); the third volume, in two parts, is subtitled *Twelve Etudes for Small Organ.* Much of his writing places great technical demands on the organist.

His "Toccata satanique," from *Organbook II,* illustrates typical features in his music, including elements of aleatoric style and the need for an assistant to add and subtract stops.

Adaptations of idioms associated with popular music are found in his *Sweet Sixteenths,* which he describes as "A Concert Rag for Organ." Predictably, a dancing pedal part, syncopations and swinging chromaticisms abound in the piece; it is heard to best effect on a large, eclectic organ with an assistant (standing or seated next to the organist) playing a brief obligato line above the principal part. Albright's "Evening Dance," from *1732: In Memoriam Johannes Albrecht* (commissioned by Robert Anderson), illustrates playful use of rhythm and associations with country music in asking the organist in places to think about a "sharp Banjo sound" or "Loud fiddle sound," and even, in one passage, to possibly whistle the melody. Albright is represented by several publishers.

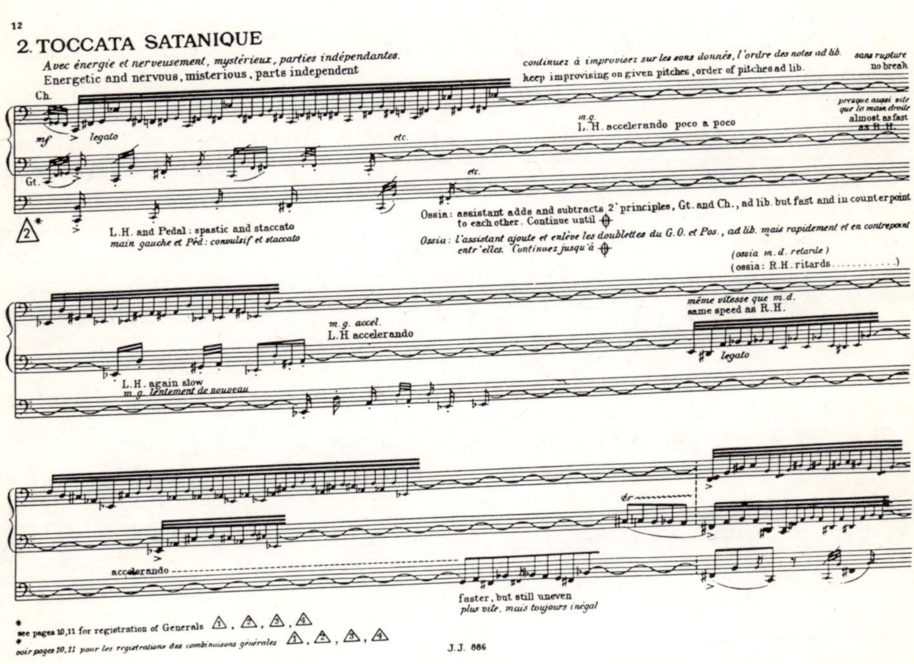

Page 12 of "Toccata satanique", from *Organbook II* by William Albright. By permission of Editions Jobert, Paris.

Measures 1–35 of "An Evening Dance", from *1732: In Memoriam Johannes Albrecht* by William Albright.

L.G.

The Organ

"If you are walking past a church and hear the organ playing, go in and listen. If you are lucky enough to be allowed to sit on the bench, try it with your small fingers and wonder at the omnipotence of the music." So wrote Robert Schumann in the *Musikalischen Haus- und Lebensregeln (Musical rules for house and life)*. The composer and writer Michael Praetorius praised the instrument in 1619 as follows: "In short, the organ has and comprehends in itself alone all other instruments of music, large and small, however they may be called." Though these two opinions come from ages centuries apart, they show how strongly this instrument of instruments has captivated people.

The two-thousand-year-long development of the organ has encountered many obstacles and sometimes taken wrong turns. Today it is inseparable in our thoughts from the galleries of churches—indeed the association between church and organ is generally accepted—but this relationship occurred relatively late in its history. The earliest example of the instrument is the hydraulis—Ktesibios of Alexandria's much-quoted water organ, dating from around 246 B.C. We can get an idea of this organ from theoretical writings and from the very few surviving examples: the air was collected in a container covered over with water, compressed and then conducted to the pipes, which were arranged on the chest in two to four registers according to pitch, and sounded when the key was pressed and a register was engaged at the same time. It was therefore closely related to the later medieval organ and must have persisted for several centuries, because it is even mentioned in the works of writers like Cicero, Petronius, Pliny and Suetonius. It was not played for religious worship, however, but for dancing and entertainment in the circus and elsewhere. A working model can be seen in the St. Louis Museum in Carthage, and a model reconstructed from fragments is to be found in the museum at Aquincum, near Budapest.

In the Eastern Roman Empire we have evidence of the organ's course through the first centuries after Christ, but in the West it is first heard of again in the middle ages. It is said that the Byzantine emperor Constantine V presented Pippin with an organ in about 757 and that Pope John VIII asked the Bishop of Freising in 880 for a monk who could build an organ for him and play it. In this way the organ was introduced into the Christian church in the 9th century through the monastic orders, and soon after, in 951, Winchester Cathedral boasted of an organ with no less than 400 pipes.

It is not entirely clear why an instrument which was not allowed in Christian churches for centuries because of its "pagan" associations was now being used for worship. It was of course a valuable asset that an organ could be built in different sizes to suit both small and large churches, but presumably a determining factor was that phenomenon which belongs exclusively to the organ: a note, once struck, cannot be influenced by the player but will continue to sound in the set pitch and in the same timbre without allowing the organist to introduce dynamic change or expressive nuance. This means that it is not susceptible to such personal feelings as a player may experience while interpreting the music, and suppresses subjective emotionalism to give more scope to the detached, spiritual aspect. This characteristic fits the organ better than any other instrument for use in Christian worship, and the history of church music demonstrates that these considerations have repeatedly emerged and repeatedly been resolved in favor of the organ but often against the use of other instruments.

The instruments built in the 9th century in Rome, Freising, Cologne, Aachen, Strasbourg and many other cities had as yet no facility for registration, and all the pipes activated by a key sounded together. Only at the beginning of the 15th century were devices similar to our stops installed, to permit single rows of pipes to be opened and shut. The range was about three octaves and the ranks of pipes arranged chromatically, as in the positive organ. Later they were arranged on other principles in different and often symmetrical ranks. In the 11th century for the first time we meet the *portative organ*, a small instrument of one to two-and-a half octaves, which could be carried about and played (one line only) with the right hand, while the left hand worked the bellows to provide the air. The *positive* [or small stationary] *organ* had a single manual and at most two to three rows of pipes, while the *regal*—a tiny portative organ—had only reed pipes. These miniature organs were initially used solely for secular music and only later found in churches. Organs with one, two or three-manual keyboards were further improved in the 14th century with the coupler which linked two manuals, and around 1350 with the pedals as well. Pedal boards which had already been built to relieve the burden on the player's hands now became independent and acquired their own registers. Finally towards the end of the 14th century the positive manual was added, and placed on the parapet of the loft behind the player (hence the name *Rückpositiv*) who sat facing the main instrument. Similarly in Renaissance times the regal was incorporated into the main organ at chest level, as "Brustwerk".

All the mechanism of the organ was visible from the outside. In a single-manual organ the Great organ was in the middle, flanked to right and left by the two pedal towers, while in a two-manual organ the Great and Swell organs were arranged vertically. Then the Positive organ was added behind as an arbitrary architectural feature and the Brustwerk enlivened the substructure. All the pipes were enclosed in a cupboard, the doors of which could be shut in front of the façade row. When the doors were open they were often seen to be richly decorated with paintings, like the still surviving organ in St. Valerie's church at Sion in the Valais (1380) and in St. Valentin's at Kiedrich (c.1500). The oldest surviving organ (1370) was at Sundre in Gotland and now stands in the Historical Museum in Stockholm. The panels of the housing allowed the sound to be directed down into the church. In Renaissance and Baroque times they were artistically carved into screens instead, and the ranks of pipes were partly arranged in a concave or convex pattern, to give the façade an effect of greater depth. In this period the outward beauty of the organ was acknowledged, if we may believe Arnold Schlick when he wrote in 1511 in his *Spiegel der Orgelmacher und Organisten (Mirror of organ builders and organists)*: "Whereas the organ primarily rings out to be heard and to praise God, yet it is nonetheless an ornament of the church when the organ has a right aspect and conduces to worship through proper figures and paintings."

At the beginning of the 16th century all types of pipes as we know them today were available in basic form and were being used in organs, so that the instrument could develop into its large form with four manuals and more than 50 stops, once a problem of space had been resolved: The Gothic organ was to be found either in the "swallow's nest"—a small gallery, usually on the lateral side of the nave—or at the side of the sanctuary. Now that more choristers and instrumentalists were to be positioned near the organ, it was removed to a loft at the west end of the church, where it could be seen to balance the high altar at the east end. To this day the loss of the better acoustics obtained from its position on the lateral wall is to be deplored.

Now that the organ had come into being in its full grandeur of size and sound, it developed various national characteristics, especially in Holland, Spain, Italy, France and north and south Germany, and in the high Baroque period the art of organ building reached a high point which has remained a model to the present day. Soon after, with the beginning of Viennese musical classicism, the organ ceased to exist as an organically developed entity, as it could not keep pace with the development of the orchestra. Innumerable attempts were made to imitate orchestral instruments on the organ and to produce the effects of crescendo, diminuendo and distance, but the organ thereby betrayed its own nature and became a caricature of itself. The "working principle," based on juxtaposing individual sections of contrasting sound quality on an equal footing, disappeared, as did the specific intonation which allowed the inner voices to stand out in polyphonic textures. Finally the mechanical action with its ability to influence the production of the note also vanished. (The intonation of the note is in fact influenced by opening the valve mechanically at the touch of finger, so that the process of vibration, i.e., producing the note in the pipe with all its overtones, flows faster or slower.) The artistic decline of the organ was not only accelerated by the conception of orchestral sound with its limitless wealth of nuance as the new contemporary ideal, but also by the technical possibilities of pipe pneumatics and later of electricity.

In this century there has been renewed interest in the historical origins of the art of organ building. The first suggestions for reforming the instrument came from Albert Schweitzer who, in conjunction with organ builders and musicologists, promoted attempts to understand the organ again as an "instrumental entity" and to utilize once more its distinct and inalienable basic structure. The success of this organ movement is manifested in countless new instruments.

How does an organ work? We have seen that one can always draw conclusions about the internal construction of the instrument from its outward appearance or façade. The Principal [or Diapason] pipes usually stand in the first row to form the façade, with horizontal trumpet pipes of Spanish origin included among them today, which are both architecturally and audibly superb. They leave one to guess about the mechanism behind, and together with the wooden walls of the lower structure also conceal the complicated arrangements for conveying the action of keys and stops to the wind chests, and the appliances designed to achieve an even wind pressure. The organ can be described as a keyboard instrument in which the wind makes the pipes speak to create the tones. It therefore consists of the following principal parts:

pipework with substructure (chests)
wind supply
action
console

The pipework is divided into individual stops, by which term is meant a rank of pipes—56 for a keyboard of four-and-a-half octaves, 30 for a pedal board of two-and-a-half octaves—which form an entity, because each individual tone they produce has the same sound character. Each of the stops can be individually operated to sound or be silent. The names of the stop derives from the musical characteristic of each rank of pipes and many take their names from a wind instrument with similar sound (and not vice versa, in an effort to make the organ imitate the sound of that wind instrument!). So we have Flute, Cor de Nuit, Trumpet, Weidenpfeife

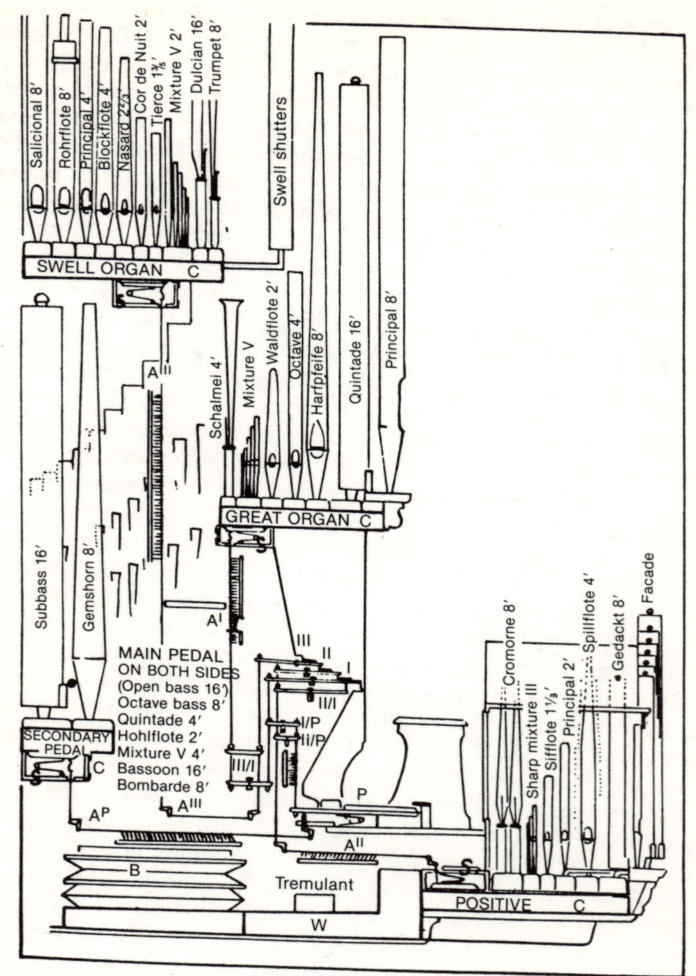

Section of a three-manual organ with Great organ, Positive, Swell organ and Pedal. (Drawing by kind permission of Dr. Walter Supper.) Each manual and the pedal board in the console (I,II,III,P) are linked by the action (AI,AII,AIII,AP) with the sliders (S) and thus with the chests (C). On the chests the individual stops are indicated. (II/I,III/I,I/P,II/P) indicate the couplers, i.e., the linking of two manuals or one manual and pedal board. B is the bellows, and W a wind channel with a tremulant built onto it.

[Salicional], Krummhorn, Dulcian, Bombarde and Bassoon. Others are named after the way they are built: Gedackt (covered), Spitzflöte (pointed flute), Rohrgedackt etc., while the musical backbone of every organ is the Principal or Octave stop. The various tone colors and dynamics are determined by the materials

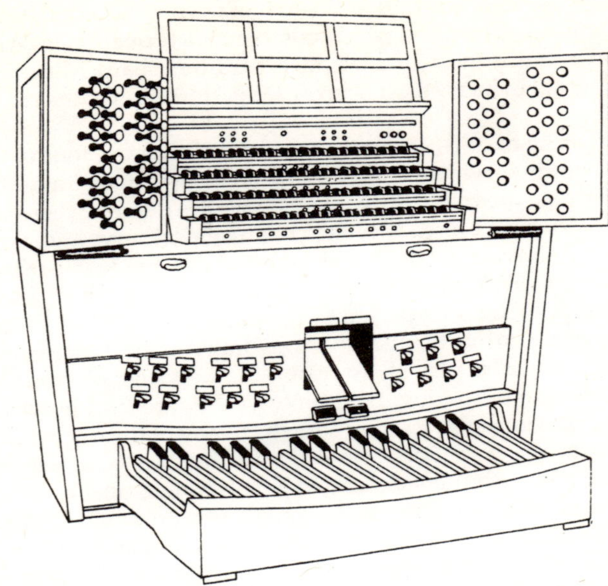

Console of a four-manual organ in the Great Minster in Zurich. The stops are arranged on both sides of the four keyboards, and above the pedal board are two pedals which can be moved to work the swell shutters. The hookdown pedals above the pedal board and the buttons under the manuals are the couplers and combination pistons used to help with registration changes.

used, the method of construction and the dimensions of the individual pipes. The main materials are wood, an alloy of tin and lead known as "organ metal", and copper. In building there is a primary difference between flue pipes (the column of air in the pipes is turned into vibrations through the current reaching the flue) and reed pipes (a metal tongue makes the vibration, and the note grows stronger and modulates through the schallot). Both kinds are found in a whole range of variations within the basic form. Finally the dimensions establish the relationship between the sizes of the individual pipes in a stop, which decrease in size as the sound goes higher. The width determines for instance the relationship of the diameter of one pipe to that of the one an octave lower.

The numbers in feet given with the name of the stops—16, 8, 4, 2, 2 2/3, 1 3/5 etc.—give the length of the lowest pipe in a stop (= bottom C) with open, cylindrical pipes. 8′ therefore means the normal position, i.e., with an 8′ stop one can play at the same pitch as on the piano, for instance, and the A next above middle C sounds in both cases at the same pitch. According to the laws of physics a pipe half as long sounds an octave higher, and one twice as long an octave lower, so that with a 16′ stop one is playing an octave lower on the same notes, with a 4′ stop an octave higher and with a 2′ stop two octaves higher than written or than would be the case with a 8′ stop. In this lies one reason for the opulence of the organ's sound, though other contributory factors are the overtone stops like quint, tierce and septième, which produce only the fifth, third or seventh of the note struck, or their respective octaves, and the mixture stops which combine such overtones. When they are drawn, as for instance the Cornet, Grave Mixture, Sharp Mixture or Cymbel, several pipes sound in intervals of octaves, fifths, thirds, sevenths etc. from the one note struck.

This multiplicity of stops, from a home organ with three, four or five stops to a four-manual instrument with 60 to 70, is assembled in various "organs". Their combinations determine musical style, while their names describe their position in the total structure, as we have already seen in this historical survey: Rückpositiv, Brustwerk (behind the player, or before his chest above the keyboard), Hauptwerk, Seitenwerk, Oberwerk, Kronwerk and Pedalwerk. Each organ is played on its own manual, but the pedal organ is played by the pedal board. The different organs can be coupled together, so that for instance stops drawn in the third manual also sound when the first manual is played. To obtain the best possible sound-effects each organ is enclosed in a housing, open only in the direction in which the sound should go, usually outwards into the church. To any of the organs can be added a swell mechanism, using shutters operated from the console, to increase the sound smoothly from *piano* (shutters closed) to *forte* (shutters open).

The *chests* on which the pipes stand contain wind conduits divided like a cross, with pallets connected to the keys and sliders, to close and open whole ranks of pipes which are linked to the stops on the console. This mechanism constitutes the core of every organ and is essential for the sound, the decisions of the player and the smooth functioning of the instrument.

The *wind supply* is provided through bellows, pressure regulators and wind channels, which carry the wind needed to make the pipes sound from the feeders (electric or, more rarely, hand-driven) through the bellows to the chests. A tremulant can cause the wind supply to fluctuate unevenly, so making the sound more interesting.

The *action*, which connects the key to the valve or slider in the chest directly under the pipes, employs thin wooden rods and occasionally also ropes. Trackers serve for lateral links and angles for changes of direction, so that the whole contraption is like an old-fashioned bell pull. Electric current is also used for this transmission in unfavorable climate or restricted space. The *console* comprises the manuals, pedal board and stops, with couplers and other aids on larger instruments to enable the player to change registration without an assistant. The optional combinations of various systems provided for this purpose make it possible to set chosen registration in advance, and to cancel one registration and install another by pressing a button when a quick change of tone color or dynamics is called for. At the console the organist must decide which stop he wants to draw for the work he is about to play. There are no set precedents, nor can there be, for every organ sounds differently, every auditorium makes the same stop sound different and every organ builder offers different possibilities of combining or contrasting registration, according to his artistic ideas. It should be possible to perform compositions on small and large instruments alike, for which purpose the most basic directions such as Full Organ, Mixtures, Reed Stops, Principals, etc. may be given. It is more important for the organist to present a composition according to his sense of style, in such a musical shape that its form and expression can be heard and felt, than it is to master it technically. "Only when faced with restrictions is mastery revealed" (Goethe) is quite particularly applicable to the organist who spends his life searching in vain for the ideal organ, while having to play whatever instrument is available to him.

Glossary of Terms

Agogic (Gr.) Subtle change of tempo, i.e., a minor, expressive modification of the basic tempo, not notated in the music

Alberti bass Repeated broken chords, giving a somewhat monotonous effect, mostly for left-hand accompaniment. Named after the Venetian composer, Domenico Alberti (c.1710 or 1717–1740).

Aleatory (Lat. alea = dice) Method of composing which allows considerable freedom for the interpreter, resulting in chance effects.

Anticipation see **Imitation**.

Antiphon Liturgical alternation between two singers or choirs. Also a short piece sung before and after the psalms.

Arpeggio The notes of a chord played in quick succession [indicated by a wavy line].

Attacca (Ital. = join) Indicates that the next section should follow immediately.

Augmentation See **Fugue** (p. 253).

Basso continuo see **Continuo.**

Bicinium (Lat.) 16th-century two-part instrumental or vocal composition, usually part of a partita.

Cadence Harmonic closing phrase.

Cadenza In a concerto with orchestra, used from the middle of the 18th century on to denote a freely improvised section for the soloist.

Canon Strictest form of imitation: a single part occurs at various times and at various pitches, thereby forming a piece in several parts. In other words, all the parts of a composition use one and the same tune, not at the same time or pitch, but one after the other and at set intervals. Precursor of the fugue. The following example by Michael Praetorius is of a canon in unison, i.e., each part begins on the same note. At the pause marks all three parts may finish together.

Cantus Firmus (Latin = fixed song. abbrev.: c.f.) Fixed part in a polyphonic composition, often a chorale, but may also be a freely invented theme.

Canzona (Ital. = song) Italian instrumental form, derived from the French chanson. Polyphonic, imitative structure. Precursor of the fugue (q.v.).

c.f. see **Cantus firmus**

Chaconne Dance in slow triple time. Usually denotes a set of variations based on it. For structure, see **Passacaglia.**

Chorale In organ music: a) Gregorian chorale—a single-line liturgical chant used in the Catholic church; b) German chorale—Protestant hymn consisting of several melodic sections or chorale lines.

Chorale variations Instrumental variants and changes (mostly polyphonic) which either use a counter melody to the chorale, leaving its melody unchanged, or elaborate on the chorale cantus firmus itself.

Church modes or **ecclesiastical modes** Denote the key system in use before 1600, i.e., before the establishing of our major and minor scales. They correspond to the diatonic series of white notes on the keyboard, from the tonic to its octave, and were named as follows:

1st mode: d-d^1 dorian
2nd mode: A-a hypodorian
3rd mode: e-e^1 phrygian
4th mode: B-b hypophrygian
5th mode: f-f^1 lydian
6th mode: c-c^1 hypoloydian
7th mode: g-g^1 mixolydian
8th mode: d-d^1 hypomixolydian

Added later were aeolian (a-a^1) and ionian (c-c^1) with the related hypoaeolian and hypoionian, from which the gradual transition from the aeolian to our minor, and from the ionian to our major, becomes clear.

Ciacona see **Chaconne.**

Clausula (Latin = close) Melodic cadence (q.v.)

Cluster Several neighboring notes sounded together, either chromatically at semitone intervals, or diatonically, using either white or black keys.

Color To decorate or ornament.

Comes (Lat. = companion) Repetition of the theme at another pitch. See **Fugue.**

Concerto grosso Italian concerto form used by Vivaldi, Corelli, etc. Movements: Allegro—andante—allegro. Also indicates the formal structure of a piece. Developed from rondo form, it contrasts grosso (= tutti, ripieno) and solo (= concertino). In the grosso the whole instrumental force plays, and in the solo the soloist(s). Form: A—tutti, B—solo, with new thematic material, A—tutti, C—solo, with new thematic material, A—tutti. Countless orchestral concertos were transposed for organ, with tutti and solo sections executed on differently registered manuals.

Continuo, basso continuo (abbrev. b.c.), **figured bass, thorough bass** A bass part using figures to indicate the harmonic framework of an instrumental or vocal work. The "thorough bass age" is the period from about 1600 to 1750. The church continuo instrument usually was the organ, but otherwise the harpsichord or clavichord, together with the lute and a bass instrument, e.g., viola da gamba, cello, double bass, bassoon or trombone.

Counterpoint 1) Counter-melody to a theme (see **Fugue**). 2) The subject of counterpoint deals with the composition of polyphonic (q.v.) works in which each part is and remains independent. *Double counterpoint* exists where the parts are interchangeable, i.e., the upper part may also become the lower.

Development Section of a compound work in which themes and motifs are elaborated. See **Fugue** and **Sonata.**

Diminution Reduction in the note values of, for instance, the cantus firmus of a canon or fugue. Also indicates a style of ornamentation whereby a melodic line is reduced into smaller note values. See **Fugue.**

Dux (Lat. = leader) Statement of the theme in its original form. See **Fugue.**

Electronic music Music produced by sound generators (oscillators) and usually recorded on tape, to which conventional instruments may be added.

Exposition The presentation of themes in the first section of a compound work. See **Fugue** and **Sonata.**

Figuration Describes a way of embellishing a part, built on a melody and broken into small motifs. Also similar treatment of harmonies.

Figured bass see **Continuo.**

Fugato and **fughetta** Describe forms or sections in fugal style which are however not strictly carried through.

Fugue (Lat. = flight) So called because in it several voices "pursue" each other. Evolved from the canon (q.v.) which is the strictest form of developing several similar parts out of one part. The parts of a fugue are:

Exposition, in which the theme is presented, by itself, in one part (dux, q.v.).

A second part answers, usually at the interval of a fifth (comes, q.v.);

a third restates the theme as dux, etc. The first part reappears in counterpoint to the comes, i.e., its theme is also executed as a counterpart to it and is called "combined counterpoint" if it later always appears together with the theme, which will then be appropriately transposed into another key. When all the parts in the fugue—usually three or four—have stated the theme, the exposition ends with a cadence and leads into the

Development. In this section the themes are broken up by free interludes, appear in other keys and change from major to minor or vice versa:

Finale (or recapitulation). Here the theme is restated in the original key or at the dominant. Special contrapuntal devices are often used in the fugue, e.g., augmentation of the theme:

diminution of the theme:

inversion of the theme's intervals, so that for instance a descending fifth replaces an ascending one:

retrograde of the theme, so that it reads from back to front:

stretto, whereby the comes begins before the dux has finished:

These technical devices can also be combined in various permutations, as for instance by inverting the intervals in a retrograde version of the theme:

The classical masters made plentiful use of these possibilities, and showed their mastery of this form by combining the various parts so as to obey the laws of harmony. The examples quoted previously come from J. S. Bach's Fugue in C major, BWV 545, but the changes to the theme given here do not all appear in the original.

A *Double Fugue* has two themes, developed either sequentially or simultaneously. No. I in this example is the first theme, originally developed alone, and followed by the development of the second theme—here No. II—but in the closing bars both themes appear together, one above the other, as seen in this example from the fugue in the Toccata in F major, BWV 540:

Triple and *quadruple fugues* treat three and four themes respectively, but are rarer.

Gregorian chorale Denotes the liturgical melodies to Latin texts used in the Roman Catholic church. Named after Pope Gregory the Great (590–604) who is thought to have been the first to collect them. See **Chorale.**

Homophonic (Gr. = the same sound) Also used to describe a work with one leading part above subordinate accompanying parts, as opposed to polyphonic.

Head imitation See **Imitation.**

Hymn Early Christian song used in worship.

Imitation Repeating (imitating) motifs or parts of themes in different parts or voices of a polyphonic composition. The German term *Vorimitation* (head imitation) refers to the practice, often found in organ music, of introducing or "anticipating" such a theme at the beginning before its main entry as the cantus firmus [Ed.].

Introit (Lat. = entrance) Used in the liturgy for the singing of psalms, in larger organ works for the first part or introduction, and in Protestant churches for the music played at the beginning of the service.

Inversion of a theme. See **Fugue.**

Manualiter To be played on manuals only.

Melisma Ornamentation of the melody, coloratura.

Modal Setting which is melodically or harmonically related to a mode (See **Church modes**).

Motif Short phrase used as a melodic ingredient in a composition and frequently recurring. Often forms part of a theme.

Orchestrion Mechanical instrument with reeds and percussion, first built by Johann Nepomuk Mälzel in 1800 to imitate orchestral wind instruments. Developed and enlarged in the 19th century.

Organo pleno (Ital. = full organ) Baroque-period term for the full registration of the organ, e.g., Principal 8′, 4′ and 2′, and Mixture.

Organ chorale Chorale arrangement with the chorale as cantus firmus in the soprano. Prime examples are to be found in Bach's *Orgelbüchlein (Little Organ Book)*.

Ostinato An "obstinate" figure, thus a phrase which constantly recurs. It is of great importance as a continuously repeated bass in a passacaglia (q.v.)

Partita In organ music a set of movements composed as variations on a theme, usually a chorale.

Passacaglia Set of variations on a continuously recurring bass (See **Ostinato**) which proceeds in a slow, triple dance rhythm—the original "passacaglia". Our example is taken from J. S. Bach's passacaglia in C minor. The first three lines offer some typical variations coinciding with the ostinato. The recurring bass may also appear in the upper parts and be modified as in the bass itself. The ringed notes form the theme which is the framework of that part.

Passage work Quickly moving runs, broken chords, scales and arpeggios etc., often whole, thematically significant sections of a work.

Passamezzo (Ital. = half step, thus also step in half-time) Old Italian dance used as the theme for a series of variations in the same way as a passacaglia.

Pedal point (Fr. = point d'orgue) A sustained bass note, over which melodic and harmonic progressions evolve. Mostly used at the end of a piece to heighten effect.

Polyphonic (Gr. = many-voiced) Music in which several parts move independently of each other.

Positive see section on The Organ, above.

Post-serial Reaction against the extremes of serial technique. Absolute freedom in all aspects of composition such as aleatory, improvisation, free activity and live electronic music.

Preamble (Praeambulum) Early term for

Prelude An unstructured piece of music. Often imitative treatment of a theme or motif in the manner of a toccata. A prelude often precedes a fugue, passacaglia, etc.

Psalm tones Various manners of singing (chanting, reciting) the psalms, classified according to the church modes (q.v.).

Recercare see **Ricercare.**

Recapitulation see **Sonata.**

Reprise = recapitulation.

Retrograde version of a theme. See **Fugue.**

Ricercare Instrumental work comparable to (and sometimes based on) a vocal motet. An early form of strictly imitative writing, in several parts. Precursor of the fugue (cf. Frescobaldi).

Serial A method of composition in which pitch, length of note, dynamics and tone color are organized in "rows".

Sonata Does not describe any definite form in organ music. It underwent many changes from simple early Baroque pieces and Bach's three-movement trio sonatas on the one hand to the sonatas by Mendelssohn, Reger and 20th-century composers on the other. The classical sonata form of exposition with two themes, development and recapitulation is scarcely found in organ music.

Stretto Method of composing, in which parts and themes overlap. See **Fugue.**

Supporting chords Appear in or under passage work as structural focal points.

Theme Basic musical idea of a composition, out of which the content of the piece develops.

Tiento 16th-century Spanish term for a mainly imitative work, thus comparable to a ricercare though often also similar to a free prelude or praeambulum.

Toccata A free, predominantly improvisatory piece, often alternating passage work with fugal and homophonic sections. Since Bach also used to describe a work to be played at a consistently high speed.

Tone row technique Takes its name from the *Methode der Komposition mit 12 nur aufeinander bezogenen Tönen (Method of composition with 12 tones of equal value)* developed by Arnold Schoenberg in 1920. These 12 tones form a "row".
Tutti (Ital. = all) Used in contrast to solo (see **Concerto grosso**). Also means "all registers of the organ together".
Verset The small verses which are set to music for alternate vocal and instrumental performances, for instance in the psalms, the Magnificat, etc.
Voluntary Used to describe a completely free instrumental piece which may employ several themes in imitative and toccatalike style.
Vorimitation: *see* **Imitation**

List of Publishers

American Institute of Musicology; Hänssler-Verlag, Neuhausen-Stuttgart
Artia, Prague
Astoria Verlag, Berlin
Bärenreiter-Verlag, Kassel
Billandot Editeur, Paris
A. Böhm u. Sohn, Augsburg
Boosey & Hawkes, London, New York
S. Bornemann, Paris
Bote & Bock, Berlin
Breitkopf & Härtel, Wiesbaden
Brockhoff, Münster
J. & W. Chester Ltd., London
M. Combre, Paris
A. Coppenrath, Altötting
Deutscher Verlag für Musik (DVfM), Leipzig
Doblinger, Vienna and Munich
Durand & Cie., Paris
Editions Jobert, Paris
Editions Musicales Transatlantiques, Paris
Elkan-Vogel, Inc., Bryn Mawr, Pennsylvania
M. Eschig, Paris
Faber Music, London
H. T. Fitzsimmons, Chicago
R. Forberg, Bonn
H. Gerig, Cologne
H. W. Gray & Co., New York
Hal Leonard Publishing Corporation, Milwaukee, Wisconsin
J. Hamelle, Paris
W. Hansen, Copenhagen
Heinrichshofen's Verlag, Wilhelmshaven
G. Henle, Munich
Heugel & Cie., Paris
Hinrichsen Ltd., London
Ione Press, Inc., Boston
Fr. Kistner & C. F. Siegel & Co., Cologne
A. Leduc, Paris
H. Lemoine & Cie., Paris
F.E.C. Leuckart, Munich
Merseburger, Berlin
Möseler, Wolfenbüttel
Müller see Süddeutscher Musikverlag
Musica, Budapest
Musika, Moscow
Novello & Co., London
Österreichischer Bundesverlag, Vienna
Orbis, Prague
Oxford University Press, London, New York
C. F. Peters, Frankfurt-am-Main, New York
Philippo Editeurs, Paris
Piedmont Music Company, New York
F. Pustet, Regensburg
Ricordi, Milano, New York
Salabert, Paris
G. Schirmer, New York
Schola Cantorum, Paris
B. Schotts Söhne, Mainz
C. L. Schultheiss, Tübingen
Schwann, Frankfurt-am-Main
H. Sikorski, Hamburg
N. Simrock, Hamburg
Süddeutscher Musikverlag Willy Müller, Heidelberg
Tischer & Jagenberg, Cologne
Universal Edition, Vienna
J. Weinberger, Vienna
G. Zanibon, Padua

Index of Composers and Works